Praise for
Rediscovering the Issues Surrounding the 1974 Concordia Seminary Walkout

Some may think that the LCMS "Great War" in the mid-1970s was merely a contest between domineering but incompatible leaders, tragically put into play by the inescapable question of whether to accommodate secular shifts in wider society. But if we fail to acknowledge that the combat was really over truth, we miss the entire point of the fight. This book testifies that genuine Lutheran faith vigilantly holds itself accountable to truth as articulated in Scripture and the Confessions.

Mark Mattes
Lutheran Bible Institute Chair in Theology, Grand View University, Des Moines, Iowa

With the fiftieth anniversary of Seminex on the horizon, these essays are a welcome reassessment of a controversy that rocked American Lutheranism. Seminex not only shaped the LCMS and ELCA, it also had a ripple effect throughout the former Synodical Conference churches and American Christianity in general. This book succeeds at making the controversy understandable for a broad audience without sacrificing doctrinal and historical analysis. It is sure to foster fruitful discussions about the origins, significance, and consequences of Seminex.

Dr. Timothy R. Schmeling
Professor of Exegetical and Historical Theology
Bethany Lutheran Theological Seminary, Mankato, Minnesota

A half century ago, friends of the former Lutheran Synodical Conference looked on with shock and dismay as turmoil plagued Concordia Seminary and culminated in the Walkout. *Rediscovering the Issues* provides a valuable contribution to the books and articles that recall those difficult days. It addresses the theological issues that had been brewing in the LCMS for decades before the event. Now we look on with hope.

Rev. Dr. Mark Braun
Professor Emeritus, Wisconsin Lutheran College, Milwaukee

The Concordia Historical Institute Monograph Series exists to publish and disseminate significant and engaging research connected with the history of the confessional Lutheran Church in North America, especially that historical research making use of the material held by the archive and library of Concordia Historical Institute, as well as material held by the archives and libraries of other entities of The Lutheran Church—Missouri Synod.

Daniel N. Harmelink, Series Editor
John C. Wohlrabe Jr., Lawrence R. Rast Jr, John W. Sias, Associate Editors

PREVIOUS VOLUMES

Seminex in Print: A Comprehensive Bibliography of Published Material and Selected Archival Resources for Historical Research. Compiled by David O. Berger with Daniel Harmelink (2021)

The Emigration of the Saxon Lutherans in the Year 1838 and Their Settlement in Perry County, Missouri by J. F. Koestering (2022). Translated by Brian Lutz and G. H. Naumann. Revised for publication by Matthew Carver

REDISCOVERING THE ISSUES
SURROUNDING THE 1974 CONCORDIA SEMINARY WALKOUT

EDITED BY
KEN SCHURB

concordia
historical
institute

monograph
series

CONCORDIA PUBLISHING HOUSE · SAINT LOUIS

Published by Concordia Publishing House
3558 S. Jefferson Ave., St. Louis, MO 63118-3968
1-800-325-3040 • cph.org

Library of Congress Cataloging-in-Publication Data

Names: Schurb, Ken, editor.

Title: Rediscovering the issues surroundings the 1974 Concordia Seminary Walkout / edited by Ken Schurb.

Description: Saint Louis, MO : Concordia Publishing House, [2023] | Includes bibliographic references. | Summary: "Essays on the historical events and theological issues leading up to the Concordia Seminary Walkout in 1974 and subsequent Seminex controversy"-- Provided by publisher.

Identifiers: LCCN 2023004186 (print) | LCCN 2023004187 (ebook) | ISBN 9780758674234 (paperback) | ISBN 9780758674241 (ebook)

Subjects: LCSH: Lutheran Church—Missouri Synod—Doctrines. | Lutheran Church—Missouri Synod—History. | Concordia Seminary (Saint Louis, Mo.)—History. | Christ Seminary-Seminex—History.

Classification: LCC BX8061.M7 R44 2023 (print) | LCC BX8061.M7 (ebook) | DDC 284.1/322—dc23/eng/20230531

LC record available at https://lccn.loc.gov/2023004186

LC ebook record available at https://lccn.loc.gov/2023004187

4 5 6 7 8 9 10 11 12   32 31 30 29 28 27 26 25 24 23

CONTENTS

ABBREVIATIONS

A Statement	*A Statement of Scriptural and Confessional Principles* (see below, pp. 265–77).
AC	Augsburg Confession.
ACDC	Advisory Committee on Doctrine and Conciliation.
ACDC	*Report of the Advisory Committee on Doctrine and Conciliation.* N.p., 1976.
AE	*Luther's Works: American Edition.* Volumes 1–30: Edited by Jaroslav Pelikan. St. Louis: Concordia Publishing House, 1955–76. Volumes 31–55: Edited by Helmut T. Lehmann. Philadelphia: Fortress Press, 1957–86. Volumes 56–82: Edited by Christopher Boyd Brown and Benjamin T. G. Mayes. St. Louis: Concordia Publishing House, 2009–.
AELC	Association of Evangelical Lutheran Churches.
ALC	American Lutheran Church.
ALPB	American Lutheran Publicity Bureau.
Anatomy	Marquart, Kurt E. *Anatomy of an Explosion: Missouri in Lutheran Perspective.* Concordia Seminary Monograph Series 3. Edited by David P. Scaer and Douglas Judisch. Fort Wayne: Concordia Theological Seminary Press, 1977; 4th printing, 2017.
Ap	Apology of the Augsburg Confession.
Blue Book	"Report of the Synodical President to The Lutheran Church—Missouri Synod In compliance with Resolution 2-28 of the 49th Regular Convention of the Synod, held at Milwaukee, Wisconsin, July 9–16, 1971," in Zimmerman (see listing below).
CCM	Commission on Constitutional Matters.
CHI	Concordia Historical Institute.
CHIQ	*Concordia Historical Institute Quarterly.*
CJ	*Concordia Journal.*

Concordia Seminary	The institution in St. Louis, Missouri, which the majority of students and faculty members left in February 1974.
Concordia Theological Seminary	
	The institution in Fort Wayne, Indiana (in Springfield, Illinois, at the time of the Walkout).
Convention Workbook	Convention workbooks from national conventions of the LCMS, identified by year. Archived at https://www.lcms.org/convention/national/archives
Crisis	Montgomery, John Warwick, editor. *Crisis in Lutheran Theology: The Validity and Relevance of Historic Lutheranism vs. Its Contemporary Rivals*. 2 volumes. 2nd edition. Minneapolis: Bethany Fellowship, 1973. Reprint, Irvine, CA: New Reformation Publications, 2017. Volume 3. Irvine, CA: New Reformation Publications, 2017.
CTCR	Commission on Theology and Church Relations.
CTM	*Concordia Theological Monthly.*
CTQ	*Concordia Theological Quarterly.*
Danker	Danker, Frederick W. *No Room in the Brotherhood*. St. Louis: Clayton Publishing House, 1977.
ELCA	Evangelical Lutheran Church in America.
ELIM	Evangelical Lutherans in Mission.
Exodus	Board of Control, Concordia Seminary, St. Louis. *Exodus from Concordia: A Report on the 1974 Walkout*. St. Louis: Concordia College, 1977.
Faithful I	[Concordia Seminary Faculty]. *Faithful to Our Calling Faithful to Our Lord: An Affirmation in Two Parts by the Faculty of Concordia Seminary*. Part I: *A Witness to Our Faith: A Joint Statement and Discussion of Issues*. St. Louis: Concordia Seminary Office of Seminary Relations, [1973].
Faithful II	[Concordia Seminary Faculty]. *Faithful to Our Calling Faithful to Our Lord: An Affirmation in Two Parts by the Faculty of Concordia Seminary*. Part II: *Personal Confessions of Faith and Discussion of Issues*. St. Louis: Concordia Seminary Office of Seminary Relations, [1973].
FC Ep	Epitome of the Formula of Concord.
FC SD	Solid Declaration of the Formula of Concord.
FFC	Fact Finding Committee.
Heritage	August R. Suelflow, ed. *Heritage in Motion: Readings in the History of The Lutheran Church—Missouri Synod, 1962–1995*. St. Louis: Concordia Publishing House, 1998.

ILCW	Inter-Lutheran Commission on Worship.
K-W	*The Book of Concord: The Confessions of the Evangelical Lutheran Church*. Edited by Robert Kolb and Timothy J. Wengert. Philadelphia: Fortress Press, 2000.
LC	Large Catechism.
LCA	Lutheran Church in America.
LCMS	The Lutheran Church—Missouri Synod.
LCUSA	Lutheran Council in the Unites States of America.
LQ	*Lutheran Quarterly*.
LSB	*Lutheran Service Book*. St. Louis: Concordia Publishing House, 2006.
LW	*The Lutheran Witness*.
LWF	Lutheran World Federation.
Memoirs	Tietjen, John H. *Memoirs in Exile: Confessional Hope and Institutional Conflict*. Minneapolis: Fortress Press, 1990.
Moving Frontiers	Meyer, Carl S., ed. *Moving Frontiers: Readings in the History of The Lutheran Church—Missouri Synod*. St. Louis: Concordia Publishing House, 1964.
Pieper	Pieper, Francis. *Christian Dogmatics*. Translated by Walter W. F. Albrecht et al. 3 volumes. St. Louis: Concordia Publishing House, 1950–53.
PIM	Partners in Mission.
Proceedings	Convention proceedings from national conventions of the LCMS, identified by year. Archived at https://www.lcms.org/convention/national/archives.
Res.	Resolution.
SA	Smalcald Articles.
SC	Small Catechism.
Spr	*The Springfielder*.
Tappert	Tappert, Theodore G., ed. *The Book of Concord: The Confessions of the Evangelical Lutheran Church*. Philadelphia: Fortress Press, 1959.
ULCA	United Lutheran Church in America.
Watershed	Baker, Tom. *Watershed at the Rivergate: 1,400 vs. 250,000*. Sturgis, MI: N.p., 1973.
WCC	World Council of Churches.
Zimmerman	Zimmerman, Paul A. *A Seminary in Crisis: The Inside Story of the Preus Fact Finding Committee*. St. Louis: Concordia Publishing House, 2007.

CONTRIBUTORS

Roy Askins is editor of *The Lutheran Witness*.

Armand Boehme is associate pastor of Trinity Lutheran Church, Northfield, Minnesota.

Robert Dargatz is assistant pastor of Immanuel Lutheran Church, Orange, California, and former Religion Division chairman at Concordia University Irvine.

Matthew Harrison is assistant pastor of Village Lutheran Church, Ladue, Missouri, and president of The Lutheran Church—Missouri Synod.

Raymond Hartwig is the immediate past secretary of The Lutheran Church—Missouri Synod and a former member of the Concordia Historical Institute Board of Governors.

Cameron MacKenzie is Ellis Professor of Historical Theology and former department chairman at Concordia Theological Seminary, Fort Wayne, Indiana. He has served as Book Review editor of *Concordia Historical Institute Quarterly* and as a member of the Concordia Historical Institute Board of Governors.

Timothy Maschke is associate pastor of St. Paul Lutheran Church, Grafton, Wisconsin, and former chairman of the Department of Theology at Concordia University Wisconsin.

Scott Murray is senior pastor of Memorial Lutheran Church, Houston, Texas, and third vice president of The Lutheran Church—Missouri Synod.

Martin Noland is pastor of Grace Lutheran Church, San Mateo, California, and former executive director of Concordia Historical Institute.

John Pless is assistant professor of pastoral theology and missions at Concordia Theological Seminary, Fort Wayne, Indiana.

Ken Schurb is administrative assistant to the president of the Central Illinois District of The Lutheran Church—Missouri Synod and Book Review editor of *Concordia Historical Institute Quarterly*. He is a former member of the Concordia Historical Institute Board of Governors.

Dean Wenthe is president of the Concordia University System and immediate past president of Concordia Theological Seminary, Fort Wayne, Indiana.

John Wohlrabe Jr. is assistant pastor of Our Savior Lutheran Church, Whitefish Bay, Wisconsin, and second vice president of The Lutheran Church—Missouri Synod. He is president of the Concordia Historical Institute Board of Governors and editor of *Concordia Historical Institute Quarterly*.

ACKNOWLEDGMENTS

Concordia Historical Institute gratefully acknowledges the help of many people with the present book. Special funding for this volume has been made possible by the Eugene E. and Nell S. Fincke Memorial Trust; in thankfulness for this gift, this book is produced to the glory of God and in honor of Ewald J. Otto, Edwin C. Weber, Charles H. Burmeister, Alfred W. Briel, and Walter C. Dissen—majority members who served on the Concordia Seminary Board of Control at the time of the Walkout. The Fincke Memorial Trust can provide funding for additional historical research and publication on subjects related to this event. Concordia Historical Institute welcomes such proposals. Please contact the executive director or one of the other members of the CHI Monograph Series Committee for more information on proposal guidelines and possible funding assistance.

Those who contributed chapters and other portions of this book have rendered a noteworthy service to the church at large, not only scholars and pastors but also other church workers and laypeople. Particular mention should be made of Dr. Scott Murray, who stepped in and wrote a second chapter when the need arose. Dr. John Wohlrabe originally conceived of this book. He and Dr. Daniel Harmelink have rendered exceptional service to this project. Mr. Mark Bliese of Concordia Historical Institute provided invaluable research and reference services. Mrs. Dawn Weinstock and her colleagues at Concordia Publishing House made major efforts to ensure that this book appeared in a timely fashion. As always, Mrs. Läna Schurb was of great help to the undersigned.

Permission to quote has been granted by those who own the rights to a variety of sources. We acknowledge American Lutheran Publicity Bureau, Clayton Publishing House (Kathie Danker), Concordia Historical Institute, Concordia Publishing House, Concordia Seminary, *Currents in Theology and Mission, dialog,* Eclipse Press (Randi Lundell), ELCA Archives, English District of the LCMS, Evangelical Lutheran Church in America, Evangelical Theological Society, Mrs. Barbara Johnston, The Lutheran Church—Missouri Synod, Lutheran Education Association, Lutheran Laymen's League, *Lutheran Quarterly,* Dr. John Warwick Montgomery, and *The Wall Street Journal.*

Ken Schurb
Editor

HISTORICAL INTRODUCTION
Matthew C. Harrison

In the spring of 1948, the distinguished Lutheran theologian Hermann Sasse of Erlangen University in Germany wrote to Missouri Synod president John Behnken. LCMS representatives were about to travel to Germany to engage in discussions with "big-name" German Lutheran theologians at a place called Bad Boll. Sasse was concerned. Realistically, he warned: "No theological discussion can stop the development that has been moving forward for a quarter of a millennium in the sphere of German Protestant territorial churches, and whose logical end is general unionism." In effect, Sasse observed dolefully, it had come to pass that in Germany, "*Lutheran* and *Reformed* are names for [mere] theological schools within the Protestant Church." Ecclesiastical leaders were to blame:

> For several centuries now, we theologians, bishops, members of consistories and, above all, professors, have learned the great art of hiding our true thoughts behind our words, practicing the same with ever-increasing virtuosity. In front of the congregation, one confesses with the tone of heartfelt conviction the birth of Christ from the Virgin Mary . . . but privately one opposes it as mythology.

Therefore, Sasse emphasized,

> we must fight for the dogmatic heritage of our Church, insofar as it is truly the teaching of the infallible, divine Word and not merely a human legacy, and not be content to concede equal rights in the Church to false doctrine, in the hope that one day, it will disappear of its own accord.[1]

Sadly, Sasse's warning was not well-heeded. German theologians from the state churches and universities who participated in the Bad Boll conferences would have an influence on LCMS participants, particularly attendees from Concordia Seminary, St. Louis. At stake were such things as the true

---

1   "Letter to J. W. Behnken from Hermann Sasse Regarding the Bad Boll Conferences—May 14, 1948," trans. Albert B. Collver III with Charles P. Schaum, *CHIQ* 93 (Winter 2020): 33–34 (emphasis added).

teaching of the divine Word, the doctrine of the church, the integrity of the Lutheran confession, and the simple honesty of churchmen. The influence of Bad Boll became one of the factors that led to the disruption known as "the Walkout" at Concordia Seminary in 1974.

As the fiftieth anniversary of the Walkout approaches, we acknowledge that much has already been written about it.[2] However, we now have the advantage of a half century's perspective as we examine the causes and issues involved in this event. Was it a battle for the Bible?[3] Or was it primarily a contest between two men, Jacob A. O. Preus and John H. Tietjen, revolving around the historical-critical method's approach to biblical interpretation and the understanding of what constituted unionism?[4] Was it primarily a political institutional power struggle? Or was there more to it?[5]

The present book will not answer all these questions. Its purpose is to discuss, from a confessional Lutheran perspective, the important doctrinal issues at hand. This volume consists of chapters written by LCMS theologians, each addressing a different doctrinal issue. The book is directed toward church workers and laypeople, for use in Bible studies or discussion groups. There will be some overlap between chapters and issues, but the astute reader will note that much more was involved than a battle for the Bible and the political machinations between two church leaders.

The Concordia Seminary Walkout did not just happen out of thin air in 1974. Therefore a brief history of events leading up to it may be helpful.

In many ways, the agitation and protest that broke out within the LCMS during the 1970s had been building for more than fifty years. Initially, it arose as a German Lutheran church body faced growing anti-German sentiment during World War I (1914–18) and as it underwent Americanization in the following years. The need was felt to present Lutheranism in a more positive light. Already in 1914, members of the Missouri Synod's English District—formerly an English-speaking church body that was a counterpart to the "German" Missouri Synod, but since 1911 assumed into this Synod as a nongeographic district—joined other eastern Missouri Synod Lutherans in

---

2   See *Seminex in Print: A Comprehensive Bibliography of Published Material and Selected Archival Resources for Historical Research*, compiled by David O. Berger with Daniel N. Harmelink, Concordia Historical Institute Monograph Series 1 (St. Louis: Concordia Publishing House, 2021).

3   Harold Lindsell, *The Battle for the Bible* (Grand Rapids: Zondervan, 1976).

4   Danker; see also James E. Adams, *Preus of Missouri and the Great Lutheran Civil War* (New York: Harper & Row, 1977).

5   *Memoirs*; see also James C. Burkee, *Power, Politics, and the Missouri Synod: A Conflict That Changed American Christianity* (Minneapolis: Fortress Press, 2011).

forming the American Lutheran Publicity Bureau (ALPB).[6] By the end of 1917, the ALPB launched its own monthly periodical in English called *The American Lutheran*.

After the United States became involved in the war, the Missouri Synod began commissioning military chaplains and supporting camp pastors for U.S. troops preparing to embark for Europe. Still, the Synod was reluctant to work with other Lutheran church bodies with which it was not in fellowship in an organization called the National Lutheran Commission. Eastern Missouri Synod Lutherans, including many involved in the ALPB, protested this reluctance. They wanted closer cooperation with other Lutherans. The issue was resolved when the war ended and Missouri Synod military ministry disbanded.[7]

Unrest developed again, however. During the Great Depression, *The American Lutheran* published articles taking issue with various LCMS administrative policies. This led to politicking at the 1935 synodical convention, the defeat of incumbent president Friedrich Pfotenhauer, and the election of the Synod's first American-born president, John Behnken.[8]

Further discontent and outward protest came with the drafting and synodwide dissemination of what has been called the "Statement of the 44." It was signed by forty-four LCMS clergymen, five of whom were professors at Concordia Seminary. The initial meeting to draft the statement was called for by the ALPB Editorial Board, and it coincided with their meeting at the Stevens Hotel in Chicago on September 6–7, 1945. The "Statement of the 44" included twelve theses, each saying "We affirm . . ." and "We therefore deplore . . . ." The theses deplored legalism, a lack of love, a misapplication of Romans 16:17 to all who do not hold the doctrinal positions of the Synod, and actions related to church fellowship.[9]

---

6   See Richard O. Johnson, *Changing World, Changeless Christ: The American Lutheran Publicity Bureau, 1914–2014* (Delhi, NY: ALPB Books, 2018), 1–3.

7   Alan Graebner, "World War I and Lutheran Union: Documents from the Army and Navy Board, 1917 and 1918," *CHIQ* 41 (February 1968): 49–57.

8   Johnson, *Changing World*, 59–74. See John C. Wohlrabe Jr., "The Missouri Synod's Unity Attempts during the Pfotenhauer Presidency, 1911–1935" (STM thesis, Concordia Seminary, St. Louis, 1982), 156–76, https://scholar.csl.edu/cgi/view content.cgi?article=1058&context=stm.

9   This portion of the present introduction is dependent on John C. Wohlrabe Jr., "The Role of the Seminaries in the LCMS, 1847–2001," *CTQ* 85 (July/October 2021): 215–39; reprinted by permission in *CHIQ* 94 (Fall 2021): 33–55. For the "Statement of the 44," see *Moving Frontiers*, 422–24; online at http://www .projectwittenberg.org/etext/lcms/ST44/ST44.htm; Carl S. Meyer, *Log Cabin to Luther Tower* (St. Louis: Concordia Publishing House, 1965), 247; *Speaking the*

Following World War II, the LCMS became involved in extensive disaster relief in Europe. In conjunction with that, it began a series of theological discussions with German Lutheran theologians, initially meeting in 1948 at a resort located in Bad Boll, Germany.[10] The discussions exposed LCMS attendees, including St. Louis faculty members, to modern German scholarship in Luther studies and historical criticism of the Bible.[11] This theology made a profound impact at Concordia Seminary.

Another theological emphasis growing within the LCMS, especially on the St. Louis seminary campus, was the push for union with American Lutheran church bodies with which the Missouri Synod was not in fellowship. Beginning in 1917, Missouri Synod representatives began meeting with representatives from various church bodies in what became known as the Intersynodical Movement. Although the Missouri Synod did not reach doctrinal agreement with these other synods, this movement led to the formation of a church body called the American Lutheran Church (ALC) in 1930. Discussions with the ALC throughout the middle part of the twentieth century involved several members of the St. Louis faculty. An interest in Lutheran unity pervaded the seminary campus.[12]

In 1958 Martin Scharlemann, director of Concordia Seminary's School for Graduate Studies, published exploratory essays concerning inspiration and revelation. The perceived rejection of the inspiration and inerrancy of Scripture elicited strong reactions.[13] Although Scharlemann apologized to the Synod at its 1962 convention,[14] the historical-critical method would be championed by others at Concordia Seminary.

Attempting to deal with growing controversies over both church fellowship and the inroads of historical criticism, the LCMS at its 1959 convention not only passed a "Statement on Scripture," but in Resolution 9 it also resolved

---

Truth in Love: Essays Related to A Statement, Chicago, 1945 (Chicago: The Willow Press, [1946?]), *passim*; several articles in *CHIQ* 43 (November 1970); Jack Treon Robinson, "The Spirit of Triumphalism in The Lutheran Church—Missouri Synod: The Role of the 'A Statement' of 1945 in the Missouri Synod" (PhD diss., Vanderbilt University, 1972), 132–50.

10 See above, p. 1.

11 See Scott R. Murray, *Law, Life, and the Living God: The Third Use of the Law in Modern American Lutheranism* (St. Louis: Concordia Publishing House, 2002), 67.

12 Meyer, *Log Cabin*, 229.

13 Beginning with the November 1959 issue, the Scharlemann controversy dominated the pages of an independent publication called *The Confessional Lutheran* until well after the Synod's 1962 convention. See 1962 *Convention Workbook*, 164–65.

14 1962 *Proceedings*, 106–7.

that "every doctrinal statement of a confessional nature adopted by Synod as a true exposition of the Holy Scriptures is to be regarded as public doctrine (*publica doctrina*) in Synod," and "Synod's pastors, teachers, and professors are held to teach and act in harmony with such statements."[15] This would have included the Synod's *Brief Statement* of 1932. However, the Synod's Commission on Constitutional Matters (CCM) reported to the next (1962) synodical convention that Resolution 9 was unconstitutional, conflicting with Article II of the Synod's constitution.[16] The Synod urged its pastors, teachers, and professors to teach according to doctrinal statements adopted by the Synod.[17] However, many faculty members of Concordia Seminary did not consider this a requirement for them in their teaching office.

To address matters relating to doctrinal unity and to advise and prepare special studies on theological matters, the Synod in 1962 established the Commission on Theology and Church Relations (CTCR).[18] Plenty of opportunity for theological clarification presented itself when the 1965 convention adopted the so-called "Mission Affirmations." These "affirmations" expanded "mission" to include more than the proclamation of God's Word and the administration of His Sacraments. They held that "mission" involved any and all acts of mercy that Christians do for others, even social and political action.[19] The Mission Affirmations were supported by many on the St. Louis faculty.

Many pastors, teachers, and laypeople within the Missouri Synod were expressing concern with what was being taught at Concordia Seminary. Shortly before the 1969 LCMS convention, seminary president Alfred Fuerbringer announced his retirement, preparing the way for John Tietjen's election as president. Tietjen (1928–2004) had received a doctorate from Union Seminary, New York, with a dissertation on which he based his book *Which Way to Lutheran Unity?*[20] He came to St. Louis after serving as executive director of publicity for the Lutheran Council in the United States of America (LCUSA), a pan-Lutheran group organized in 1966. LCUSA sought to pave the way for a union between the ALC, the LCA, and the

---

15   Resolution 9, Committee 3, 1959 *Proceedings*, 189, 191.

16   1962 *Proceedings*, 187.

17   Res. 3-17, 1962 *Proceedings*, 106.

18   Res. 6-03, 1962 *Proceedings*, 123–24.

19   Res. 1-01A to 1-01F, 1965 *Proceedings*, 79–81.

20   John H. Tietjen, *Which Way to Lutheran Unity: A History of Efforts to Unite the Lutherans of America* (St. Louis: Concordia Publishing House, 1966).

LCMS. Lutheran union had been a special interest of Alfred Fuerbringer. John Tietjen would now keep it as a focus at Concordia Seminary.

The 1969 Missouri Synod convention soon thereafter elected J. A. O. Preus (1920–94) as president of the Synod. Preus came to the synodical presidency after serving as president of the Synod's seminary in Springfield, Illinois. Preus had received a doctorate in classics and was already involved in his life's work of translating writings by the sixteenth-century Lutheran theologian Martin Chemnitz. Preus took an orthodox approach to Lutheran theology. As president-elect, he recommended against altar and pulpit fellowship with the ALC, but the 1969 convention declared it nonetheless.[21]

Not long after the Synod's 1969 convention, a few St. Louis faculty members expressed concerns about what was being taught at the seminary. Among them was Martin Scharlemann, who wrote President Preus on April 9, 1970, suggesting an official inquiry.[22] (It might be noted, however, that even after the Walkout, in 1975, Scharlemann wrote Hermann Sasse expressing his support for Sasse's *Letters to Lutheran Pastors* on Holy Scripture, particularly where Sasse rejected the position that Scripture is inerrant in every respect.[23] Although otherwise orthodox Lutherans like Sasse and Scharlemann could retain the dogmatic context of the faith without a strict doctrine of inerrancy, most cannot, and certainly not members of following generations.)

On April 20, 1970, Preus wrote the seminary Board of Control that he intended to appoint a Fact Finding Committee (FFC).[24] He appointed Karl Barth, LCMS South Wisconsin District president; Elmer Foelber, former editor at Concordia Publishing House; H. Armin Moellering, a parish pastor with a doctorate in classics; Paul Streufert, fourth vice president of the Synod; and, as chairman, Paul A. Zimmerman, president of Concordia Lutheran Junior College, Ann Arbor, Michigan. This panel interviewed Concordia Seminary professors between December 11, 1970, and March 6, 1971. Tape recordings of the interviews were transcribed, and each faculty member had the opportunity to make additions or corrections to his transcript. The FFC submitted its report, based largely on these interviews, to President Preus on June 15, 1971,[25] shortly before the Synod's 1971 convention in Milwaukee.

---

21 1969 *Proceedings*, 22, 32.

22 *Exodus*, 22–23; see *Exodus*, 151–53, for Scharlemann's entire letter.

23 See Martin H. Scharlemann, St. Louis, to Hermann Sasse, North Adelaide, Australia, [July 1975], copy of typescript, CHI, Martin Henry Scharlemann, Series 1, General Correspondence, Folder 120.

24 *Exodus*, 23–24.

25 Zimmerman, 35, 41–43, 65. The entire FFC report is in Zimmerman, 155–96.

The convention directed Concordia Seminary's Board of Control to receive the FFC report from President Preus and take appropriate action. It also required Preus to report to the Synod on this matter within one year.[26]

Storm winds whipped up during that year. In February 1972, President Preus wrote President Tietjen regarding an Old Testament professor at the seminary, Arlis Ehlen, directing that he teach "no course in which he will have opportunity to advocate his higher critical views concerning biblical interpretation." In a roundabout response, President Tietjen told the student body and included in a seminary news release his declaration that it would be impossible for Dr. Ehlen or any other professor to teach at the seminary level without using the historical-critical method.[27] A few days earlier, Preus had sent the Synod a letter regarding the Ehlen case. He appended to it *A Statement of Scriptural and Confessional Principles*, a document that he had offered to the Board of Control to assist it in dealing with theological issues at the seminary.[28] The faculty responded a month later that *A Statement* had "a spirit alien to Lutheran confessional theology" and that it made "binding dogma out of mere theological opinion."[29]

On September 1, 1972, Preus reported to the Synod, as directed by the Milwaukee convention. The "Report of the Synodical President," called the "Blue Book" because of the color of its cover, ran to 160 pages in small type. It contained lengthy quotations from the transcripts of the FFC interviews with St. Louis faculty members, in which the various professors were identified not by name but by letters of the alphabet.[30] For example, though the Blue Book did not say so, President Tietjen was "Prof. I." One week after the appearance of the Blue Book, Tietjen released to the Synod a 35-page document, "Fact Finding or Fault Finding," in which he used the language of computer programming to characterize the work of the FFC as "garbage in, garbage out."[31]

Late in 1972, the Concordia Seminary faculty published a fuller statement of its position: *Faithful to Our Calling, Faithful to Our Lord: An Affirmation in Two Parts.* Part I was *A Witness to Our Faith: A Joint Statement*

---

26   Res. 2-28, 1971 *Proceedings* (quoted in *Exodus*, 29).

27   Quoted in *Exodus*, 32–33. See *Memoirs*, 98.

28   *A Statement* appears below, pp. 265–77.

29   Quoted in *Exodus*, 31. See "Response of the Faculty of Concordia Seminary, St. Louis," *LW*, April 30, 1972, 28–31.

30   The Blue Book is included in Zimmerman, 199–444. See *Exodus*, 34–36.

31   See *Exodus*, 36–38.

Photograph by Paul Ockrassa

Seminex students and professors gathered in DuBourg Hall on the campus of St. Louis University listen as Dr. John Tietjen reads the letter from Concordia Seminary's Board of Control informing him of his dismissal as president (October 1974).

and Discussion of Issues. Part II consisted of individual statements by almost all the seminary's professors.

The Synod's next convention, in New Orleans, Louisiana, came about a half-year later, in July 1973. It adopted three key resolutions:

- Res. 2-12, in which the Synod understood its constitution as permitting it to adopt doctrinal statements "as definitive of the Synod's position" and "binding upon all its members"[32]

- Res. 3-01, in which the Synod adopted *A Statement* as such a doctrinal statement[33]

- Res. 3-09, "To Declare Faculty Majority Position in Violation of Article II of the [Synod's] Constitution," that is, contrary to Scripture and the Lutheran Confessions[34]

After the convention, the Concordia Seminary Board of Control, with conservatives now in the majority, had the responsibility of dealing with the faculty, starting with President Tietjen.[35] The board temporarily suspended him on January 20, 1974. The next morning, the majority of the seminary's

---

32   1973 *Proceedings*, 115; see 1973 *Proceedings*, 111–15.

33   1973 *Proceedings*, 127–28.

34   1973 *Proceedings*, 133–39.

35   Res. 3-09 and Res. 3-12A, 1973 *Proceedings*, 139, 140.

students declared a moratorium on attending class. Later that day, a majority of faculty members announced that they identified with President Tietjen's position and considered themselves also suspended, so they refused to teach.[36] Students not attending classes in late January participated instead in Operation Outreach, fanning out across the Synod to rally support for the faculty.[37] At its February 17–18, 1974, meeting, the Board of Control determined that faculty members would be terminated if they did not resume teaching on February 19.[38]

On February 19, 1974, the majority of faculty and students literally walked out of Concordia Seminary—hence, the term "Walkout."[39] They considered themselves to be Concordia *Sem*inary *in Ex*ile, *Seminex*. The institution founded by those who walked out eventually became known as Christ Seminary—Seminex.

Reconciliation attempts followed the Walkout. The seminary Board of Control reached out to the former faculty and students.[40] Recognizing the need to address matters in the Synod more broadly, already in January 1974 President Preus had appointed an Advisory Committee on Doctrine and Conciliation (ACDC), which consisted of a chairman and fourteen members, a seven-member "conservative caucus" and a seven-member "moderate caucus." Before the ACDC was finished, and before the next synodical convention, the Synod hosted a theological convocation in April 1975 that was attended by more than three hundred people. The convocation featured essays from representatives of both sides, as well as small-group discussion sessions, but no agreement was reached.[41]

Following the Walkout, the presidents of several LCMS Districts placed Seminex graduates to fill pastoral vacancies, then ordained them. The Synod's 1975 convention resolved that District presidents who would not comply with the Synod's bylaws on placement and ordination of pastors should resign or they would be removed.[42] Eventually, three District presidents resigned and four were removed from office.[43] This led in late 1976 to

---

36 *Exodus*, 92–98, 100–101.

37 *Exodus*, 105–8. "Fact Sheets" used by students in Operation Outreach appear in *Exodus*, 177–83.

38 The board's resolution is in *Exodus*, 185–86.

39 *Exodus*, 115–19.

40 Zimmerman, 129–31.

41 *Memoirs*, 247.

42 Res. 5-02A, 1975 *Proceedings* (*Heritage*, 184–86; see *Heritage*, 186–87).

43 Zimmerman, 131–33.

Photograph by Paul Ockrassa

Dr. John Tietjen addresses students and the press at Seminex shortly after being removed from the presidency of Concordia Seminary (October 1974).

the formation of a new church body, the Association of Evangelical Lutheran Churches (AELC). It consisted of approximately 250 congregations that left the LCMS.[44] A bit more than a decade later, the AELC merged with the ALC and LCA to form the Evangelical Lutheran Church in America (ELCA).

After the Walkout, and after the CTCR made a report in 1975 on *The Inspiration of Scripture*, the 1977 LCMS convention adopted a resolution that held the historical-critical method to be inappropriate in application to Holy Scripture as the inspired Word of God.[45] Also at that convention, the Synod declared a state of "fellowship in protest" with the ALC, a prelude to its 1981 declaration that fellowship with the ALC did not exist.[46]

In some ways, 1977 marked the end of an era. In the fall of that year, LCMS vice president Theodore Nickel announced that he had sustained charges filed against John Tietjen for allowing false doctrine and that Tietjen

---

44 Zimmerman, 134–35.

45 *The Inspiration of Scripture* (St. Louis: LCMS, 1975); Res. 3-11, 1977 *Proceedings* (*Heritage*, 40–41).

46 Res. 3-02A, 1977 *Proceedings* (*Heritage*, 120–21); Res. 3-01, 1981 *Proceedings* (*Heritage*, 127–28).

was no longer a clergy member of the Synod.[47] LCMS conventions after 1977 ceased to be engulfed with issues urgently related to the Walkout.

Digging Deeper

Concordia Seminary, St. Louis, Board of Control. *Exodus from Concordia: A Report on the 1974 Walkout.* St. Louis: Concordia College, 1977.

Marquart, Kurt E. *Anatomy of an Explosion: Missouri in Lutheran Perspective.* Concordia Seminary Monograph Series 3. Edited by David P. Scaer and Douglas Judisch. Fort Wayne, IN: Concordia Theological Seminary Press, 1977; 4th printing, 2017.

Suelflow, August R., ed. *Heritage in Motion: Readings in the History of The Lutheran Church—Missouri Synod, 1962–1995.* St. Louis: Concordia Publishing House, 1998.

Zimmerman, Paul A. *A Seminary in Crisis: The Inside Story of the Preus Fact Finding Committee.* St. Louis: Concordia Publishing House, 2007.

---

47 Zimmerman, 138–39.

Chronology

1932   LCMS adopts *Brief Statement*

1945   "Statement of the 44"

1948   First of the Bad Boll (Germany) conferences

1958   Martin Scharlemann and Horace Hummel present papers favorable to the historical-critical method to the faculty of Concordia Seminary

1959   LCMS meets in convention in San Francisco, California; resolves that *Brief Statement* and others adopted by the Synod should be regarded as *publica doctrina*

1962   LCMS meets in convention in Cleveland, Ohio; sustains CCM opinion that doctrinal statements cannot be placed on a level with the Lutheran Confessions; receives apology from Martin Scharlemann

1965   LCMS meets in convention in Detroit, Michigan; adopts Mission Affirmations

1967   LCMS meets in convention in New York City; adopts *Theology of Fellowship*

1969   John H. Tietjen becomes president of Concordia Seminary

        LCMS meets in convention in Denver, Colorado; elects Jacob A. O. Preus as president; approves fellowship with ALC

1970   FFC interviews Concordia Seminary professors starting December 11, ending March 6, 1971

1971   LCMS meets in convention in Milwaukee, Wisconsin

1972   **March 3:** President Preus writes the Synod about the Arlis Ehlen case; releases *A Statement* (see below, pp. 265–77)

March 6: President Tietjen states that seminary-level instruction must use the historical-critical method of biblical interpretation

September 1: Appearance of President Preus's report to the Synod on Concordia Seminary (the "Blue Book")

1973   **January:** Appearance of Concordia Seminary faculty majority's *Faithful to Our Calling, Faithful to Our Lord* and CTCR report *Gospel and Scripture*

July 6–13: LCMS meets in convention in New Orleans, Louisiana; reelects President Preus, adopts Res. 2-12, 3-01, 3-09 (see below, pp. 103–4)

August 28–29: Beginnings of ELIM

1974   **January:** President Preus appoints Advisory Committee on Doctrine and Conciliation (ACDC)

January 20: Tietjen suspended from the office of Concordia Seminary president

February 19: Student, faculty, and staff walk out from Concordia Seminary

April–October: LCMS Board for Missions staff walk out (see below, pp. 123–43)

1975   **March:** Appearance of CTCR report *Inspiration of Scripture*

July 4–11: LCMS meets in convention in Anaheim, California; authorizes removal from office of District presidents who ordain uncertified Seminex graduates

1976   Appearance of *ACDC*; four LCMS District presidents are removed; three LCMS District presidents resign

December: Formation of AELC

1977   **July 15–22:** LCMS meets in convention in Dallas, Texas; disapproves historical-critical method for studying the Bible; declares "fellowship in protest" with ALC; distinguishes between synodical doctrinal statements and resolutions

September 28: LCMS vice president Theodore Nickel announces that Tietjen is no longer a clergy member of the Synod

CHAPTER ONE

GOSPEL AND SCRIPTURE

Ken Schurb

Instead of recognizing that the Bible is the only source and norm of the church's doctrine while the biblical Gospel of Christ forms the heart of the Christian faith, Concordia Seminary professors and others came to think of the Gospel as the norm of theology. They were even using the Gospel to allow ruling out certain contents of Scripture as historical, true, and authoritative. Such "Gospel reductionism" compromises Scripture and endangers both the Gospel message and the comfort it brings to sinners.

Introduction

The Bible can make people uncomfortable. Such discomfort can come to Christians. Sooner or later you will find something in it, such as accounts of various miracles, that "no educated person" should believe. Or you encounter ethical teachings, such as on marriage and sexuality, that "no enlightened person" would follow. What do you do with these? Set them aside? If not, why not?

Why should people believe the Bible? Why *do* people believe the Bible? Are these two questions asking the same thing?

Let's approach this subject through a slice-of-life example: "I said so." Parents often say this to their children. Frequently they say it to support some rule: "Do this . . . because I said so." Sometimes they say "I said so" concerning a factual matter, probably after children have asked "Why?" for the twentieth time. Either way, with the words "I said so," parental authority is asserting itself.

Why do children accept this answer? Usually they have no alternative, so there can be frustration and anger on their part. Then why don't children conclude that their parents are rejecting them by saying "I said so"? Because the parents have shown their love for their children by other words and actions. Wise parents know not to tell their children only "I said so."

During the years leading up to the 1974 Walkout, something like this had been on the minds of Concordia Seminary faculty members and others in the LCMS, as well as others in American Lutheranism. They were thinking not about parents and children, but of God communicating with sinners. A Concordia Seminary professor wrote: "To say we must bow to what God has said, no matter what he has said, is to blur the distinction between Law and Gospel."[1]

Professors went further. They said in effect that as they studied Scripture, if they weren't "hearing" God say that He loved them (the Gospel) in some aspect of the text, they need not heed other things the text said. This would be like a child hanging on every word when his or her parents say "I love you" but—at best—losing interest when they say other things. Except for the "I love you," why should children care?

An example of this came when another St. Louis professor told LCMS president J. A. O. Preus's Fact Finding Committee (FFC) that one need not insist that Adam and Eve were historical people and their fall into sin was a real historical event, for some have difficulty relating the biblical account of the fall to the Gospel.[2] Similar things were said or written by professors at Concordia Teachers College, River Forest, Illinois, and at Valparaiso University.[3] In Lutheran circles outside the Synod, but within earshot of Missouri representatives, it was even being claimed that it was *un-Lutheran* to hold that Adam and Eve were real historical people and that the fall really took place![4]

A word about terms: the Latin word for a carpenter's square used to draw right angles is *norma*. This word came to be used for any rule or standard. Following the Formula of Concord, classical Lutheran theology referred to Scripture as the *norma* (in English, *norm*) for doctrine. For example, President Preus's September 1972 Blue Book report to the Synod employed this term: "The question is whether the Scriptures are the norm for our faith and life or

---

1   Quoted in FFC report (Zimmerman, 177).

2   FFC report (Zimmerman, 177).

3   *Watershed*, 20. See Walter R. Bouman, "The Teaching of Religion: A Theological Analysis," in *The Teaching of Religion: Twenty-Second Yearbook* (River Forest, IL: Lutheran Education Association, 1965), 43; and Walter E. Keller, "Necessary and Relevant to What?" *The Cresset* 36 (February 1973): 22.

4   Robert Preus, "Gospel Fundamentalism," *Affirm* 2 (August 1972): 3.

whether the Gospel alone is that norm."[5] Using the Gospel to reduce what is to be accepted in Scripture was referred to as *Gospel reductionism.*[6]

The 1973 LCMS convention defined Gospel reductionism:

> The first and usual meaning is that where the "Gospel" is established as the "governing principle" instead of the Scriptural Word, then such "Gospelism" reduces to a minimum the content of Christian belief and discards whatever does not seem to serve it directly.

The Synod quoted a *Lutheran Witness* article from President Preus, that a

> limitation of the *normative* authority of Scripture to its Gospel content or function is what we call "Gospel reductionism." By this we mean a reducing of all doctrine to the one doctrine of the Gospel and making the Gospel (often undefined) the only *norm* for all doctrine and life.[7]

More than a year before the convention, in May 1972, the Concordia Seminary faculty and President Preus had agreed that the relationship between Scripture and the Gospel stood out as the basic issue amid mounting tensions within the LCMS. Today this fact may surprise people who presume that the main concern at the time was historical criticism or the nature of Scripture. But Gospel reductionism gave historical criticism of Scripture "cover" within the Missouri Synod. It allowed such criticism of the biblical text to seem Lutheran. The question kept arising: Does the Gospel let a reader of Scripture make judgments as to which of its contents are historical, true, and authoritative?[8]

Historical Background

The roots of this controversy go back into the 1800s. However, we will join the story in the first half of the twentieth century.

---

5   "Preface" in Blue Book (Zimmerman, 203).

6   See John Warwick Montgomery, "Current Theological Trends in The Lutheran Church—Missouri Synod," *Crisis* 1:120; see also Montgomery, "The Unbridgeable Chasm: Gospelism or the Scriptural Gospel?" *Crisis* 1:140–47.

7   Resolution 3-09, 1973 *Proceedings*, 136, quoting J. A. O. Preus, "From the President: Two Kinds of Biblical Authority," *LW*, April 22, 1973, 29 (italics in Preus). See CTCR, *Gospel and Scripture* (St. Louis: LCMS, 1972), 4, 10; "A Summary of the Findings" in Blue Book (Zimmerman, 226); Scott R. Murray, *Law, Life, and the Living God: The Third Use of the Law in Modern American Lutheranism* (St. Louis: Concordia Publishing House, 2002), 103–7.

8   Robert Preus, "Gospel Fundamentalism," 3.

Karl Barth

After World War I, the Swiss theologian Karl Barth (1886–1968) ushered in a period of new ("neo"-) orthodoxy. He thought that Jesus is God's only true revelation. Standing in the Reformed tradition of Calvin or Zwingli rather than that of Luther, Barth asserted that God had basically spoken not two words (Law and Gospel), but one. He wrote: ". . . the Law is nothing else than the necessary *form of the Gospel*, whose content is grace."[9] The very fact that God speaks to limited human beings is grace, Barth said.

Going back to the sixteenth century and controversies with Lutherans over the bodily presence of Christ in the Lord's Supper, the Reformed had held that the finite is incapable of the infinite. In that controversy, Reformed theologians had insisted that the finite body of Christ can be in only one place at a time. Similarly, on the assumption that the finite is incapable of the infinite, Barth held that the Word of God is not truth in the form of finite human speech—statements such as are found in the Bible. The Bible simply witnesses to Jesus as Word of God, Barth claimed; it is not itself the Word of God. It *becomes* the Word of God for people when the Holy Spirit does His work on them. And since the Word comes to people alongside of Scripture but not through it, the integrity of this Word stands independent from the historical reports in Scripture. However many faults the Bible may have, Barth comforted himself that none of them could harm the Word of God or Barth's own faith.[10]

Werner Elert

Against Barth's ordering of "Gospel and Law," the Lutheran theologian Werner Elert (1885–1954) of Erlangen, Germany, emphasized Law and Gospel, in that order. In fact, Elert wanted to make Law and Gospel the controlling theme of theology.[11] Ironically, in his determination to emphasize Law and Gospel, he ended up in one way like Barth. Elert was highly critical of the teaching of Luther and Lutheran orthodoxy that the Bible was verbally inspired by God. He did not want to see the Scriptures regarded as a set of laws, as if all their contents were the same. Also, he wanted to retain what one analyst called a "kernel of experience." That is, he wanted people to recognize

---

9   Karl Barth, "Gospel and Law," trans A. M. Hall, in *Community, State, and Church: Three Essays* (New York: Doubleday Anchor Books, 1960), 80 (italics original).

10 See Robert D. Preus, "The Word of God in the Theology of Karl Barth," *CTM* 31 (February 1960): 105–15; Jack D. Kilcrease, "The Challenge of Karl Barth's Doctrine of the Word of God," *CTQ* 84 (January–April 2020): 59–81.

11 See Werner Elert, *Law and Gospel*, trans. Edward H. Schroeder (Philadelphia: Fortress Press, 1967).

the Bible's authority through their experience. Although one does not have to reject the verbal inspiration of Scripture to satisfy Elert's basic concern for the Gospel, Elert himself did so.[12]

Bad Boll

Representatives of the Missouri Synod met Elert and other noted German Lutheran theologians in annual theological discussions held at the Bad Boll resort in Germany after World War II. Elert was at these meetings in 1948 and 1949, as was Edmund Schlink of Heidelberg. In a book on the Lutheran Confessions, Schlink had written that Scripture is the norm because God saves through the message, the Gospel, that Scripture proclaims.[13] A question of what Scripture *is* was answered in terms of what it *does*.

Overall, "at Bad Boll no agreement was reached on the doctrine of Holy Scripture."[14] However, the Missouri Synod representatives returned home with much to think about.

American Lutheranism

Missouri Synod representatives were not the only ones impressed by German Lutheran theologians. Most of American Lutheranism was too, including a great many in the ALC. The ALC had been involved with the Missouri Synod in church fellowship talks for most of the 1960s. Representatives of the two church bodies discussed, among other topics, "the authority of Scripture." An essay with that very title was delivered at Concordia Seminary in 1968 by Kent Knutson (1924–73), an ALC seminary professor who shortly thereafter became the president of the ALC. He said: "In the Scriptures God speaks to us in His judgmental and His redemptive word, and we hear Him speak. That is the power. That is the authority."[15] Here again, biblical authority was cast strictly in terms of what the Scriptures do.[16]

---

12 See Lowell C. Green, "The Relationship of Werner Elert and America," *CHIQ* 70 (Summer 1997): 87 (quoting Karlmann Beyerschlag) and 93 n. 17.

13 Edmund Schlink, *Theology of the Lutheran Confessions*, trans. Paul F. Koehneke and Herbert J. A. Bouman (Philadelphia: Fortress Press, 1961; repr., St. Louis: Concordia Publishing House, [2003]), 10.

14 Martin Hein, *An Evaluation of Bad Boll 1948 and 1949*, trans. J. T. Mueller (N.p.: LCMS, n.d.), 11.

15 Kent S. Knutson, "The Authority of Scripture," *CTM* 40 (March 1969): 164.

16 See also ALC theologian Gerhard Forde, "Law and Gospel as the Methodological Principle of Theology," in *Theological Perspectives* (Decorah, IA: Luther College Press [1966]), 50–69.

In The Lutheran Church—Missouri Synod

Fact Finding Committee Report

The FFC reported similar understandings among Concordia Seminary professors. One said that Scripture "is authoritative because of what it does to people."[17]

The same thinking was expressed in other ways. A professor said he would allow the position that the flood of Noah was perhaps a local event, not world-encompassing, if the holder of this view "does not negate the divinely intended sense of the passage, which is to teach sin and grace."[18] Another, answering how to determine whether to take some biblical point literally, replied: "You have to determine how does it relate to the Gospel."[19] Still another, responding to a question about whether a clear biblical report of a miracle could be interpreted as a legend later added to the text, said he would ask the interpreter, "What does this do to the Gospel?" This professor did not want to set Scripture and Gospel at odds with each other, he said, yet he added that for himself as a Lutheran "the final, the ultimate step, the touchstone of anything is the Gospel."[20]

The FFC summarized that various professors saw the Gospel as not only the heart of the faith but also as the yardstick for biblical interpretation. They did not feel a need to reject any interpretation of a text in Scripture unless they thought the interpretation harmed the Gospel. They would grant a great deal of latitude to read the text in a nonliteral or nonhistorical way as long as the Gospel remained unaffected, as with the fall or the flood. These accounts did not have to be taken as factual, so long as the interpretation retained the message of sin and grace.[21]

The FFC contrasted this view with the Synod's position, which it summarized as follows: While "one approaches the Scriptures expecting to hear the Good News of Jesus Christ and to relate all that he reads there to Him," still, the Gospel "does not determine the meaning of the Biblical text. Whatever the text says is the meaning of the text." That meaning "is to be accepted as such because it is the Word of God." Whether a text should

---

17   FFC report (Zimmerman, 174).

18   Prof. M [Walter Wegner], Blue Book (Zimmerman, 304).

19   FFC report (Zimmerman, 177).

20   Prof. O [Edgar Krentz], Blue Book (Zimmerman, 306).

21   See "Table of Divergent Positions Held by Various Members of the Faculty," Blue Book (Zimmerman, 234).

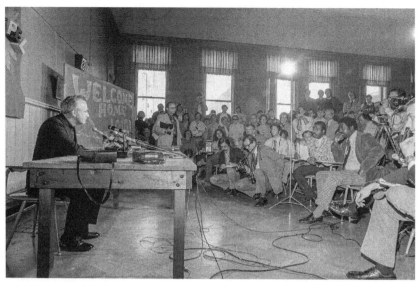

Photograph by Paul Ockrassa

Dr. John Tietjen conducts a press conference at Seminex in the days following his dismissal as president of Concordia Seminary (October 1974).

be taken literally or in some other way is determined by the text itself—its grammar, context, etc.[22]

The FFC pointed out related issues:

1. *The church as potential determiner of doctrine.* Why should interpreters not question teachings of Scripture such as Christ's virgin birth or His resurrection? One professor said that these are safeguarded by the Lutheran Confessions. So, the FFC wondered, were the Confessions in effect displacing the Bible as the prime source of the Christian faith?[23] In the Blue Book, a professor was quoted concerning the virgin birth:

> As I wrestle with this question, I am tremendously helped by the ancient tradition of the church, which has always

---

22 See "Table of Divergent Positions Held by Various Members of the Faculty," Blue Book (Zimmerman, 234). For elaboration, compare Ralph A. Bohlmann, *Principles of Biblical Interpretation in the Lutheran Confessions*, rev. ed. (St. Louis: Concordia Publishing House, 1983). Contrast Edward H. Schroeder, "Is There a Lutheran Hermeneutics?" in *The Lively Function of the Gospel: Essays in Honor of Richard R. Caemmerer on Completion of 25 Years as Professor of Practical Theology at Concordia Seminary, St. Louis*, ed. Robert W. Bertram (St. Louis: Concordia Publishing House, 1966), 81–97.

23 FFC report (Zimmerman, 189). See *ACDC*, 65.

said we have found it desirable, wise, necessary to affirm the virgin birth. . . . At some point in some way I have to fall back on my faith, my belief.[24]

2. *Old Testament prophecy concerning Christ.* A professor told the FFC that "Abraham put his full confidence in his salvation in the Lord's action in some shape or form," not necessarily trusting that his Offspring would be the God-man Deliverer.[25] An Old Testament professor said that there are no prophecies pointing *directly* to Christ—in every case there was an earlier fulfillment, but New Testament authors took these to be *ultimately* fulfilled in Christ.[26] A professor wrote that scholars today generally "begin with the Old Testament materials by themselves and . . . emphasize their open-endedness" instead of looking to the New Testament to point out fulfillments of Old Testament prophecy.[27] Here, the FFC observed, professors recognized that their approach did not match that of the Lutheran Confessions, which holds that Old Testament believers were saved by faith in the coming Christ (Ap IV 57; FC SD V 23).[28]

3. *"This-worldly" expressions of the Gospel.* Social action was Gospel in a certain sense, a professor said.[29] A pastoral conference heard from a professor that Gospel wasn't fully Gospel without social action.[30] The Gospel "cannot be formulated in terms enduringly valid," John Tietjen wrote shortly before he became president of Concordia Seminary in 1969, for "the world's needs should determine the form and shape in which the gospel is expressed."[31]

---

24 Prof. G [Herbert Mayer], Blue Book (Zimmerman, 252).

25 Prof. S [Arthur Repp], Blue Book (Zimmerman, 318). See an article by another professor, Norman C. Habel, "The Gospel Promise to Abraham," *CTM* 40 (June, July–August 1969): 26–35.

26 FFC report (Zimmerman, 184). See Prof. B [Alfred von Rohr Sauer], Blue Book (Zimmerman, 319–20).

27 FFC report (Zimmerman, 184), quoting Arlis John Ehlen, "Old Testament Theology as *Heilsgeschichte*," *CTM* 35 (October 1964): 540.

28 Blue Book (Zimmerman, 312).

29 Prof. S [Arthur Repp], Blue Book (Zimmerman, 273).

30 Blue Book (Zimmerman, 274), quoting "The Meaning of Gospel," Eastern Missouri Pastoral Conference, 1968.

31 Blue Book (Zimmerman, 274, 275), quoting John H. Tietjen, "The Gospel and the Theological Task," *CTM* 40 (June, July–August 1969): 119, 120.

A Statement of Scriptural and Confessional Principles

In March 1972, President Preus released guidelines to help the St. Louis seminary's board sort through theological issues. This *Statement of Scriptural and Confessional Principles* included subsection IV.C. "The Gospel and Holy Scripture."[32] It pointed to justification by grace for Christ's sake as the heart of the Christian faith and upheld "the prophetic and apostolic writings of the Old and New Testaments" as "the only rule and norm" by which to judge teachings and teachers (FC Ep Rule and Norm 1). *A Statement* summarized:

> The Gospel which is the center of our theology is the Gospel to which the *Scriptures* bear witness, while the Scriptures from which we derive our theology direct us steadfastly to the *Gospel* of Jesus Christ.

A Statement rejected certain ideas, including that "acceptance of the Bible as such, rather than the Gospel, is the heart and center of Christian faith and theology, and the way to eternal salvation." It also rejected any thought that "Christians need not accept matters taught in the Scriptures that are not a part of the 'Gospel.'"[33]

Opponents of *A Statement* found that last point particularly objectionable, as if it were saying that "the message which Christians must accept to be true Christians, is *more* than Christ alone" but rather believing whatever the Bible says.[34] Putting the best foot forward for Gospel reductionism, St. Louis professor Edward Schroeder wrote in April 1972: "It is hard to read" the critics of Gospel reductionism "without hearing them pushing their convictions about Biblical inspiration as a *requirement* before God will really be pleased with a person. Clearly they do not want to be saying that," Schroeder allowed, yet he continued with his impression.[35] The faculty as a whole cautioned against casting the Bible as a law to be obeyed in its message to the 1972 graduates, "A Parting Peace," warning also about prizing one's faith for

---

32 *A Statement* included the terms "material" and "formal" principles, on which see the note at the end of this chapter.

33 *A Statement*, part IV.C and points 1 and 4 (italics original; cf. below, p. 268). Compare Robert D. Preus, *The Theology of Post-Reformation Lutheranism: A Study of Theological Prolegomena* (St. Louis: Concordia Publishing House, 1970), 331, 410–11.

34 Paul G. Bretscher, *After the Purifying: Thirty-Second Yearbook* (River Forest, IL: Lutheran Education Association, 1975), 63 (italics original).

35 Edward H. Schroeder, "Law-Gospel Reductionism in the History of The Lutheran Church—Missouri Synod," *CTM* 43 (April 1972): 236 (italics original).

its correctness.[36] What is important is not how many amazing things one believes; faith should not become a good work.[37]

The faculty complained that Preus's *Statement* "puts the Gospel and the Holy Scriptures into a false opposition."[38] One professor had told the FFC that "right now what we need like a hole in the head is to distinguish the Scripture from the Gospel."[39] He wanted the two to have the same boundaries, as it were. (A later book likewise argued that Scripture should not be "regarded as broader than the Gospel."[40]) The professor said he meant "Gospel" broadly speaking, including all the articles of faith.[41]

The rub came, however, when people encountered items in the Bible that they deemed to be unrelated to the Gospel—such as an historical Adam and Eve, a world flood, various miracles, etc. Could such things be set aside? Were they in a sense not even *Scripture*? "A Parting Peace" had cautioned about retaining "all sorts of facts, but not as Gospel facts, hence not the facts of Scripture."[42]

People were noticing what the St. Louis faculty was saying. In December 1972, Concordia Theological Seminary professor David Scaer warned about shifting the basis of theology "from what Scripture says to what the Gospel allows."[43]

Faithful to Our Calling, Faithful to Our Lord

At about the same time as Scaer was issuing his warning, the Concordia Seminary faculty released *Faithful to Our Calling, Faithful to Our Lord: An Affirmation in Two Parts*. Part II consisted of statements by individual professors, but Part I was a "Joint Statement and Discussion of Issues." Its "Preamble" asked rhetorically, "Is the Gospel alone sufficient as the ground of faith and the governing principle for Lutheran theology?"[44]

---

36 See Zimmerman, 270, 278.

37 Robert W. Bertram, *Faithful* II, 19–20. See Zimmerman, 299–300.

38 "Response of the Faculty of Concordia Seminary, St. Louis," *LW*, April 30, 1972, 30. See *Memoirs*, 54, 55, 132–33 *et passim*.

39 Prof. R [Robert Bertram], Blue Book (Zimmerman, 268); *Memoirs*, 38.

40 Bretscher, *After the Purifying*, 63.

41 Prof. R [Robert Bertram], Blue Book (Zimmerman, 268, repeated on 277); *Memoirs*, 39. Similar: Prof. I [John Tietjen], Blue Book (Zimmerman, 276).

42 Zimmerman, 299.

43 David P. Scaer, "The Law-Gospel Debate in the Missouri Synod," *Spr* 36 (December 1972): 159.

44 *Faithful* I, 3.

Various "discussion" topics followed. In these, the most memorable single statement made by the faculty was: "The Gospel gives the Scriptures their normative character, not vice-versa."[45] The phrase "normative character" was a novelty at that time, and it still is. Keeping in mind that a *norm* is a *standard*, we can see how remarkable the faculty's statement was. It was not simply saying that the Holy Spirit's work through the biblical Gospel causes people to accede to Scripture as standard. It said the Gospel makes Scripture a standard.[46]

Returning to the parent-and-child comparison, it can readily be seen that parents' "I love you" leads children to accept other things that parents say, everything about which they may say, "I said so." Likewise, the Gospel in Scripture moves Christians to accept whatever God says in Scripture. But the faculty claimed that the Gospel gives Scripture its normative character. That would be as if parents saying "I love you" is what gives them the parental authority to say "I said so."

Yet parents are not the only people who can tell children that their parents love them. And the Gospel is contained in writings other than the Bible. So would the Gospel in a devotional resource such as *Portals of Prayer* give that devotional "normative character"? If so, what would this "normative character" amount to? Could a human writing such as *Portals of Prayer* become the standard for Christian teaching?

This example helps us to see the trouble with the faculty's attempt to base Scripture's normative authority strictly on the fact that it contains the Gospel. Any Gospel proclamation would be of equal rank with Scripture. No specific writing, Scripture or any other, could be identified as *the* norm or standard for theology. So, would one have to spot the genuine Gospel only on an "I'll know it when I hear it" basis?[47]

Gospel and Scripture

Just under six months before the Synod's 1973 convention, the CTCR mailed out the report *Gospel and Scripture*, which had been drafted by one

---

45   *Faithful* I, 21. See a similar statement by the faculty in *Faithful* I, 28, and by President Tietjen in *Faithful* II, 7.

46   See the later ACDC discussions by the moderate caucus (*ACDC*, 41, 75) and the conservative caucus (*ACDC*, 46, 53). See also Jack D. Kilcrease, *Holy Scripture*, vol. 2 of Confessional Lutheran Dogmatics, ed. Gifford A. Grobien (Fort Wayne, IN: Luther Academy, 2020), 108–9.

47   See J. Valentinus Andreae, "Prerequisite of Lutheran Loyalty: *Sola Scriptura* and the Word-of-God Character of the Bible," *Sola Scriptura: An International Voice of Authentic Lutheranism* 1 (July–August 1970): 21.

of its members, Pastor Harry Huth.[48] His outline drew on a sentence from Edmund Schlink that "the Gospel is the norm in [the St. Louis faculty had said *of*] Scripture and Scripture is the norm for the sake of the Gospel."[49] Strengthening Schlink's statement, the CTCR divided its report into two halves:

- *Gospel as Norm in the Scriptures*: Since the "Scriptures [are] given to us for the sake of the Gospel," a doctrine or practice that runs contrary to the Gospel cannot agree with Scripture. However, the Gospel is itself taught in Scripture. It is the Bible's chief teaching, but not a principle from which other points of doctrine are derived. The Gospel does not permit anyone to limit or disregard Scripture's contents.[50]

- *Scripture as Norm of the Gospel*: The Gospel is not true or powerful by reason of the fact that it is recorded in Scripture. God gave people the Gospel before anyone wrote it down. However, today we must go to the Bible to determine whether the Gospel we teach is the Gospel as taught by God there.[51] If our Gospel is not *that* Gospel, it will not be true and it will not have power.

The CTCR summarized:

> Lutheran theology has always affirmed the authority of the Bible on a two-fold basis: (1) That as Gospel the Sacred Scriptures are the power of God unto salvation through which the Holy Spirit begets the faith that grasps Christ and sets men free from sin and death ["causative authority"]; (2) That as God's inspired Word the Sacred Scriptures regulate the faith that is believed, taught, and confessed in the church ["normative authority"].

Neither of these is to be played off against the other. "Can the source [Scripture] deny the central thought [the Gospel], or the central thought [the Gospel] nullify the source [Scripture]?"[52]

---

48 See Karl L. Barth, *Just a Chip Off the Old Blog* (Milwaukee: PIP Printing, 2008), 43–44. Huth is named as author of *Gospel and Scripture* in Robert Preus, "Biblical Authority in the Lutheran Confessions," *CJ* 4 (January 1978): 24 n. 7. A summary of *Gospel and Scripture* by CTCR executive Ralph A. Bohlmann appeared in *LW*, January 7, 1973, 18–19.

49 Schlink, *Theology of the Lutheran Confessions*, 6. Compare *Faithful* I, 28.

50 *Gospel and Scripture*, 7; see *Gospel and Scripture*, 7–14.

51 See *Gospel and Scripture*, 14–20.

52 *Gospel and Scripture*, 21. See Harry A. Huth, "A Response to Dr. Kramer's Gospel—Scripture Relationship," in *Heritage*, 28–32.

Scripture and the Lutheran Confessions

The biblical teaching on faith bears on our topic. The object of saving faith is the Gospel of Christ, not the Law. Galatians 3:12: "The law is not of faith." The Law is God's Word, one of the two main topics in Scripture. But faith as it saves does not have as its object the Law, or the entire Bible.[53] It believes Christ, in whom there is grace and truth, and so receives Him (John 1:12 and 17). Furthermore, faith in Christ is God's gift (Ephesians 2:8–9; Philippians 1:29). It is not a good work and no cause for pride (Luke 18:9–14). Justification is *through* faith, not *on account of* it. The St. Louis faculty had good reason to make these points.

In the Bible, no one started speaking the Gospel by making a case for biblical inerrancy. The faculty observed this too, but the insight was hardly new. A half-century before the Walkout, Concordia Seminary president Francis Pieper wrote:

> In dealing with an unbeliever we cannot begin with an attempt to convince him of the divine authority of Scripture. We must first bring him to the knowledge of his sins and to faith in Christ, the Redeemer from sin.[54]

After people are converted to Christ by the Holy Spirit through the Gospel, they will want to have the same attitude toward Scripture that Jesus had.[55]

When people are justified by faith, it is in their new nature to take God at His word in everything He says.[56] In this sense, they believe all that is laid down and written in the Scriptures (Acts 24:14; see Deuteronomy 32:46). When Jesus told Peter to put his boat out and let his nets down, Peter did not say he would listen to Jesus only regarding salvation. He responded, "At Your word I will," not "What does this have to do with the Gospel?" Peter was not trying to find God's *real* Word within the sayings of Jesus (Luke 5:1–11). Elsewhere Jesus said, "Whoever is of God hears the words of God" (John 8:47).

St. Paul's proclamation centered on Christ crucified (1 Corinthians 2:2), but this in no way conflicted with his declaring "the whole counsel of God"

---

53 See Pieper 2:423–24.

54 Pieper 1:137–38.

55 See Jacob A. O. Preus, *It Is Written* (St. Louis: Concordia Publishing House, 1971).

56 Pieper 2:423–24. See Martin Chemnitz, *Loci Theologici, Part II*, trans. J. A. O. Preus, Chemnitz's Works 8 (St. Louis: Concordia Publishing House, 2008), 915–18, 927–32; and Johann Gerhard, *On Justification through Faith*, trans. Richard J. Dinda, ed. Joshua J. Hayes and Heath R. Curtis, gen. ed. Benjamin T. G. Mayes, Theological Commonplaces (St. Louis: Concordia Publishing House, 2018), 115, 122, 242–45; also Eugene F. Klug, "Saving Faith and the Inerrancy of Scripture," *Spr* 39 (March 1976): 202–11.

(Acts 20:27). Paul pointed out that he proclaimed the Gospel in accordance with Scripture (1 Corinthians 15:3–4; see Acts 17:2; 26:22–23; 28:23). His hearers did not have to fall back on their own belief as the authority. The church, he wrote, is "built on the foundation of the apostles and prophets, Christ Jesus Himself being the cornerstone" (Ephesians 2:20). In fact, the "noble" Bereans took Paul's message and held it up against the standard of the Scriptures "to see if these things were so" (Acts 17:11). Paul was preaching the Gospel, but they did not think his words gave the Old Testament its authority. Instead, they used Scripture as their standard to evaluate even the Gospel proclamation of the apostle.

Speeches at the apostolic council in Jerusalem demonstrate two ways of evaluating a teaching in the church. Peter in effect asked whether the teaching of the circumcision party did violence to the Gospel. It did (Acts 15:7–11; this criterion was also employed by the Lutheran Confessions, e.g., SA II II 1; II III 2; II IV 3). Then James assessed the Judaizers' teaching by citing Scripture. What they taught could not be part of the Gospel, nor could it be permitted in the church, because it was not based on Scripture and opposed Scripture (Acts 15:13–21). The Formula of Concord recognized "the prophetic and apostolic writings of the Old and New Testaments" as "the pure, clear fountain of Israel, which alone is the one true guiding principle [or *norma*], according to which all teachers and teachings are to be judged and evaluated" (FC SD Rule and Norm 3).[57] As Luther wrote in the Smalcald Articles: "the Word of God—and no one else, not even an angel—should establish articles of faith" (SA II II 15; see Galatians 1:8).[58] Luther did *not* write: "The articles of faith shall establish the Word of God, and nothing else, not even the Bible."[59]

The Lutheran Confessions acknowledged that Scripture as a whole is to be divided into two main topics: "the law and the promises" (Ap IV 5), or Law and Gospel. This distinction stands out as "an especially glorious light" (FC Ep V 2) for understanding the Bible.[60] Article V of the Formula of Concord noted that while *Gospel* most properly means the comforting Good News of Christ and forgiveness (FC Ep V 7), Scripture also sometimes uses the word more broadly, even to include the Law (FC Ep V 6). Both Law and Gospel have content. Each teaches something (what is right and God-pleasing;

---

57   K-W, 527.

58   K-W, 304. Compare Ap XXIV 92.

59   Kurt E. Marquart, "The Swing of the Pendulum: An Attempt to Understand the St. Louis 'Affirmations and Discussions,' " in *Truth, Salvatory and Churchly: Works of Kurt E. Marquart*, ed. Ken Schurb and Robert Paul (N.p.: Luther Academy, 2018), 3:54.

60   K-W, 121, 500.

that Christ has paid for all sins—FC Ep V 3, 5) and does something (condemns; comforts and raises up—FC Ep V 4, 7). The Augsburg Confession noted that faith in Christ believes "the effect of the [saving] history, namely, this article of the forgiveness of sins"—yet not to the exclusion of the history itself, which it also believes (AC XX 23).[61]

Recall our parent-and-child comparison. Parents often say "I said so" in reference to rules of conduct. Sometimes they might say this about factual matters that do not impinge directly on their relationship with their children. In these cases, parents are speaking with their authority as parents when they say, "I said so." And there are also times when a child needs reassurance of a parent's love. Then the best thing the child can hear from that parent is "I love you. I'm telling you." There the parent's "I love you" is reinforced by an "I said so." Here, too, the parent gives an authoritative word, in this case a word of good news.

In Scripture the God who never lies (Titus 1:2) proclaims His Good News. Although "we can affirm nothing about the will of God without the Word of God" (Ap XV 17), in the Gospel God Himself makes the greatest affirmation sinners can hear, proclaiming forgiveness in the Christ who atoned for sins and delivers from death (FC SD V 19–20).[62] Article IV of the Apology of the Augsburg Confession observed that "a human being, particularly in the terrors of sin, cannot be sure of the will of God (namely, that he ceases to be angry) without a sure Word of God."[63] Think of the absolution, in which pastors go out of their way to make it clear that the forgiveness they are pronouncing is not their own, but God's. It matters who is saying this! It makes a huge difference that this forgiving message comes from the Lord Himself. "It is God who justifies. Who is to condemn?" (Romans 8:33–34). God's "I love you" is reinforced by His "I said so."

The Gospel taught in Scripture is not *undercut* but is *underscored* by God's authoritative speech in Scripture. This Gospel comes to sinners from *the* Author, God Himself. In the words of a hymn:

By grace I'm saved, grace free and boundless;
My soul, believe and doubt it not.
Why stagger at this word of promise?
Has Scripture ever falsehood taught?[64]

---

61   K-W, 57. See Ap IV 50–51 (K-W, 128).

62   K-W, 225, 584–85. See the Preface to the Book of Concord 22 (K-W, 14) and LC V 31 (K-W, 469–70).

63   K-W, 161 (compare Ap IV 262 in Tappert, 145); see Ap XII 88 (K-W, 202).

64   "By Grace I'm Saved," *LSB* 566:1. See also "Salvation unto Us Has Come," *LSB* 555:7.

What Happened

1973 Convention

At its 1973 convention, in Res. 3-09, "To Declare Faculty Majority Position in Violation of Article II of the [Synod's] Constitution," the LCMS said much concerning Gospel and Scripture.[65] It noted that for the St. Louis faculty majority, the norm of theology was not the Scriptures but rather "the 'Gospel' abstracted from them." The resolution added that making the Gospel the "governing principle" of theology, as the faculty majority insisted, amounted to a step in the erosion of biblical authority.

It is an illusion to expect to hold on to the Gospel under such circumstances, the resolution added, especially when modern historical criticism is applied to the Bible. It affirmed that an emphasis on the Gospel is certainly salutary. But if the Gospel we believe and teach is not firmly rooted in Scripture, the Synod said, other teachings of human origin "are bound to intrude." The Gospel itself can become clouded. The resolution observed that for all the stress on the Gospel in *Faithful* I, the faculty in that work had not mentioned vicarious satisfaction, substitutionary atonement, or imputation of Christ's righteousness. Not only had these terms been absent, so was the theology to which the terms refer. Even "the hope of eternal life in heaven" got short shrift.

Nor was that all. "With this there is a definite, studied avoidance of Christ's avowal concerning the Old Testament Scriptures that 'they are they which testify of Me.' "[66] Here, some elaboration is in order. *A Statement*, adopted in 1973, contained a subsection on "Old Testament Prophecy" (part IV.H).[67] It cited the notion that "the Old Testament, read on its own terms, does not bear witness to Jesus Christ" and rejected it (part IV.B.2).[68] This shoe seemed to fit *Faithful* I, which had been content to characterize the content of the promise in the Old Testament as Adam's "new lease" on life after the fall, Cain's mark of protection, Noah's rescue from the flood together with "a promise of God's concern for all men," and Abraham' reception of promises of a land and nation, numerous seed, and "the privilege of mediating God's blessing to other nations."[69] In an extensive critique of *Faithful* I, Kurt Marquart pointed out that while nothing could be "more gloriously

---

65 1973 *Proceedings*, 133–39.

66 1973 *Proceedings*, 136–37; quotation from 1973 *Proceedings*, 137, citing John 5:39.

67 See below, p. 271.

68 See below, p. 267.

69 *Faithful* I, 28.

Christ-centered and Gospel-oriented" than direct prophecies of Christ, the faculty shied away from them. Instead, it warned against what it called premature leaps into the New Testament to understand the Old Testament.[70]

Continuing Controversy

More than a year after the 1973 convention, a vigorous assertion of the Gospel as theology's governing principle—indeed, as *the* Word of God—appeared in the 1975 Lutheran Education Association yearbook.[71] The author, Paul G. Bretscher, was the son of a Concordia Seminary professor. He himself had studied at that seminary, eventually earning a doctorate in theology. He had written for the seminary's journal supporting the faculty majority position. Bretscher claimed that in Scripture and in Luther's catechisms "Word of God" basically means Christ and the Gospel proclaiming Christ. Occasionally Bretscher defined *Gospel* broadly, so as also to include the Law, but he emphasized that "Word of God" really refers to Scripture only insofar as Scripture brings the Gospel message. Basically, Bretscher contended that "Word of God" means Gospel, not Scripture. However, he added, Missouri Synod tradition thinks of the "Word of God" in a different way: as the Bible itself.[72]

Many answered Bretscher.[73] Several responses cited places where the Lutheran Confessions employ the terms *Word of God* and *Scripture* interchangeably (for example, AC XXVIII 35, German and Latin texts; FC SD Rule and Norm 3 and 9).[74] Also noted were places where the German text says "Word of God" and the Latin translation done at the time says "Scripture."[75]

Bretscher recognized that the Confessions sometimes did use the phrase "Word of God" in reference to the Bible. He classified this as ambiguity that

---

70 Marquart, "Swing of the Pendulum," 61, 62, quoting or referring to *Faithful* I, 30, 28.

71 See above, p. 23 n. 34.

72 Bretscher, *After the Purifying*, 12–19.

73 See Harry A. Huth, review of *After the Purifying* by Paul G. Bretscher, in *LQ* [o.s.] 27 (August 1975): 262–64; Paul A. Zimmerman, "A Vital Point," *Lutheran Education* 111 (September–October 1975): 1–2; Raymond F. Surburg, "Paul Bretscher's *After the Purifying*: A Review Article," *Spr* 39 (March 1976): 212–15; David P. Scaer, "The Law-Gospel Debate in the Missouri Synod Continued," *Spr* 40 (September 1976): 107–18; "Dr. Paul G. Bretscher's 'The Sword of the Spirit': An Evaluation by the Department of Systematic Theology, Concordia Theological Seminary, Fort Wayne, Indiana—June, 1979," *CTQ* 43 (October 1979): 327–37.

74 K-W, 96, 97, 527–28.

75 The CTCR had listed such quotes from the Lutheran Confessions in *Gospel and Scripture*, 19–20.

had not been cleared up.[76] In effect, he was acknowledging that his contention lacked support from the Confessions. At any rate, Bretscher's book forms a prime example of "Gospel and Scripture" remaining a controverted subject in the Missouri Synod after the Walkout.

The Difference This Makes

Returning to the questions with which we started this chapter—Why *should* people believe the Bible? Why *do* people believe the Bible? And are these two questions asking the same thing?—let's consider the following lessons to be learned.

Lutherans are not legalistic when they acknowledge Scripture as norm.

Although the two questions are related, they remain distinct. It is one thing to ask why people *should* believe the Bible. It is another to ask why they *do* believe it.

Recognizing an authoritative standard outside oneself has not been popular in modern or postmodern times. Yet God Himself certainly ranks as authoritative, and He should remain the authority in theology.[77] In Scripture He says what He wants to say, as He wants to say it. The Bible is His Word. This is why anyone *should* believe the Bible.

God creates saving faith through the Gospel, and as a result of this working, people believe what He says in the Scriptures. This is why Christians *do* believe the Bible.

The Bible's authority in the church is a matter not only of what Scripture *does* but also of what it *is*. Parents cause their children to recognize their authority by showing them love—among other ways through their words. Yet their authority is not based solely on their affirmations of love. Our contemporary world may not especially like this, but parents have authority by virtue of the fact that they are parents. Likewise, by bringing people the Gospel (God's "I love you" because of Christ), Scripture creates faith in Christ and acceptance of all its teachings. Yet Scripture serves as norm for Christian doctrine because it is God's own Word. In fact, it remains God's Word whether or not people recognize it as such.

---

76 See Bretscher, *After the Purifying*, 21 n. 30. For a contrasting view concerning Luther, see M. Reu, *Luther and the Scriptures* (Columbus, OH: Wartburg Press, 1944; repr., *Spr* 24 [August 1960]: 8–111), esp. 51–56.

77 See David P. Scaer, "Theses on the Law and the Gospel," *Spr* 37 (June 1973): 53–63.

The Lutheran Confessions present a parallel case concerning good works. All people *should* do good works because God has commanded these works. Christians actually *do* genuine good works—that is, they bring forth the fruit of the Spirit—because they have been renewed by the Holy Spirit through the Gospel.[78]

Remember, while it is true that a parent can tell a child, "Do this, because I said so," a parent can also say another kind of word: "I love you. I said so." It is not necessarily Law when God, even in all His authority, says something to His human creatures. Whether a word from God is Law or Gospel depends, first, on what it says.

Acknowledge Scripture as norm.

If the Scriptures are not regarded as the authority to tell us what the Gospel is, something else will take their place.

As discussed earlier, you can get the Gospel from *Portals of Prayer*, but only as *Portals of Prayer* got it from the Bible. *Portals of Prayer* can be wrong. To determine whether *Portals of Prayer* really is teaching the Gospel, we must compare it not with our own ideas or those of any other human being but rather with what God Himself teaches in Scripture.

The basis of theology should be not whatever the Gospel allows. We can persuade ourselves that the Gospel allows all sorts of things. Instead, the basis of theology should be what the Scriptures teach. As the Formula of Concord says concerning the person of Christ: "In this case we have the clear, certain testimonies in the Scripture, which we should simply believe and to which we should not raise any objections" (FC SD VIII 53).[79]

This does not add another condition for salvation. The Gospel, not something else, is the Gospel. But the Gospel will not remain the Good News that it is if people proclaim it according to some standard other than Scripture.

Don't use one thing God says to deny another.

During the sixteenth century, Ulrich Zwingli maintained that if Christ has a body, as Scripture says, it must be in one place and not on countless altars as the Lord's Supper is celebrated. Further, Zwingli thought that even if Christ's body were present, it would profit nothing and would have nothing to do with the Gospel of salvation. Luther responded that he needed to stick to God's Word, which does not lie, and the Lutheran Confessions followed

---

78 See Harry A. Huth, "Fact Finding or Fault Finding?" *Affirm* 2 (January 1973): 4–5, 7.

79 K-W, 626.

suit. One thing God said would not be used to deny another. Luther and the Lutheran Confessions stayed with the Lord's words: "This is My body."[80]

The St. Louis faculty placed great importance on an interpreter connecting various points of theology to the Gospel. Trouble arose, however, when they and others found difficulties in relating to the Gospel certain matters such as historicity or authorship of biblical materials, and so deemed these matters dispensable.[81]

It can become subjective and slippery to claim that various things Scripture says are unrelated to the Gospel, let alone unnecessary. For instance, Jesus said that "in the resurrection they neither marry nor are given in marriage" (Matthew 22:30). Is this statement related to the Gospel? Some might say no, for knowledge about marital status in the resurrection will not save anyone. Yet the statement describes the future heavenly home of all sinners for whom Christ died and rose, the place He is preparing. That *is* related to the Gospel. Overall, as the CTCR put it: "Every question about what Scripture says or teaches is already a 'Gospel question' simply because it is a question about Scripture given to us by God *for the sake of the Gospel!*"[82] (See Romans 15:4.)

We at times may have difficulty seeing the connections between the Gospel and a given biblical point. In any case, such difficulties do not release us from the authority of the biblical text.[83] Don't use one thing God says to deny another. Any difficulties should be left to Him.[84]

The Gospel does not float above the biblical text.

The faculty majority along with others liked to point out that the truth of the Gospel was not dependent on biblical inerrancy, for the Gospel had been proclaimed even before it was written down. However, they went on to conclude that the truth of the Gospel is unrelated to biblical inerrancy—as

---

80 See FC Ep VII 11–14 (K-W, 505), also Robert David Preus, "1973 Reformation Lectures: How Is the Lutheran Church to Interpret and Use the Old and New Testaments?" *The Lutheran Synod Quarterly* 14 (Fall 1973): 16–18.

81 *ACDC*, 52.

82 *Gospel and Scripture*, 14 (italics original).

83 Especially the last point was made by Martin Scharlemann, a Concordia Seminary professor who stood against the faculty majority, in a May 18, 1972, lecture and also in a question-and-answer session with students on October 24, 1973: audio archived at https://scholar.csl.edu/synodhistory/SynodicalHistory/Year/32/ and https://scholar.csl.edu/synodhistory/Synodical_History/Year/17/.

84 See Robert D. Preus, "Luther and the Doctrine of Justification," *CTQ* 48 (January 1984): 1–15.

if Gospel proclamation today could go on unimpeded, regardless of what anyone makes of discrepancies in Scripture.[85] However, John Warwick Montgomery noted:

> The irony of this attempt [by the faculty] to make Christian belief rest on "the promise of a faithful God" and not on a reliable scriptural revelation is, obviously, that *apart from the Bible we do not know what God's promises are.*[86]

Luther and the Lutheran Confessions roundly condemned "enthusiasm," that is, religion apart from God's external Word. Disconnecting the Gospel from the biblical text results in a form of enthusiasm.[87]

Scripture as norm means that Christians, individually or collectively, are not the authority for the Gospel.

It makes a massive difference what determines the content of theology: an inspired Scripture that stands above me, or my own thoughts or piety assisting me at least in part to figure out what I can accept as "Word of God for me."[88]

Neither the individual Christian nor the church collectively can serve as a guarantor for the Gospel or as its protector. Not even the Lutheran Church! For "it is downright 'un-Lutheran' to state that we hold to any tenet of Lutheran theology, including the Gospel, simply because it is Lutheran."[89]

The Gospel can be defended historically.

Gospel reductionism discourages defending the Gospel by recourse to the Bible or the history it recounts. Therefore Gospel reductionism leaves inquirers about Christianity to conclude, in Montgomery's characterization, "that only 'personal experience' will validate Christian claims and the soundness of the law-gospel distinction."[90] But a case *can* be made for Christ historically, answering baseless objections. This effort does not require unbelievers to regard biblical books as God's own Word, only as generally reliable historical sources. The Holy Spirit's power is then unleashed through the Gospel set

---

85   Moderate caucus, *ACDC*, 66; compare conservative caucus, *ACDC*, 57.

86   Montgomery, "Unbridgeable Chasm," *Crisis* 1:143 (italics original).

87   SA III VIII 3–13 (K-W, 322–23). See E. F. Klug, "Missouri Mules," *Affirm* 2 (December 1972): 7; also Res. 3-09, 1973 *Proceedings*, 136.

88   See Horace D. Hummel, "Gospel and Bible," *Affirm Occasional Papers* (Spring 1973): 29.

89   Scaer, "Theses on the Law and the Gospel," 60.

90   Montgomery, "Gospel Reductionism," *Crisis* 3:112.

forth in the biblical books to convert people and bring them to the same attitude toward Scripture that Jesus Himself had. Yet none of this is possible if all I can tell inquirers is that I have faith in what I have faith in.

Be like Abraham!

Once God told Abraham, *Kill your son.* If anyone in the Bible might have had occasion to ask God, "What does this have to do with the Gospel?" it would have been Abraham at that time. Yet Abraham did not try to get around God's words, even though they flew in the face not only of "divine and natural law but also the most important article of the faith, regarding the promised seed, Christ, who was to be born of Isaac." Abraham "honored God by believing him," taking the Lord's words as they came, regardless of his own reason (FC SD VII 46, reflecting on Genesis 22:1–18). He kept trusting God's promises (Hebrews 11:17–19) while heeding everything the Lord had said.[91] No Gospel reductionism here!

For Discussion

1. In your own words, how does *A Statement of Scriptural and Confessional Principles* summarize the relationship between Gospel and Scripture?

2. What is Gospel reductionism? Give examples.

3. In what way can it be said that Christians believe the Scriptures? In what way should this not be said?

4. Why should people believe the Bible? Why do they believe the Bible? What results might follow if these questions are not distinguished from each other?

5. Does the distinction between Law and Gospel allow a reader to determine that something in Scripture may not be as the Bible says it is? Why or why not? Consider Abraham in Genesis 22:1–18.

6. Choose one of the other theological lessons in the section "The Difference This Makes." Tell what you think of it.

7. Evaluate the statement: "To say we must bow to what God has said, no matter what he has said, is to blur the distinction between Law and Gospel."

---

91 K-W, 601. Compare Luther, *This Is My Body* (1527), AE 37:26, 127–28, cited in Armand John Boehme, "A Study in Luther's Anti-Sacramentarian Writings," *Spr* 38 (March 1975): 303–14.

Digging Deeper

Bohlmann, Ralph, [and] Robert Bertram. "Holy Scripture and the Gospel" 10:00 AM–10:00 AM [sic] and 11:00 AM–11:00 AM [sic]. Audio recording archived at https://scholar.csl.edu/synodhistory/Synodical_History /Year/13/and https://scholar.csl.edu/synodhistory/Synodical_History /Year/14/. Accessed 9/6/2022.

Bretscher, Paul G. *After the Purifying: Thirty-Second Yearbook*. River Forest, IL: Lutheran Education Association, 1975.

CTCR. *Gospel and Scripture: The Interrelationship of the Material and Formal Principles in Lutheran Theology*. St. Louis: LCMS, 1972.

Marquart, Kurt E. "The Swing of the Pendulum: An Attempt to Understand the St. Louis 'Affirmations and Discussions.'" Pages 31–74 in *Essays Historical and Historic*. Volume 3 of *Truth, Salvatory and Churchly: Works of Kurt E. Marquart*. Edited by Ken Schurb and Robert Paul. N.p.: Luther Academy, 2018.

> **NOTE:** LCMS discussions of Gospel and Scripture during the first half of the 1970s sometimes spoke of "material" and "formal" principles.[92] However, only occasionally did anyone discuss the terms themselves.[93] In his FFC interview, Prof. R (Robert Bertram) said he did not know the origin of the distinction between formal and material principles.[94] Additional historical work has been done since on these terms and their background.[95]

---

92 See *A Statement* subsection IV.C. "The Gospel and Holy Scripture" (below, pp. 267–68).

93 E.g., Huth, review of *After the Purifying*, 263–64; Walter E. Keller, Kenneth F. Korby, Robert C. Schultz, and David G. Truemper, "A Review Essay of *A Statement of Scriptural and Confessional Principles*," *The Cresset* 36 (March 1973): 15.

94 Blue Book (Zimmerman, 268); *Memoirs*, 38.

95 See Eric M. Heen, "The Distinction 'Material/Formal Principles' and Its Use in American Lutheran Theology," *LQ* [n.s.] 17 (Autumn 2003): 329–54; Charles P. Schaum and Albert B. Collver III, *Breath of God, Yet Work of Man: Scripture, Philosophy, Dialogue, and Conflict* (St. Louis: Concordia Publishing House, 2019).

CHAPTER TWO

THE NATURE OF SCRIPTURE

Martin R. Noland

The basic problem at Concordia Seminary from 1951 to 1974 was two different views of the nature of the Holy Scriptures. One view, which is the one taught by the Bible and the *Book of Concord*, is that the Holy Scriptures are the Word of God. The other view, which arose in the seventeenth century and is the dominant view in universities today, is that the Holy Scriptures are merely human writings and have limited truthfulness because of the "primitive worldview" of their authors.

Introduction

People become Christians, and churches are started, when they believe the testimony of the apostles and prophets concerning Jesus Christ, trusting that it is true, relevant, and applicable to them personally. Reflecting on his missionary work in Thessalonica, St. Paul wrote the new Christians there: "We also thank God constantly for this, that when you received the word of God, which you heard from us, you accepted it not as the word of men but as what it really is, the word of God, which is at work in you believers" (1 Thessalonians 2:13). What happens, though, when Christians lose confidence that the Bible is the Word of God?

This is not just a matter for theological debate; it is a matter of eternal life and death. People become Christians when they believe that God has forgiven their sins on account of Christ. But who says that Jesus is their Savior? Who says that God forgives their sins on account of Christ? These essential doctrines of the Gospel cannot be discovered through science or even through the natural knowledge of God. Although revealed in prophecy, the Gospel was a mystery until the coming of John the Baptist and Jesus. The Gospel is a mystery to us, and others, until it has been "disclosed and through the prophetic writings made known to all nations, according to the command of the eternal God, to bring about the obedience of faith" (Romans 16:26). These "prophetic writings" are none other than the Old and New Testaments of Scripture.

How do we know that the Bible is the Word of God and that it is true? The apostles and prophets who wrote the Bible were assisted in that task by the Holy Spirit. This is the Holy Spirit's special work. The Nicene Creed says that He "spoke by the prophets." Jesus explicitly promised the Holy Spirit's assistance to His apostles with these words: "The Holy Spirit, whom the Father will send in My name, He will teach you all things and bring to your remembrance all that I have said to you" (John 14:26). Because of the apostles' intent to tell the truth, and even more because of the assistance of the Holy Spirit, you can believe that the apostles' accounts of Jesus' words and deeds in the Gospels and Epistles are true. St. Paul observed that every part of the Bible was the work of the Holy Spirit when he said, "All Scripture is breathed out by God and profitable for teaching, for reproof, for correction, and for training in righteousness" (2 Timothy 3:16). Therefore all of Scripture is God's Word, true, relevant, and applicable to everyone in every place and every time.

For anyone who grew up in the LCMS or another church body that teaches that the Bible is God's Word, what I have just stated may seem obvious. What is a mystery is how a Christian could believe in Christ yet deny that the Bible is God's Word in some or all its parts. But we should not be surprised. St. Peter warned: "False prophets also arose among the people [of Israel], just as there will be false teachers among you, who will secretly bring in destructive heresies" (2 Peter 2:1); and St. John admonished: "Beloved, do not believe every spirit, but test the spirits to see whether they are from God, for many false prophets have gone out into the world" (1 John 4:1).

Historical Background

How did large segments of the Christian world come to think that some, most, or all of the Bible is not God's Word? It ended up taking more than just a few alleged contradictions here and there in the Bible to overturn its authority. What really caused that "revolution" was an alternate philosophy that replaced the Christian faith and its theology. This was provided in the early seventeenth century by the philosopher Edward Herbert (1583–1648), the First Baron Herbert of Cherbury in England.[1] In 1624, Herbert published his book *De Veritate*, which set forth his philosophy about common or natural religion. He developed his ideas in more detail in *Religione Laici*

---

1   See Henning Graf Reventlow, *The Authority of the Bible and the Rise of the Modern World* (Philadelphia: Fortress Press, 1985), 185–93.

(1645), a book in which the beginnings of a criticism of the divine authority of the Bible became evident.[2] Herbert's ideas of "natural religion" became one of the chief bases for Deism, which soon challenged the cultural dominance of Christianity in Europe and North America.[3]

Herbert's books and ideas were esteemed highly by the English philosopher Thomas Hobbes (1588–1679), the first well-known European Bible critic.[4] In his controversial book of political philosophy titled *Leviathan* (1651), Hobbes denied the Mosaic authorship of the Pentateuch. Although Hobbes conceded that some parts of the Pentateuch came from Moses, he argued that it was composed long after his death.[5] Hobbes wrote similarly of Joshua, Judges, Ruth, 1 and 2 Samuel, Job, and Jonah and their alleged authors.

The second well-known European philosopher to deny the Mosaic authorship of the Pentateuch went further than Hobbes by asserting that Moses wrote none of it. This was the Dutch philosopher Benedict Spinoza (1632–77). While he was studying at the Jewish High School in Amsterdam, Spinoza's textbooks included the commentaries of Abraham ben Meir Ibn Ezra, a medieval Jewish critic of the Pentateuch.[6] In his own writings, Spinoza not only denied the Mosaic authorship of the Pentateuch, he also asserted that "prophecy" and "miracles" amounted to mere natural phenomena and should be explained as such.[7] He set forth a new system of biblical interpretation which argued that the Bible *contains* the Word of God, but that *not all* of Scripture is God's Word.[8] According to Spinoza, only those statements in the Bible which are in agreement with the "Divine Law" are God's Word.[9]

---

2 Reventlow, *Authority of the Bible*, 191.

3 E.g., Anthony Collins's 1713 treatise "A Discourse on Free-Thinking," in E. Graham Waring, *Deism and Natural Religion: A Source Book*, Milestones of Thought (New York: Frederick Ungar, 1967), 64–65 n. 1.

4 Reventlow, *Authority of the Bible*, 206.

5 Thomas Hobbes, *Leviathan: Or the Matter, Forme, and Power of a Commonwealth Ecclesiastical and Civil*, Collier Classics in the History of Thought (New York: Collier Books/Macmillan, 1962), 277–81 (ch. 33).

6 Benedict de Spinoza, *A Theological-Political Treatise and A Political Treatise*, trans. R. H. M. Elwes (n.p.: G. Bell & Son, 1883; repr., New York: Dover, 1951), xi.

7 Spinoza, *Theological-Political Treatise*, 13–42 (on prophecy) and 81–97 (on miracles). On Spinoza's denial of miracles and the supernatural, see Jonathan I. Israel, *Radical Enlightenment: Philosophy and the Making of Modernity, 1650–1750* (Oxford: Oxford University Press, 2001), 218–29.

8 Spinoza, *Theological-Political Treatise*, 98–119 (on interpretation) and 165–74 (on the definition of the "Word of God").

9 Spinoza, *Theological-Political Treatise*, 171–72.

Although he was labeled a heretic and excommunicated from the Dutch synagogue, Spinoza's books and treatises succeeded in their purpose of replacing the role of Scripture with philosophy in a portion of European society.[10]

The next stage in the development of biblical criticism came out of two organized groups of English thinkers. One group was known as the "Great Tew Circle." It was named after the village in Oxfordshire where its members met in the 1630s. A similar group, active from the late 1630s until the 1680s, was found in Cambridge. It became known as the "Cambridge Platonists." Through emphasis on the supremacy of reason, both groups undermined the Protestant principle that Scripture is the rule and norm of faith and life, and they became an inspiration for the Deist movement that followed them.[11]

Deism *rejected* revelation and asserted a belief in God's existence without any reliance on revealed religion.[12] So Deism held that the Bible was nothing more than speculation by its authors about God and unusual phenomena, that it was merely a human product subject to the same prejudices and ignorance of the people of its era. Deists did not believe that the Holy Scriptures were the "Word of God" in any way, shape, or form.

The present chapter especially follows the way Lutheran theology was changed by the German "Enlightenment," which is known in that language as the *Aufklärung*. Although he had some predecessors, Christian Wolff (1679–1754), a German philosopher at the University of Halle, is typically credited with the rise of theological rationalism, natural theology, and moral philosophy in Germany, overturning both Lutheran orthodoxy and Pietism.[13] The theologian Hermann Samuel Reimarus (1694–1768) is usually credited with the initial development of biblical criticism in Germany.[14] At various times professor at Jena, Wittenberg, and Hamburg, Reimarus distinguished what Jesus said and did on the one hand from how He is portrayed in the New

---

10 Israel, *Radical Enlightenment*, 173–74; the author traces Spinoza's influence throughout this excellent book.

11 See Frederick C. Beiser, *The Sovereignty of Reason: The Defense of Rationality in the Early English Enlightenment* (Princeton: Princeton University Press, 1996), 84–183.

12 "Deism," Wikipedia, https://en.wikipedia.org/wiki/Deism. Accessed 4/9/2022. For a thorough treatment of Deism, see Beiser, *Sovereignty of Reason*, 220–328, and Reventlow, *Authority of the Bible*, 223–414. See also Waring, *Deism and Natural Religion, passim*.

13 See Margaret C. Jacob, *The Secular Enlightenment* (Princeton: Princeton University Press, 2019), 167–72.

14 See Hans W. Frei, *The Eclipse of Biblical Narrative: A Study in Eighteenth and Nineteenth Century Hermeneutics* (New Haven: Yale University Press, 1974), 114–16.

Testament on the other. He effectively accused the New Testament authors of fraud on a grand scale. In his book *Wolfenbüttel Fragments*, published posthumously in 1774–78 by Gotthold Lessing (1729–81), Reimarus absolutely rejected miracles and revelation in the Holy Scriptures. His other writings defended the ideas of "natural religion" along the lines of Wolff.

Johann Salomo Semler (1725–91), professor of theology at the University of Halle, and Johann David Michaelis (1717–91), professor of theology at the University of Göttingen, were the first German theologians to approach the New Testament from a more "historical viewpoint."[15] This meant that they approached the New Testament writings as they would any other historical documents, thus ignoring or rejecting (1) the divine authority of the traditional canon of Scripture, (2) the inspiration and inerrancy of the text of the Old and New Testaments, and (3) the identification of the Word of God with Scripture. The "traditional canon" was in two parts. First, it included all the Old Testament books accepted as God's Word by the Jewish religious leaders in Jesus' day and by Jesus Himself. Second, it included all the New Testament books accepted as God's Word by the early church in the first and second centuries after Christ's birth. If God was not the ultimate author of the New Testament, then how were the stories about Jesus and the apostles developed or composed? One early theory from the eighteenth century was that the writers came under the influence of "myths."

At the beginning of the nineteenth century, the most influential philosopher in Germany was Georg Wilhelm Friedrich Hegel (1770–1804). Hegel constructed a unified philosophy and philosophy of religion that claimed to see God's revelation in all of history, not just in biblical history. Hegel is the source of the modern idea of "progressive" truth, in which older ways of thinking about God are believed to have become irrelevant to "modern man." Hegel believed that the old ideas meet the new ideas, they struggle "dialectically," and the result is a synthesis of the two which is the "new truth." Under Hegel's influence, Ferdinand Christian Baur (1792–1860), a theologian at the University of Tübingen, argued that the New Testament was developed and composed out of the struggles in primitive Christianity between the "school of Peter" (which made a basic statement of Christianity, or thesis) and the "school of Paul" (which in some respects stood in opposition, an antithesis), resulting in the Catholic church (a synthesis of the first two). More radical was the work of David Strauss (1808–74), professor for a time also at Tübingen. His widely influential *Life of Jesus* (1835–36) argued that all

---

15 See Werner Georg Kümmel, *The New Testament: The History of the Investigation of Its Problems*, trans. S. McLean Gilmour and Howard C. Kee (Nashville: Abingdon Press, 1972), 62–73.

Photograph by Paul Ockrassa

Students and faculty move through the Concordia Seminary quadrangle where crosses with the names of the terminated faculty members had been planted (February 19, 1974).

of Jesus' miracles were mythical and that none of the supernatural elements in the New Testament had any basis in historical truth or evidence.

Although Strauss was removed from his professorship, the German culture and church increasingly accepted his way of thinking. Albrecht Ritschl (1822–89), a Protestant theologian at the Universities of Bonn and Göttingen, developed his own theology of "value." He argued that though Jesus was not God "historically," yet Jesus is "valued as God" by the community He founded. The "Ritschl school" rejected miracles, mysteries, and the supernatural in the Bible and soon came to include a great number of significant Protestant theologians in Germany and everywhere Lutherans were found.[16] An alternative to the "Ritschl school" in the late nineteenth and early twentieth century was the "history of religions school," whose best-known figure is Ernst Troeltsch (1865–1923).[17] The theologians of this school sought to understand Judaism and Christianity within the overall history of religion. This approach is still used in universities today.

---

16   See Claude Welch, *Protestant Thought in the Nineteenth Century*, vol. 2: *1870–1914* (New Haven: Yale University Press, 1985).

17   See Ernst Troeltsch, *Religion in History*, trans. James Luther Adams and Walter F. Bense (Minneapolis: Fortress Press, 1991), especially pp. 73–108.

After the initial work on the *Life of Jesus* by Strauss, others stepped into the fray, offering their own opinions about the "real Jesus." This approach to the Gospels initially came to an end when Martin Kähler (1835–1912) and Albert Schweitzer (1875–1965) published devastating critiques of the "lives of Jesus" literature as hopelessly speculative.[18] This did not prevent later theologians—for example, Rudolf Bultmann (1884–1976)—from teaching and writing about new types of biblical criticism and new "lives of Jesus."

The first half of the twentieth century did not offer much new in biblical criticism, though any prominent theologian had to deal with the legacy that is outlined here. Karl Barth (1886–1968), a Reformed professor of theology at the Universities of Göttingen, Münster, Bonn, and Basel, was the most influential Protestant theologian of that century, and his influence extended into the Missouri Synod. Barth argued that "natural religion" and "natural theology" is impossible because God's sole revelation is in Jesus Christ and the Word of God. Barth redefined the term "Word of God" to mean the believer's experience of God's speech. Barth did not equate the "Word of God" with Scripture, though he asserted that the Bible *becomes* the Word of God for faith, and for faith alone, despite the faults and errors of Scripture. He accepted the assured "findings" of "higher criticism" and did not believe in biblical inerrancy. Barth argued that the Word of God has three related modes: revelation, Scripture, and proclamation. In Barth's threefold scheme, Scripture is *not normative* for proclamation and preaching as it was for Luther, Calvin, and their followers, but proclamation cannot properly occur in isolation from Scripture.[19]

In The Lutheran Church—Missouri Synod

The founding fathers of the Missouri Synod who had attended universities in Germany, such as C. F. W. Walther (1811–87), were fully aware of how almost all the German Protestant university professors in the nineteenth century denied that some, most, or all of the Bible was God's Word. (There were a few well-known exceptions among the German theologians, such as Ernst Wilhelm Hengstenberg, 1802–69). The immediate successors to Walther and his peers, such as Francis Pieper (1852–1931), all spoke and

---

18 See Martin Kähler, *The So-Called Historical Jesus and the Historic Biblical Christ*, trans. Carl E. Braaten (Minneapolis: Fortress Press, 1988); and Albert Schweitzer, *The Quest of the Historical Jesus: A Critical Study of Its Progress from Reimarus to Wrede*, trans. W. Montgomery (New York: Macmillan, 1968).

19 For a fair-minded assessment of Barth's view of Scripture, see Robert Preus, "The Word of God in the Theology of Karl Barth," in *Doctrine Is Life: The Essays of Robert D. Preus on Scripture*, ed. Klemet Preus (St. Louis: Concordia Publishing House, 2006), 39–52.

read German natively. They were able to keep abreast of currents in theology in both German-speaking and English-speaking spheres. However, Missouri Synod professors with native German linguistic ability began dying out after World War II, and the men who replaced them were not so fluent in the German language. They were not as likely to read, cite, or quote from their own predecessors because of the language barrier. This may be one reason many of the Synod's theologians from 1950 to 1974 promoted or accepted changes in their doctrine of Scripture.

Another reason is the influence of imposing intellectual personalities, foremost among whom was Jaroslav Pelikan (1923–2006), professor at Concordia Seminary from 1949 to 1953. In his book *From Luther to Kierkegaard: A Study in the History of Theology*, published in 1950 by the Synod's own Concordia Publishing House, Pelikan argued that the "existential philosophy of Søren Kierkegaard had performed a great service toward a solution of the problem of a philosophy for Lutheran theology."[20] For Kierkegaard, the object of faith was not a proposition, such as Gospel promises or Scriptures, nor even a teacher such as Jesus, but rather the fact that God has existed.[21] For Kierkegaard, each individual—not reason, society, or religious orthodoxy—has the duty of giving meaning to his or her own life and living that life "authentically." This contrasted with the Bible, which asserts that God has given meaning to human life and each individual person, and that the quest for meaning and purpose can be satisfied only in a relationship of faith in Jesus Christ. Pelikan's commendation of existential philosophy should have drawn questions from the Synod's doctrinal reviewers, but they apparently were so impressed by his credentials that they let it pass.

More serious was Pelikan's statement: "We may not think philosophically as though [Immanuel] Kant had never lived. There is no going behind the critical philosophy [of Kant] and its validated results."[22] What did the philosopher Kant say about religion? In *Religion within the Limits of Reason Alone*, he described faith in miracles, faith in mysteries (such as the Trinity and the virgin birth), and faith in the means of grace to be three types of "illusory faith" that reason cannot accept.[23] If there was no going behind Kant's critical philosophy

---

20 Jaroslav Pelikan, *From Luther to Kierkegaard: A Study in the History of Theology* (St. Louis: Concordia Publishing House, 1950), 118.

21 On Kierkegaard's theology, see "Theology of Soren Kierkegaard" at https://en .wikipedia.org/wiki/Theology_of_S%C3%B8ren_Kierkegaard. Accessed 4/9/2022.

22 Pelikan, *From Luther to Kierkegaard*, 119.

23 Immanuel Kant, *Religion within the Limits of Reason Alone*, trans. T. M. Green and H. H. Hudson (New York: Harper & Row, 1960), 182 (book 4, after part 2, "General Observations").

and its results, then there were no miracles in Bible times, no virgin birth, no Trinity, no divine nature of Jesus, no prophecy, no worldwide flood, and no six-day creation. Nor do the means of grace really forgive sins and offer eternal life to those who believe. And those denials are just for starters.

Pelikan was a forerunner of a critical approach to the Missouri Synod's traditions in doctrine and biblical studies, but he was only on the St. Louis faculty for four years. The real damage was done by Richard Caemmerer Sr. (1904–84), who taught at Concordia Seminary from 1940 to 1974, then at Seminex from 1974 to 1984. His influence is seen in the accolades given by his peers, associates, and former students in a volume produced in his honor: *The Lively Function of the Gospel*.[24] Serious damage was caused by Caemmerer's 1951 *Concordia Theological Monthly* article "A Concordance Study of the Concept 'Word of God,' "[25] which argued that the "Word of God" is not equal to Scripture, though it acknowledged both the "inspiration" of Scripture and the "dynamic quality" of Christian theology. This position was akin to Karl Barth's doctrine of the Word of God.

Other evidence of early "slippage" in the doctrine of Scripture or its interpretation can be found in *CTM* during the 1950s and 1960s. A. C. Rehwaldt's 1955 article "Natural Science with Reference to Genesis 1" argued that the word "day" in the six-day creation had no duration.[26] Matters had gone much further with an unsigned 1962 article: *"A Brief Statement*: Guidelines and Helps for Study."[27] It alleged several weaknesses in the *Brief Statement*, a theological document adopted by the Missouri Synod in 1932, including the use of Romans 3:2 to support the doctrine of biblical inspiration, the document's general stance on Scripture, and its failure to place the teaching Scripture under the category "Means of Grace." This article also observed that the *Brief Statement* was adopted prior to the scholarship of Karl Barth, Gerhard Kittel, Rudolf Bultmann, and contemporary Near Eastern and Old Testament studies, and suggested that it was outmoded by 1962.

Finally, biblical "inerrancy" was undermined by Arthur Carl Piepkorn, one of the most respected members of the Concordia Seminary faculty, in his

---

24   Robert Bertram, ed., *The Lively Function of the Gospel: Essays in Honor of Richard R. Caemmerer on Completion of 25 Years as Professor of Practical Theology at Concordia Seminary, St. Louis* (St. Louis: Concordia Publishing House, 1966).

25   Richard Caemmerer Sr., "A Concordance Study of the Concept 'Word of God,' " *CTM* 22 (March 1951): 170–85.

26   A. C. Rehwaldt, "Natural Science with Reference to Genesis 1," *CTM* 26 (May 1955): 341–59.

27   Anon., *"A Brief Statement*: Guidelines and Helps for Study," *CTM* 33 (April 1962): 210–23.

1965 article "What Does 'Inerrancy' Mean?"[28] Piepkorn wrote: "It does not seem to this writer that we are serving the best interests of the church when either we continue formally to reaffirm the inerrancy of the Sacred Scriptures or even continue to employ the term."[29] Piepkorn asserted that one reason for not reaffirming "the inerrancy of Sacred Scriptures is its ultimate theological irrelevance."[30]

Yet what could be more theologically relevant than Luther's affirmation of Scripture's inerrancy at the Diet of Worms, over against the errors in the religious opinions and theological writings of the scholastic theologians and other churchmen? At the diet, Luther quoted directly from St. Augustine's *Epistle 82* to Jerome. Luther stated:

> This is my answer to those also who accuse me of rejecting all the holy teachers of the church. I do not reject them. But everyone, indeed, knows that at times they have erred, as men will; therefore, I am ready to trust them only when they give me evidence for their opinions from Scripture, which has never erred. This St. Paul bids me to do in 1 Thess. 5:21, where he says, "Test everything; hold fast what is good." St. Augustine writes to St. Jerome to the same effect, "I have learned to do only those books that are called the holy Scripture the honor of believing firmly that none of their writers have ever erred. All others I so read as not to hold what they say to be the truth unless they prove it to me by holy Scripture or clear reason."[31]

Against Piepkorn's erring position, Robert Preus quoted the same passage from Augustine's *Epistle 82* and defined inerrancy in this way:

> In calling the sacred Scriptures inerrant we recognize in them, as words taught by the Holy Spirit, that quality which makes them overwhelmingly reliable witnesses to the words and deeds of the God who has in His inspired spokesmen and in His incarnate Son disclosed Himself to men for their salvation.... [This definition agrees] with what the church catholic has believed and confessed through her entire history.[32]

After being published in the autumn 1965 *Bulletin of the Evangelical Theological Society*, Robert Preus's article on biblical inerrancy was republished

---

28 Arthur Carl Piepkorn, "What Does 'Inerrancy' Mean?" *CTM* 36 (September 1965): 577–93.

29 Piepkorn, "What Does 'Inerrancy' Mean?" 588.

30 Piepkorn, "What Does 'Inerrancy' Mean?" 589.

31 *Defense and Explanation of All the Articles* (1521), AE 32:11.

32 See Robert Preus, "Notes on the Inerrancy of Scripture," in *Doctrine Is Life*, 116.

by *CTM* in 1967.[33] By then, however, it amounted to a minority voice on the St. Louis faculty.

Scripture and the Lutheran Confessions

Scripture on Scripture

What does Scripture say about itself? First and foremost, it says that all Scriptures are *inspired*, that is, a direct product of the Holy Spirit: "All Scripture is breathed out by God and profitable for teaching, for reproof, for correction, and for training in righteousness" (2 Timothy 3:16). Notice that the apostle Paul says that inspiration is an attribute of "all Scripture." This aspect of inspiration is known as *plenary inspiration*. Another Scripture passage that teaches the same thing is from the apostle Peter: "No prophecy of Scripture comes from someone's own interpretation. For no prophecy was ever produced by the will of man, but men spoke from God as they were carried along by the Holy Spirit" (2 Peter 1:20–21). On Maundy Thursday, Jesus promised His apostles:

> The Helper, the Holy Spirit, whom the Father will send in My name, He will teach you all things and bring to your remembrance all that I have said to you. . . . When the Spirit of truth comes, He will guide you into all the truth, for He will not speak on His own authority, but whatever He hears He will speak, and He will declare to you the things that are to come. He will glorify Me, for He will take what is Mine and declare it to you. (John 14:26; 16:13–14)

Second, the Scriptures teach that they limit what should be taught in the Christian Church. St. Paul wrote: "I have applied all these things to myself and Apollos for your benefit, brothers, that you may learn by us *not to go beyond what is written*, that none of you may be puffed up in favor of one against another" (1 Corinthians 4:6, italics added). Notice that he is pointing to "what is written" as the standard and limiting factor. Scripture thus serves as a *judge, rule, and norm* of all Christian doctrine and teachers.

Third, the Scriptures teach that they are perennial and eternal truth. Jesus said, "Heaven and earth will pass away, but My words will not pass away" (Matthew 24:35).

Fourth, the Scriptures teach that their words are *healthful*. Paul wrote about "the sound words of our Lord Jesus Christ" (1 Timothy 6:3); also his readers are to "follow the pattern of the sound words that you have heard from me" (2 Timothy 1:13). The word "sound" here is a translation of the Greek *hygiainoo*, from which we get our English word "hygiene." In this context, it

---

33 *CTM* 38 (June 1967): 363–75.

means that the words of Scripture are always healthful for the soul and spirit of man, woman, and child.

Fifth, the Scriptures teach that they are *holy*. For example, Paul explained how God "promised beforehand through His prophets in the holy Scriptures" (Romans 1:2). Notice here that Paul did not write that the "word of God" is holy, but that the Scriptures themselves are holy.

Sixth, the Scriptures teach that *they cannot be repealed, annulled, or abolished*. Jesus said, "If he called them gods to whom the word of God came— and Scripture cannot be broken" (John 10:35). The word for "broken" here is a translation of the Greek *lutheenai*, which in this context means to be loosened or to be released. In other words, the application and effect of the Scriptures cannot be overturned, because God has spoken these words. About this same quality of Scripture Jesus said, "For truly, I say to you, until heaven and earth pass away, not an iota, not a dot, will pass from the Law until all is accomplished" (Matthew 5:18).

Seventh, the Scriptures teach that they have *universal scope*. Paul wrote: "The Scripture imprisoned everything [that is, everyone] under sin, so that the promise by faith in Jesus Christ might be given to those who believe" (Galatians 3:22). Notice again that Paul did not say that the "word of God" did this, but the Scriptures.

Eighth, the Scriptures teach that their central purpose is to *give eternal life* and to *give testimony about the Christ*. Jesus said, "You search the Scriptures because you think that in them you have eternal life; and it is they that bear witness about Me" (John 5:39).

Ninth, and finally, the proper application of Scripture is explained by Paul: "Whatever was written in former days was written for our instruction, that through endurance and through the encouragement of the Scriptures we might have hope" (Romans 15:4). Thus the Scriptures are to be used *in instruction*, as they are in the lessons of the liturgy, in preaching, in teaching, and in catechesis; as well as *in the encouragement of the saints* through all the above, but also through individual pastoral care and the mutual encouragement of believers (Hebrews 10:24).

Other attributes of Scripture are, indeed, taught by Scripture. These include the sufficiency, clarity, power, and unity of Scripture.[34] However,

---

34 See Johann Gerhard, *On the Nature of Theology and Scripture*, trans. Richard J. Dinda, Theological Commonplaces (St. Louis: Concordia Publishing House, 2006); Robert Preus, *The Inspiration of Scripture: A Study of the Theology of the Seventeenth-Century Lutheran Dogmaticians*, 2nd ed. (Edinburgh: Oliver & Boyd, 1957; repr., St. Louis: Concordia Publishing House, 1981); and Robert D. Preus,

the attributes described above were the primary ones being contested in the Missouri Synod during the 1960s and 1970s.

The Lutheran Confessions on Scripture

There are some people who say that theological terms of the sixteenth century cannot be found in the Bible or are not biblical. The question is, however, whether such terms have added to, detracted from, or otherwise modified the *meaning* of what Scripture says. The Lutheran Confessions teach nothing different about the Scriptures than what the Scriptures teach about themselves. These Confessions may use different words at times, yet they show that they contain nothing "that departs from the Scriptures or the catholic church, or from the Roman church, insofar as we can tell from its [ancient and patristic] writers" (AC Conclusion of Part 1).[35] To prove their "catholicity," the Lutheran Confessions at times quote theologians and councils and use terms and ideas that developed in the 1,400 years between Christ and Luther. Of course, Jesus and the apostles spoke and wrote in Hebrew, Aramaic, and Greek, while the Lutheran Confessions were written in German and Latin.

Lutherans who are confused in this matter need to read the Large Catechism, which states: "We know that God does not lie. My neighbor and I—in short, all people—may deceive and mislead, but God's Word cannot deceive" (LC IV 57).[36] The German there reads: "*Gottes Wort kann nicht fehlen,*" which literally means "God's Word can do no wrong." The Latin reads: "*verbum Dei nec potest errare nec fallere,*" which literally means "It is not possible for God's Word to err or to deceive." This is the biblical and historical Christian doctrine of the *inerrancy* of Scripture, which Luther at this point in the Large Catechism deduces immediately from the proposition "God does not lie" (see Titus 1:2). Luther learned about the doctrine of inerrancy in part by studying the writings of St. Augustine, who was the preeminent teacher of the order of the Augustinian Friars, to which Luther belonged before the Reformation.

The editors and confessors of the 1580 *Book of Concord* affirmed the inerrancy of the Scriptures in its Preface, in which they stated that they confessed "in accordance with the pure, infallible, and unchangeable Word of God" (Preface to the Book of Concord 16).[37] They also appealed to the Reformed Christians to "give themselves over to and turn toward the infallible truth of

---

The Theology of Post-Reformation Lutheranism: A Study of Theological Prolegomena (St. Louis: Concordia Publishing House, 1970).

35 K-W, 59.

36 K-W, 464.

37 K-W, 10.

the divine Word" (Preface to the Book of Concord 20).[38] *Infallibility* is really the same attribute of the Scriptures as inerrancy. It explains what the Scriptures are incapable of doing. In other words, the Scriptures are incapable of erring or deceiving when they are heard or read, because they are without any errors. The Formula of Concord states, quoting Luther, that "the Word of God is not false or deceitful" (FC Ep VII 13).[39] The Large Catechism puts it most simply: "... believe the Scriptures. They will not lie to you ..." (LC V 76).[40]

The Confessions teach that the Scriptures are *inspired by the Holy Spirit*. In its article on justification, the Apology of the Augsburg Confession observes: "It is truly amazing that the opponents remain unmoved by so many passages from Scripture. ... Surely they do not think that these words fell from the Holy Spirit inadvertently, do they?" (Ap IV 107–8).[41]

The Confessions teach that the Scriptures are the *judge, rule, and norm*. The Formula of Concord states:

Photograph by Paul Ockrassa

John S. Damm, who had been terminated as academic dean of Concordia Seminary, and John Tietjen, who had been suspended as president, in DeMun Park on the east side of campus, watching for representatives of Eden Seminary, who had offered their campus as a temporary location for the students and faculty who walked out (February 19, 1974).

---

38   K-W, 13.

39   K-W, 505.

40   K-W, 474.

41   K-W, 138.

We believe, teach, and confess that the only rule and guiding principle according to which all teachings and teachers are to be evaluated and judged are the prophetic and apostolic writings of the Old and New Testaments alone.... Holy Scripture alone remains the only judge, rule, and guiding principle, according to which, as the only touchstone, all teachings should and must be recognized and judged, whether they are good or evil, correct, or incorrect. (FC Ep Rule and Norm 1, 7)[42]

The Confessions teach that the Scriptures are the *perennial and eternal truth*. The Formula of Concord states that "... we base our teaching on God's Word as the eternal truth ..." (FC SD Rule and Norm 13).[43]

Finally, the Confessions frequently refer to the Scriptures as *divine*. In one place, the Formula of Concord specifies in a parenthetical statement that "God's Word" is "the prophetic and apostolic writings" (FC SD Rule and Norm 16).[44] The Preface to the Book of Concord calls Scripture "divine, prophetic, and apostolic."[45]

What the LCMS Teaches on the Nature of Scripture

In its fellowship discussions with the ALC, the Missouri Synod drew up a doctrinal statement mentioned earlier: *A Brief Statement of the Doctrinal Position of the Missouri Synod*. The Synod's 1932 convention had adopted it to make, as the title suggested, a brief biblical statement of the Missouri Synod doctrinal position. In 1938 the Synod accepted it once again as a basis for possible church fellowship with the ALC. The *Brief Statement* included the Synod's long-standing position on Scripture:

1. We teach that the Holy Scriptures differ from all other books in the world in that they are the Word of God. They are the Word of God because the holy men of God who wrote the Scriptures wrote only that which the Holy Ghost communicated to them by inspiration, 2 Tim. 3:16; 2 Peter 1:21. We teach also that the verbal inspiration of the Scriptures is not a so-called "theological deduction," but that it is taught by direct statements of the Scriptures, 2 Tim. 3:16; John 10:35; Rom. 3:2; 1 Cor. 2:13. Since the Holy Scriptures are the Word of God, it goes without saying that they contain no errors or contradictions, but that they are in all their parts and words the infallible truth, also in those parts which treat of historical, geographical, and other secular matters, John 10:35.

---

42   K-W, 486–87. Cf. FC SD Rule and Norm 3 (K-W, 527).

43   K-W, 529.

44   K-W, 530.

45   K-W, 14.

53

2. We furthermore teach regarding the Holy Scriptures that they are given by God to the Christian Church for the foundation of faith, Eph. 2:20. Hence the Holy Scriptures are the sole source from which all doctrines proclaimed in the Christian Church must be taken and therefore, too, the sole rule and norm by which all teachers and doctrines must be examined and judged. — With the Confessions of our Church we teach also that the "rule of faith" (*analogia fidei*) according to which the Holy Scriptures are to be understood are the clear passages of *the Scriptures themselves* which set forth the individual doctrines. (Apology. Triglot, p. 441, Paragraph 60; Mueller, p. 684).[46] The rule of faith is not the man-made so-called "totality of Scripture" ("*Ganzes der Schrift*").

3. We reject the doctrine which under the name of science has gained wide popularity in the Church of our day that Holy Scripture is not in all its parts the Word of God, but in part the Word of God and in part the word of man and hence does, or at least, might, contain error. We reject this erroneous doctrine as horrible and blasphemous, since it flatly contradicts Christ and His holy apostles, set[s] up men as judges over the Word of God, and thus overthrows the foundation of the Christian Church and its faith.[47]

In 1971, members of the Synod may have been surprised, even shocked, to find that not only did the majority of Concordia Seminary faculty members *not* teach in agreement with the *Brief Statement*, the majority also rejected the *principle* of teaching in agreement with synodical doctrinal statements.[48]

The faculty majority made its position still clearer late the next year with its release of its statement *Faithful to Our Calling, Faithful to Our Lord.*

- With respect to miracles, the faculty majority stated: "To edify the Church, we ought to focus on this central meaning of the miracle accounts for us instead of dwelling on the authenticity of isolated miraculous details."[49] I respond: The empty tomb was an isolated detail of the Easter miracle. Does the factuality of that detail concern us?

- With respect to the doctrines of inerrancy and inspiration, the faculty majority stated: "Any tendency to make the doctrine of inspiration

---

46 The reference here is to Ap XXVII 60 (K-W, 287).

47 *Brief Statement of the Doctrinal Position of the Missouri Synod* (St. Louis: Concordia Publishing House, n.d.), 3–4 (italics original), online at https://www.lcms.org/about /beliefs/doctrine/brief-statement-of-lcms-doctrinal-position. Accessed 4/9/2022.

48 Blue Book (Zimmerman, 398–401). See below, "Doctrinal Resolutions and Statements," pp. 99–104.

49 *Faithful* I, 19.

or the inerrancy of the Scriptures a prior truth which guarantees the truth of the Gospel or gives support to our faith is sectarian."[50] I respond: Does this mean that Luther at Worms and Augustine in his *Epistle 82* to Jerome were sectarians? This statement by the St. Louis faculty majority is typical of their frequent confusion between the "formal principle" (*sola Scriptura*) and the "material principle" (*sola gratia*) of theology.[51]

- About historical accounts in Scripture, the faculty majority stated: "The fact that a given biblical episode is historical is not important in and of itself."[52] I respond: That sounds like the historical nature of Scripture is generally unimportant.

- Regarding inspiration, the faculty majority defined inspiration in this way: "The inspiration of the written Word pertains to the effective power of the Scriptures to bring men and women to salvation through the Gospel."[53] I respond: This statement is simply wrong, and the authors had no right to redefine this term. "Inspiration" is an attribute of Scripture that has always referred to its origin or source, not to its purpose or result.

- Regarding inerrancy, the faculty majority stated: "The reliability or 'inerrancy' of the Scriptures cannot be determined by twentieth century standards of factuality."[54] I respond: By what standards of factuality can the Scriptures be evaluated? The faculty majority did not say what these standards are, at least not here.

What Happened

In response to the St. Louis seminary faculty majority's position, the 1973 LCMS convention adopted a more thorough statement about the

---

50 *Faithful* I, 21.

51 For the most incisive single evaluation of the St. Louis faculty's confusion in this area, see Kurt E. Marquart, "The Swing of the Pendulum: An Attempt to Understand the St. Louis 'Affirmations and Discussions,' " in *Truth, Salvatory and Churchly: Works of Kurt E. Marquart*, vol. 3: *Essays Historical and Historic*, ed. Ken Schurb and Robert Paul (N.p.: Luther Academy, 2018), 50–57.

52 *Faithful* I, 23.

53 *Faithful* I, 36.

54 *Faithful* I, 37.

doctrine of Scripture in *A Statement of Scriptural and Confessional Principles*.[55] Part IV includes sections on "The Inspiration of Scripture," "The Purpose of Scripture," "The Gospel and Holy Scripture (Material and Formal Principles)," "The Authority of Scripture," "The Canonical Text of Scripture," "The Infallibility of Scripture," "The Unity of Scripture," "Old Testament Prophecy," and "Historical Methods of Biblical Interpretation."

The section on "The Canonical Text of Scripture" appears in response to modern theologians who claim that the original text of our Bible books is not the same as what we have in our Bibles today. These theologians claim that they can identify "pre-canonical sources" (such as a supposed "Q" source behind the books of Matthew and Luke), which they claim were the original Scriptures of the original Christian community. Their thinking is that our Bible books are highly revised editions of the originals. Such claims have never been verified through actual documents but are purely speculative.

The section on "The Infallibility of Scripture" is, perhaps, the key section in *A Statement*. It says:

> With Luther, we confess that "God's Word cannot err" (LC, IV, 57). We therefore believe, teach, and confess that since the Holy Scriptures are the Word of God, they contain no errors or contradictions but that they are in all their parts and words the infallible truth. We hold that the opinion that Scripture contains errors is a violation of the *sola scriptura* principle, for it rests upon the acceptance of some norm or criterion of truth above the Scriptures. We recognize that there are apparent contradictions or discrepancies and problems which arise because of uncertainty over the original text.[56]

A Statement goes on to reject a number of views put forth by modern theologians: "that the Scriptures contain theological as well as factual contradictions and errors" (point 1); "that the Scriptures are inerrant only in matters pertaining directly to the Gospel message of salvation" (point 2); "that the Scriptures are 'inerrant' only in the sense that they accomplish their [goal]" (point 3); that the biblical authors accepted the false ideas of their day (point 4); that when Jesus and the New Testament writers identify the authors of the Old Testament, or refer to historic Old Testament events, this does not prove that these were the real authors or that these events are true (point 5); that theological statements in the Bible that refer to historic events are true only theologically, not historically (point 6); that some of the deeds

---

55 This document may be found at https://www.lcms.org/about/beliefs/doctrine /statement-of-scriptural-and-confessional-principles. Accessed 4/9/2022. It also appears in its entirety below, pp. 265–77.

56 *A Statement*, part IV.F (below, p. 269).

and sayings of Jesus were invented by the Gospel writers (point 7); that the biblical authors sometimes invented speeches or events for literary purposes (point 8); and that "the use of certain 'literary forms'" indicates that what is described must be fictional (point 9).[57]

A Statement of Scriptural and Confessional Principles is a doctrinal statement of the LCMS. Members of the Synod are to honor and uphold it. Agencies of the Synod, including seminaries and universities, are to teach in accordance with it.

The Difference This Makes

Attributes of Scripture such as inerrancy, inspiration, perennial truth, etc., are vitally important. They undergird the *authority of Scripture* for your faith and life and for the faith and life of the Christian Church. St. Augustine understood this as he dealt with heretics and false religions in his day. Martin Luther also understood this as he dealt with heretics, erring theologians, and the papacy. We still face such challenges today, even more so in the pluralistic and atheistic society in which we live and work.

You as a Christian cannot know, with the certainty God wants you to have, that anything in the Bible is true if it was not inspired by the Holy Spirit who kept the human authors from erring. If you doubt Scripture, you cannot be sure of God's will for your life, how He wants you to live, whether your sins are forgiven, and that eternal life is your destiny. Religious doctrines or messages become mere guesses. Then Christianity is no better than the "philosophy of the day." Moreover, if you deny the inspiration, inerrancy, and authority of Scripture, you cut out the heart of the mission and evangelism of the church. For then how can you know with certainty that the Gospel proclaimed by the church is the Gospel given by God? Where churches allow attacks on Scripture to go unchallenged, the next generations in those churches drift away. Will they be lost forever?

Sadly, this is what we see in the "Seven Sisters of Mainline Protestantism."[58] Included in that list is the ELCA, whose predecessor synods failed to defend the authority of Scripture. We can see in the ELCA what the LCMS would have become if the attacks on Scripture in its midst had gone unchallenged. By God's grace, the Missouri Synod survived that controversy! What about the future?

---

57 For the precise wording of all these rejections, see below, *A Statement*, part IV.F.1–9, pp. 269–70.

58 See "Mainline Protestantism" at https://en.wikipedia.org/wiki/Mainline_Protestant. Accessed 4/9/2022.

For Discussion

1. Why do many theology professors of the Christian religion deny the authority, inerrancy, and inspiration of the Scriptures? What "benefit" do they get from such a denial? Give examples.

2. Why do many Christian laypeople deny, or refuse to defend, the authority, inerrancy, and inspiration of the Scriptures? What "benefit" do they get from such a denial? Give examples.

3. If Scripture is only partially God's Word, how can you determine which part(s) are God's Word?

4. If Scripture is in error, how can you determine which part(s) are true and which are false?

5. If Scripture is fallible, what effect does this have on Christian ethics and morality? Give examples.

6. If Scripture is fallible, what effect does this have on belief in the Gospel promises, for example, the forgiveness of sins, the souls of believers in heaven after death, the resurrection of the body, the judgment of evil and evildoers, and eternal life with Jesus and all the saints?

7. Why and how do social movements, such as ecumenism, socialism, feminism, the LGBTQ agenda, etc., cause Christians to deny or refuse to defend the authority of Scripture? Give examples.

Digging Deeper

CTCR. *The Inspiration of Scripture*. St. Louis: LCMS, 1975.

Preus, Klemet, ed. *Doctrine Is Life: The Essays of Robert D. Preus on Scripture*. Edited by Klemet Preus. St. Louis: Concordia Publishing House, 2006.

Preus, Robert. *The Inspiration of Scripture: A Study of the Theology of the Seventeenth-Century Lutheran Dogmaticians*. Second edition. Edinburgh: Oliver & Boyd, 1957. Reprint, St. Louis: Concordia Publishing House, 1981.

Scaer, David P. *The Apostolic Scriptures*. St. Louis: Concordia Publishing House, 1971. Reprint, Fort Wayne, IN: Concordia Theological Seminary Press, 1979.

CHAPTER THREE

THE HISTORICAL-CRITICAL METHOD

Timothy H. Maschke

Claims, counterclaims, and events surrounding the Walkout swirled about historical criticism of the Bible, a practice with roots in the eighteenth-century Enlightenment. Various secular approaches to biblical interpretation had developed as Scripture came to be viewed only as a human document. The Bible's divine inspiration was dismissed, its miracles were doubted, and its authority was undermined. Until the mid-twentieth century, the Missouri Synod had avoided the impact of historical criticism. Then several Concordia Seminary professors began teaching historical criticism. In the early 1970s, with the presidencies of John H. Tietjen at Concordia Seminary and Jacob A. O. Preus in the LCMS, the seminary faculty's use of historical criticism was acknowledged. The controversy erupted.

Introduction

This chapter is about the interpretation of the Bible. So important is the Bible to Christian faith and life, we should hardly be surprised that when questions arise about its credibility, reliability, and usefulness, concerns also arise among Christians.

The historical-critical method of biblical study, which raises just such questions, did not emerge from a vacuum. It resulted from an eighteenth-century phenomenon known as the Enlightenment. The LCMS was not affected (or perhaps better to say, infected) with this method until well into the twentieth century. During the 1950s, issues arose within the Synod about the usefulness and scholarly acceptance of historical criticism. But only after John Tietjen's ascent to the Concordia Seminary presidency was there an official acknowledgment that the method was being advocated at the seminary. Recognizing this matter as theological and doctrinal, Synod president J. A. O. Preus used his influence to bring it before the seminary administration and the Synod in the early 1970s. As they say, "The rest is history."

The present chapter provides background on the historical-critical method as well as on specific concerns raised within the LCMS. The method itself remains a major approach taken by many biblical scholars, in variously nuanced forms, throughout twenty-first-century biblical studies. Thankfully, the Missouri Synod's current seminary faculties do not use this method.

Historical Background

For Martin Luther, the Bible was God's living voice.[1] Especially important to Luther were the words of God's love and forgiveness for Christ's sake that he rediscovered in the New Testament. In addition, he regarded the Old Testament as filled with promises from the gracious God and Father of his Savior. Luther spoke of Scripture as "the manger in which Christ lies."[2]

Luther was an Old Testament scholar, but he revered both testaments as God's revelation of Himself to human beings. As a result, Luther worked diligently to translate both testaments into the German language. In addition, he preached on many books of the Bible and commented on numerous books of both testaments. In a sermon to parents, Luther strongly stressed the necessity of learning and understanding the biblical languages.[3] Similarly, he had admonished the German councilmen of the cities to support public education that included language study.[4]

The Lutheran Confessions and Post-Reformation Biblical Studies

The Lutheran confessors of the later sixteenth century in their expositions on the evangelical doctrines of the Church found scriptural support for all their teachings. As Ralph Bohlmann (1932–2016) explained: "The Lutheran Confessions view the Holy Scriptures as a unit. . . . And underlying the unity of message, content, and function is the unity of divine *authorship*,

---

1   *Church Postil* (1540–44), sermon for Advent 1 on Matt. 21:1–9, AE 75:51 n. 72.

2   *Preface to the Old Testament* (1523, 1545), AE 35:236.

3   *Sermon on Keeping Children in School* (1520), AE 46:213–58.

4   *To the Councilmen of All Cities in Germany* (1524), AE 45:347–78. See also W. W. Florer, "Luther's Attitude toward Language Study," *Monatshefte für Deutsche Sprache und Pädagogik* 18 (1917): 139–44. http://www.jstor.org/stable/30167848. Accessed 8/4/2021.

which gives meaning to the other aspects of Biblical unity."[5] He continued: "Grammar is of the utmost importance, as the general exegesis [biblical interpretation] of the confessions from beginning to end makes very clear. . . . The literary context and historical setting must also be carefully considered."[6] In summary, Bohlmann wrote:

> Thus the confessional conviction that the Holy Scripture is the clear literary word of God is demonstrated in their continual practice of careful and sober grammatical exegesis. In their literary interpretation of Scripture the confessional authors use every tool at their disposal to derive the one intended meaning of the text from the text itself. For the confessions, excellency of scholarly exegesis was not an option but a theological necessity.[7]

This literary and grammatical approach continued in the seventeenth and eighteenth centuries among those identified as Orthodox Lutherans, such as Johann Gerhard (1582–1637) and Abraham Calov (1612–86).[8] However, the eighteenth century also saw the rise of an approach to almost all academic studies known as the Enlightenment.

The Enlightenment

Also called the "Age of Reason," the Enlightenment was a philosophical movement that relied upon human reasoning instead of divine revelation or ecclesiastical doctrine as ultimately authoritative. One of its hallmarks was skepticism about long-held beliefs, including religious views. The word "Enlightenment" itself reflects an attitude of having superior knowledge and understanding of the world using human reason alone in comparison to the "darker" medieval and early modern periods, times in which faith was central. A 1784 essay by Immanuel Kant (1724–1804), "What Is Enlightenment?" explained that the term refers to using one's mind freely rather than following predisposed assertions of the church or other authorities. The latter would reflect only a lazy or cowardly attitude.[9]

---

5   Ralph A. Bohlmann, *Principles of Biblical Interpretation in the Lutheran Confessions* (St. Louis: Concordia Publishing House, 1968), 83 (italics original).

6   Bohlmann, *Principles of Biblical Interpretation*, 88.

7   Bohlmann, *Principles of Biblical Interpretation*, 95.

8   See Robert D. Preus, *The Theology of Post-Reformation Lutheranism: A Study in Theological Prolegomena* (St. Louis: Concordia Publishing House, 1970), 47–65, 254–362.

9   Immanuel Kant, "Was ist Äufklarung?" in the *Modern History Sourcebook*. https://sourcebooks.fordham.edu/mod/kant-whatis.asp. Accessed 8/9/2021.

Biblical scholar Johann Semler (1725–91) studied with several Enlightenment theologians.[10] Semler rejected the verbal inspiration of Scripture. He proposed two ideas that would influence historical-critical thinking and would be articulated by the St. Louis faculty after the mid-1950s. One was the idea that "the Bible merely *contains* the Word of God, that is, it cannot simply be said to *be* the Word, as conservatives, ancient and modern, confess." The second was: "Treat the Bible like any other book." This approach eliminates any established ideas of doctrine, tradition, or even biblical authority. While all students of the Bible recognize its historical and literary dimensions, those following Semler's view would never say that "the Bible is *not* 'like any other book.' "[11]

A bold assertion that contributed to the reception of historical criticism came from the German writer and philosopher Gotthold Lessing (1729–81). He spoke of "an ugly great ditch" (*der garstige breite Graben*) between history and faith.[12] Lessing claimed that there is a great gap between belief and historical "evidence," which he said was uncertain at best. Thus history even as recounted in biblical texts cannot be certain, nor can it confirm statements of faith. In addition, Lessing pointed to an historical ditch between the biblical text and its application to contemporary society. Edgar Krentz (1928–2021), chairman of the Concordia Seminary exegetical department (that is, department of biblical studies) during the years leading up to the Walkout, described this divide: "The Bible is an ancient book addressed to people of long ago in a strange culture, written in ancient languages. Historical criticism respects this historical gap and uses a method to determine as precisely as possible the significance of their words for the people then."[13] Krentz continued:

> Historical criticism puts us into the place of Jesus' first hearers by making the Bible seem *strange and foreign*. Palestine is an earthy place; Israel's prophets and Jesus do not resemble the well-laundered pictures of them prevalent in much piety and art. Historical criticism makes the

---

10 Hans Rollmann, "Semler, Johann Salomo (1725–1791)," *Dictionary of Major Biblical Interpreters* (Downers Grove, IL: IVP Academic, 2007), 910–11.

11 Horace Hummel, *The Word Becoming Flesh: An Introduction to the Origin, Purpose, and Meaning of the Old Testament* (St. Louis: Concordia Publishing House, 1979), 19 (italics original).

12 See Gotthold Lessing, "On the Proof of the Spirit and of the Power," as explained in Toshimasa Yasukata, *Lessing's Philosophy of Religion and the German Enlightenment* (New York: Oxford University Press, 2002), chapter 4, "Lessing's 'Ugly Broad Ditch,' " 56–65.

13 Edgar Krentz, *The Historical-Critical Method* (Philadelphia: Fortress Press, 1975), 61.

gap between us and the biblical world as wide as it actually is, forces us to face the peculiarity and particularity of the texts in their world, and confronts us with the Jesus who is the challenge to all cultures and securities of our world.[14]

Here we begin to see the distinction between criticism and critique. Criticism, as it related to "scientific studies" of Scripture, elevated human reason as the final authority in all matters, including biblical interpretation.

The Nineteenth Century

Julius Wellhausen (1844–1918) drew upon several earlier studies regarding the origin of the biblical text, particularly looking at the first five books of Moses. He advocated the idea that there were at least four originally distinct traditions from much later than Moses' time and that these were edited and brought together to form what have been called the five "books of Moses," the Pentateuch. His proposal is known as the "documentary hypothesis" or the JEDP theory. These letters stand for the four "sources" that were supposed to lie behind the Pentateuch: J for Yahwist (the proper name of the Lord given to Moses [J in German is pronounced like a Y]); E for Elohist (the name usually translated "God"); D for Deuteronomist (sections on God's revealed commandments); and P for Priestly (ritual laws of Israel's sacrificial system). Wellhausen's hypothesis, with various additions and modifications, remains the dominant view among scholars.

The result of these theories and hypotheses was that most scholars accepted a position of "rationalist antisupernaturalism."[15] Key figures of the era included Friedrich Schleiermacher (1768–1834), Ferdinand Christian Baur (1792–1860), and David Friedrich Strauss (1808–74). As chapter 2 of the present book notes, the latter two taught their Enlightenment ideas in Tübingen, in contrast to the relatively more conservative Lutheran theologians in Erlangen (who were committed to a progressive understanding of the Lutheran Confessions) and certainly to the more scripturally bound theologians of Lutheran Orthodoxy.

In his advocacy of historical criticism, Edgar Krentz assessed the nineteenth century thus:

> It is difficult to overestimate the significance the nineteenth century has for biblical interpretation. It made historical criticism *the* approved method of interpretation. The result was a revolution of viewpoint in evaluating the Bible. The Scriptures were, so to speak, secularized. The

---

14 Krentz, *Historical-Critical Method*, 64–65.

15 Krentz, *Historical-Critical Method*, 22.

biblical books became historical documents to be studied and questioned like any other ancient sources. The Bible was no longer the criterion for the writing of history; rather history had become the criterion for understanding the Bible. The variety in the Bible was highlighted; its unity had to be discovered and could no longer be presumed. The history it reported was no longer assumed to be everywhere correct. The Bible stood before criticism as defendant before judge. This criticism was largely . . . incapable of appreciating the category of revelation.[16]

Scriptural authority and divine revelation were not merely questioned; they were dismissed as passé and obsolete.

Such historical investigation questioned the traditional authorship of biblical texts and the truthfulness of biblical narratives. The critic sought to "get behind the text." Over the next century, additional methodologies were proposed and developed—form criticism, tradition criticism, and redaction criticism. These will be explained later in this chapter.

Coupled with these methods was a view that secular perspectives or understandings had greater importance than the biblical text. Often that mindset resulted in scholars rejecting certain events from Bible stories because they concluded, in light of modern scientific understandings of the world, that these things could not have happened. Historical critics asked: Did Moses really write the Pentateuch? Was Jonah a real historical figure? Did Jesus say the words the Bible attributes to Him? Were the books attributed to Paul written by others after Paul died? The historical critic would stand above the text with a supposed higher historical perspective as seen through modern eyes.

C. F. W. Walther (1811–87), the Missouri Synod's first president, was a student in the wake of the Enlightenment. He wrestled with many rationalist views, finally finding hope and comfort in the Christ of the Scriptures and in the Lutheran Confessions as a correct exposition of the Bible for teaching and life. In contrast to European rationalism, Walther would lead the Synod back to more conservative views of earlier Lutheran Orthodoxy.

In The Lutheran Church—Missouri Synod

For more than a century, biblical studies in the LCMS refrained from using the historical-critical method. Walther's student and successor as president of Concordia Seminary, Francis Pieper (1852–1931), in his *Christian Dogmatics* strongly criticized many Enlightenment theologians, advocating

---

16   Krentz, *Historical-Critical Method*, 30.

rather for a return to earlier biblical and confessional teachings.[17] Pieper was also the key advocate of the *Brief Statement of the Doctrinal Position of the Missouri Synod*, in which the third part "On Scripture" clearly rejected "scientific" methods of historical criticism.[18]

Inroads of Historical Criticism

During the mid-1950s, a brilliant Concordia Seminary professor, Martin Scharlemann (1910–82), started advocating the new approach to biblical studies. In 1958, he made a presentation to the seminary faculty along with his similarly gifted younger colleague, Horace Hummel (1928–2021). In "Notes on the Valid Use of the Historico-Critical Method,"[19] they laid out an approach to biblical studies that had become increasingly attractive to the academic world: historical criticism. Emphasizing the historical qualities of scriptural accounts and the nearly universal acceptance of the method among biblical scholars, they ventured that if it were used conservatively, historical criticism could be applied to Scripture without jeopardizing Lutheran doctrines. A little more than a decade later, both of them recognized the grave dangers of historical criticism and warned of its deleterious effects.

Synod leaders were upset with the novel views. LCMS president John Behnken (1887–1968; president, 1935–62), wrote in his autobiography: "Nothing during my 27 years in office caused me more heartache."[20] At the time, Concordia Seminary president Alfred Fuerbringer (1903–97; seminary president, 1953–69) defended Scharlemann. Yet in June 1962, Scharlemann stood before the Synod's convention in Cleveland, Ohio, expressing his deep regret and sorrow over his part in contributing to unrest within the Synod. The convention accepted his apology.[21] Still, concerns over the use of the historical-critical method continued throughout Oliver Harms's time as president of the Synod (1901–80; president, 1962–69).[22]

By 1963, alarm arose over a presentation made by St. Louis professor Norman Habel (1932– ; at Concordia Seminary, 1960–73) that questioned

---

17 Pieper 1:193–367.

18 Carl S. Meyer, "Historical Background of 'a Brief Statement,'" *CTM* 32 (September 1961): 538–39, identifies Pieper as the primary author.

19 Martin H. Scharlemann and Horace D. Hummel, "Notes on the Valid Use of the Historico-Critical Method" (Concordia Seminary Faculty meeting, February 7, 1958), CHI, Martin Henry Scharlemann Papers, Box 36.

20 John W. Behnken, *This I Recall* (St. Louis: Concordia Publishing House, 1964), 194–95. See also Zimmerman, 209.

21 1962 *Proceedings*, 106–7.

22 Blue Book (Zimmerman, 209–10).

the historical accuracy and reality of the first several chapters of Genesis.[23] Habel later recalled: "I first became a controversial figure when I gave an exploratory paper on Genesis 3 to the council of presidents [sic] of The Lutheran Church Missouri Synod [sic]. That paper became known as the *Green Dragon*."[24] A revision of his essay for study in pastoral conferences was published as *The Form and Meaning of the Fall Narrative*. There Habel asserted:

> ... the narrative of Gen. 2–3 is not an annalistic report of certain incidents from antiquity, but incorporates some elements which must be understood in a double or "deeper than surface" meaning. ... Perhaps we may tentatively propose the definition of "symbolic religious history" for the literary form of Gen. 2–3.[25]

In other words, the biblical narrative does not need to be taken as literally or historically accurate.

Concerns were not confined to the seminary. The same 1962 convention at which Scharlemann withdrew his papers was asked to reject a statement made in Valparaiso University's *The Cresset*, though a convention committee declined to act on the request.[26] The 1965 LCMS convention acknowledged that "antiscriptural teaching has made inroads within the Synod."[27] The same convention *Proceedings* carried an unpublished overture that repeated concerns from 1962 over reported false teachings by a religion instructor at Concordia College, Bronxville, New York, as well as documentation of a St. Louis professor teaching historical criticism.[28] The Synod itself raised similar concerns at its conventions in 1967 (New York)[29] and 1969 (Denver).[30]

---

23 Blue Book (Zimmerman, 210).

24 Norman C. Habel, "My Story—In Brief," http://normanhabel.com/?page_id=38. Accessed 9/3/2021.

25 Norman Habel, *The Form and Meaning of the Fall Narrative* (St. Louis: Concordia Seminary Print Shop, 1965), 9. Cf. Habel, *Form and Meaning of the Fall Narrative*, 5 and 29.

26 Unprinted memorial 361, 1962 *Proceedings*, 182. There was also another unprinted memorial (# 354) to investigate Concordia Seminary, St. Louis (1962 *Proceedings*, 180).

27 Res. 2-23, 1965 *Proceedings*, 99–100.

28 2-45 Un[published Overture], 1965 *Proceedings*, 201 and 202.

29 Res. 2-16 and Res. 2-32, 1967 *Proceedings*, 92 and 95–96.

30 See 1969 *Proceedings*. The following resolution titles are revealing: Res. 2-01, "To Answer Concerns re Authorship of Pentateuch and Book of Isaiah," 84; Res. 2-03 "To Reaffirm Position on Word of God," 85; Res. 2-04, "To Receive Answers to Questions Raised Regarding the Document 'A Lutheran Stance toward Contemporary Biblical Studies,' " 85; Res. 2-05, "To Receive a Response to Questions on 'The Witness of

In 1967, however, the relatively new Commission on Theology and Church Relations (CTCR) released a report, *A Lutheran Stance toward Contemporary Biblical Studies*, which suggested that some elements of historical criticism were allowable with necessary limitations.[31] This document provided a degree of "legitimacy" for the method in the LCMS and at Concordia Seminary.

During this time, the seminary claimed to be teaching the traditional historical-grammatical approach to biblical interpretation, even as it was advocating new approaches.[32] In an introduction to a special issue of the seminary's professional journal, *Concordia Theological Monthly* (*CTM*), the managing editor wrote rather cryptically about two articles in that issue: "The critical reader will find in both articles much that is new and much that is good. He will not encounter much difficulty in deciding how much of the new is good and how much of the good is new."[33] Similarly, Professor Richard R. Caemmerer (1904–84) authored a *CTM* article encouraging pastors not to be afraid of the "new hermeneutics" (interpretation), since "the scholars are for the most engaging in the preacher's task. They are grappling with a primary question: What does the record say?"[34] Under Alfred Fuerbringer's presidency at the seminary, voices expressing concern went unheeded while historical-critical views were quietly espoused and promoted.

Roland P. Wiederaenders, a vice president of the Synod from 1959 to 1973, summarized the situation then:

> ... the faculty of Concordia Seminary, which was shifting into the historical-critical method, which was beginning to question, for example, that our Lord walked on water, beginning to question the story of Jonah and other parts of Scripture. They were beginning to do that, and they were teaching it to their students. I know that, because I had contact with the students. However, when Dr. Behnken and Dr. Harms would meet with them, they said no, no, we're still in the same position.

Jesus and Old Testament Authorship,'" 85; and Res. 2-16, "To Affirm Historicity of New Testament," 87–88.

31   *A Lutheran Stance toward Contemporary Biblical Studies* (St. Louis: LCMS, n.d.), 8–10.

32   See Zimmerman, chapter 1, "Storm Clouds Gathering," especially 18–27.

33   Herbert T. Mayer, "Editorial," *CTM* 35, no. 9 (October 1964): 515. The articles were "Old Testament Theology as *Heilsgeschichte*," by Arlis J. Ehlen, at the time teaching at Colgate-Rochester Divinity School, and "Current Roman Catholic Thought on Prophetic Perspective," by Walter Rast of Valparaiso University.

34   Richard R. Caemmerer, "New Hermeneutic and Preaching," *CTM* 37 (February 1966): 110.

Nothing has changed. And we would go out and say to people, nothing has changed, when it had changed. They were using the historical-critical method, and in my opinion, they were pecking away at undermining the authority of Scripture. . . . There were other professors who were, however, continuing to promote militantly in their classes the historical-critical method. . . . They had changed, but we were told they had not changed, and that's why I say we didn't square with our people. We didn't tell them that changes had taken place.[35]

Greater Candor

Only after John Tietjen's election to the presidency of Concordia Seminary in May 1969 was there a clear admission that professors there were using the historical-critical method. Tietjen later wrote: "I did not appreciate what I thought was less than candor in the seminary's repeated claims that nothing had really changed in C[oncordia] S[eminary] teaching."[36] For things had indeed changed. During the winter and spring of 1970, Tietjen spoke at various LCMS District conventions. In his memoirs, he recalled how he "pointed out that our faculty made use of historical criticism with solid Lutheran presuppositions about the Scriptures as the Word of God and without the faith-destroying presuppositions of higher criticism."[37] However, Professor Ralph Bohlmann reported on a small-group meeting in spring 1970, at which the "chairman of the Department of Exegetical Theology stated that one reason many people in the church failed to appreciate the [historical-critical] method is that the use of the method involves the recognition of various contradictions within the Holy Scriptures."[38] At about this time, recently elected Synod president J. A. O. Preus announced that he was appointing a Fact Finding Committee (FFC) to investigate the seminary faculty.

In the fall of 1972, President Preus issued his *Report of the Synodical President*, which provided summaries as well as transcripts of the FFC's interviews with seminary professors. Among the conclusions was that some professors held or permitted positions that clearly advocated historical-critical views, including:

1. A commitment to use of historical criticism as a valid and even the preferred method for the interpretation of the Bible.

---

35 Roland P. Wiederaenders, interview by Eric W. Modean, July 16, 1977, transcript pp. 11–12, Oral History Collection of the Archives of Cooperative Lutheranism, Lutheran Council in the USA, Elk Grove, Illinois.

36 *Memoirs*, 23.

37 *Memoirs*, 25.

38 Quoted in *Exodus*, 22.

2. Allowing the possibility that many of the Old and New Testament stories are not historical.

3. An insistence that Moses was not the author of the Pentateuch, Isaiah did not pen his entire book, and Paul may not have written all the books attributed to him in the New Testament.

4. A reluctance to identify Old Testament prophecies which point directly to Jesus Christ by minimizing the predictive dimensions of prophecy in the Old Testament.

5. An acceptance that words attributed to Jesus in the gospels were in fact never spoken by Him, but were later additions or interpretations made by the Christian community after the death of Jesus.[39]

Further examples of problematic issues were related to the historical truthfulness of biblical accounts, the validity of miracle accounts, and a decided permissiveness to accept deviant interpretations.[40] Views such as these undermine the very Scriptures which the Synod holds to be true, infallible, and inerrant.

The specific findings in the report show the use of the historical-critical method at Concordia Seminary. For example, Old Testament professor Holland Jones (1920–2016) assumed Wellhausen's documentary hypothesis when he answered questions about his views regarding early Jewish history. Instead of speaking about Mosaic authorship, he said: "I am most interested in finding out what the Yahwist is saying and what he is asserting about God in His presence and activity with Israel as the Yahwist is saying this to his readers."[41] Similarly, Carl Graesser (1929–89) responded to a question about speeches in the books of Kings by stating that these were later creations by the Deuteronomist: "Because the nature of the language seems to me is quite Deuteronomic and like that of the Deuteronomic historian and also because the meaning of the temple is explained in terms of what its meaning is for the people in exile."[42] Robert H. Smith (1932–2006) boldly asserted: "Every part of the Bible may be studied according to the historical-critical method. I study primarily the New Testament by means of the historical-critical method."[43]

---

39 These points are from *Exodus*, 35, drawing from and citing "Summary of the Findings," *Report of the Synodical President*. See Zimmerman, 49–64, 155–96, and especially 55–60.

40 Blue Book (Zimmerman, 235–36, 280–380).

41 Prof. K (Holland Jones), Blue Book (Zimmerman, 295).

42 Prof. A [Carl Graesser], Blue Book (Zimmerman, 295).

43 Prof. H [Robert Smith], Blue Book (Zimmerman, 285).

The president's report summarized: "Many members of the faculty, and the administration and exegetical department, are fully committed to the use of the historical-critical method as a valid and preferred method for the interpretation of the Bible."[44] In the summer of 1971, the LCMS convention had stated that since the use of the historical-critical method seemed to be at the heart of the problems troubling the church, the CTCR should seek "To Evaluate Historical-Critical Method of Interpretation."[45]

In November 1972, CTCR executive secretary Ralph Bohlmann produced a study edition for *A Statement of Scriptural and Confessional Principles.*[46] *A Statement* had been issued by President J. A. O. Preus the previous March. Prominent among the biblical and theological issues it addressed was the use of the historical-critical method of biblical study.

Personal Encounters

As a first-year student at Concordia Seminary in the fall of 1970, I took an introductory course in exegetical theology with Holland Jones and Robert Smith. The course introduced us to historical criticism in an indirect way. While presenting a seemingly traditional grammatical and historical approach to biblical interpretation, calling it "the grammatical, critical, historical method," and then later a "grammatical-historical-critical method,"[47] elements of historical criticism were slowly introduced. The professors admitted:

> We do not usually encounter any difficulties in persuading students to perform the activities in the first unit. . . . We do customarily encounter some difficulties in persuading students to perform the activities of this second. . . . Quite honestly this rather extended introduction is an attempt to con you into cooperating enthusiastically in the activities of this unit.[48]

They proceeded to provide a brief overview of literary criticism in the nineteenth and early twentieth centuries, still calling it "historical." Under the guise of "the historical circumstances," we were instructed to discern the

---

44 Blue Book (Zimmerman, 226).

45 Res. 2-52, 1971 *Proceedings*, 129.

46 [Ralph A. Bohlmann, comp.], *Study Edition of A Statement of Scriptural and Confessional Principles* (St. Louis: N.p., 1972). For *A Statement*, see below, pp. 265–77,

47 Holland H. Jones and Robert H. Smith, *E-100 The Tools and Techniques of Biblical Exegesis*, Fall and Winter 1970 (Clayton, MO: Seminary Bookstore, 1970), 2 and 150.

48 Jones and Smith, *E-100 The Tools and Techniques of Biblical Exegesis*, 53.

stages of development which "produced the Biblical document that contains the pericope [that is, the particular passage under study] and the historical circumstances that influenced this process and effected the origin and preservation of the material contained in the Biblical book."[49]

This was a roundabout way of introducing us to form-, tradition-, and redaction-criticism as merely historical stages in the development of the biblical text. The stated purpose was to describe

> the process that produced a Biblical book or document. This task is engaged in by scholars who are interested in describing the growth of a [sic] Biblical books in such a way that a Biblical interpreter can know the time and thus discover the historical circumstances in which the Biblical materials originated, were first preserved in writing, and were given their present arrangement.[50]

Our professors were not throwing the historical-critical method at us all at once. No mention of the authorship of the Pentateuch or of the four Gospels was stated or even implied at this point.

In the second unit of the course, "Acquiring a Thorough Comprehension of the Origin and Transmission of a Selected Pericope and the Historical Circumstances in which this Occurred,"[51] we were introduced specifically to several aspects of historical criticism—form-, tradition-, and redaction-criticism—still under the euphemistic heading of doing "historical" research.

Form criticism assumes that diverse types of literature in the Bible developed out of earlier traditions that had been passed down orally. Jones noted the Old Testament scholar Herman Gunkel's conclusion "that Israel borrowed their literary forms from the Canaanite population that remained in Palestine after the conquest."[52] Our New Testament historical-critical textbook asserted something similar about the Gospels, indicating that there were various categories of folk traditions such as song or saga or fairy tale. From these, the book continued, the Gospels originated and coalesced.[53] The historical critic practicing form criticism has the challenge to identify such forms. Jones wrote: ". . . the realization that the majority of the small units of which the Bible is composed originated separately and existed for some time before they were incorporated into a written document remains the major

---

49 Jones and Smith, *E-100 The Tools and Techniques of Biblical Exegesis*, 53.

50 Jones and Smith, *E-100 The Tools and Techniques of Biblical Exegesis*, 56.

51 Jones and Smith, *E-100 The Tools and Techniques of Biblical Exegesis*, 3.

52 Jones and Smith, *E-100 The Tools and Techniques of Biblical Exegesis*, 61.

53 See Werner Georg Kümmel, *Introduction to the New Testament*, trans. A. J. Mattill Jr. (New York: Abingdon Press, 1966), 41.

contribution that form criticism has made to our knowledge of the process that produced the books and documents of the O.T."[54]

Our course continued with a lesson on tradition criticism, which evaluates the biblical data either using secular records that may have been passed down to the biblical writers or by trying to tease out, for example, some very early Gospel tradition that was at first passed down orally in Aramaic, then later in Greek in varying forms. In tradition criticism, techniques were "developed to attempt to describe the various collections of small units that had been made prior to and that were combined in the compilation in their present arrangement of the Biblical books."[55] A source or tradition supposedly behind Matthew, Mark, and Luke is identified as "Q" (from the German, *Quelle*, "source"). No manuscripts of Q have ever been found, yet critics assume its existence.[56] That various biblical books were written by Holy Spirit-directed writers was often questioned and even rejected in this course. Instead, the suggestion was that the text grew out of an earlier Jewish or Christian community.

Finally, redaction criticism (*redaction* is a form of editing) seeks to trace phrases or supposed independent elements that were thought to be edited into or out of biblical passages by individuals or the community to produce the final text in our Bibles. Smith explained that "redaction criticism is the study of the motivation and theology of the persons who gave Biblical books their present shape ... the community rather than ... any individual. The man whose name attaches [sic] to a book was thought of quite simply as the last in the chain of transmitters."[57] For example, "Matthew" would be identified as a "redactor," rather than the writer of the Gospel of Matthew.

The goal in all these aspects of the historical-critical method was to find the "kernel" of truth or facts which had been obscured over time. We ended up slighting the text as it stands for the sake of something "behind" it.

Not until a little more than halfway through the course did the phrase "historical-critical method" appear as such in the course notes.[58] Jones and Smith then told us that this method of biblical study is used nearly universally:

> Today investigators of all denominations and countries use the same historical-critical method as they study the life of Jesus and the earliest church. And today international N[ew] T[estament] scholarship tries

---

54   Jones and Smith, *E-100 The Tools and Techniques of Biblical Exegesis*, 62.

55   Jones and Smith, *E-100 The Tools and Techniques of Biblical Exegesis*, 74.

56   Kümmel, *Introduction to the New Testament*, 53–60.

57   Jones and Smith, *E-100 The Tools and Techniques of Biblical Exegesis*, 88.

58   Jones and Smith, *E-100 The Tools and Techniques of Biblical Exegesis*, 92.

Photograph by Paul Ockrassa

Students march north into "exile" with the Concordia Seminary campus (and Luther Tower) in the background (February 19, 1974).

> to listen to the documents also as God's address to the church of N[ew] T[estament] times and to the church of our times. Still conclusions vary. The reason for the variety lies in the fact that scholars differ from one another in their understanding of what it means to be Christian and what it means to be church.[59]

Yet the professors rather boldly gave us this much guidance as we encountered the variety of conclusions: "If, however, the ideas presented by such older commentaries [e.g. "written before the development of the Hist(orical)-crit(ical) method"] contradict the reports you have made in the last two assignments, they are to be rejected." The student/scholar was to stand above the biblical text passed down through previous generations of Christian scholarship. We were to assume our own subjective—or as we were taught, "scientific"—view as the more defensible interpretation. We were encouraged to step into the world of enlightened biblical scholarship, rejecting the very tradition which had nurtured our faith over the years.

In fall 1971, in an introductory course on the Pentateuch with Ralph W. Klein (1936–2021), we were assigned questions related more clearly and forthrightly to the documentary hypothesis, such as: "To which sources is this chapter [Genesis 15] assigned? What criteria are present?" Or "Analyze

---

59   Jones and Smith, *E-100 The Tools and Techniques of Biblical Exegesis*, 99–100.

the pericope according to the documentary hypothesis." Or "Read the Joseph story, giving special attention to the documentary hypothesis." And "What facts, names, ideas are unique to J? to E?"[60] Again, there was no discussion of the Mosaic authorship of these Bible books or other approaches to their interpretation. Clearly, the assumption was that historical criticism was to be used in the course.

Clear Commitment

March 6, 1972, brought a clear example of the seminary's overall commitment to the historical-critical method. Old Testament professor Arlis Ehlen (1932–2017) had strongly advocated the use of the documentary hypothesis and the historical-critical method. As matters related to the renewal of his contract and his teaching assignments for spring quarter became known in the Synod, President Tietjen released an official statement that said:

> It would not be possible to operate a department of exegetical theology at a graduate school without the use of historical-critical methodology. . . . It is not possible for Dr. Ehlen to teach any of his assigned courses at a seminary level of instruction, thus taking the text of the holy scriptures with utter seriousness, without using historical-critical methodology. . . . Nor is that possible for any other faculty member who teaches a course in biblical interpretation, regardless of the department to which he may belong.[61]

Such a bold statement left no question that the method was used at the seminary. On May 3, 1972, Professor Norman Habel made presentations before the seminary's Board of Control and the student body called "Faith and Fact." He clearly demonstrated his use of the historical-critical method.[62]

On November 21, 1972, the faculty majority responded to concerns that had been expressed by adopting a statement. *Faithful to Our Calling, Faithful to Our Lord*, a document in two parts that was released in early

---

60 Ralph Klein, *EO-100 Pentateuch*, syllabus for Fall 1971 (Clayton, MO: Seminary Bookstore, 1971), 6, 8, 9.

61 *Memoirs*, 98, notes: "Letter from author to Jacob Preus, March 5, 1972." See also *Exodus*, 32–33, which indicates that nearly the same words were given to the whole seminary student body in an official seminary news release on March 6, 1972.

62 Norman Habel, "Faith and Fact," a presentation made before the Board of Control of Concordia Seminary and before the student body on May 3, 1972, sponsored by the Commission on Seminary Concerns, available at https//scholar.csl.edu/synod history/Synodical_History/Year/20/. Accessed 8/4/2021.

1973, demonstrates the way historical criticism was regarded as necessary for good biblical interpretation.[63]

In March 1973, the CTCR produced another document that helped to delineate the differences between the historical-critical method of biblical interpretation and the traditional historical-grammatical approach.[64] A three-column chart set forth distinctions between the traditional historical-grammatical approach and the historical-critical views of "the radical position" and of a "mediating position." That latter position was held by many St. Louis seminary professors. Perhaps one example will suffice. Instead of the traditional view of direct special revelation, the mediating view presented a more indirect way of explaining the Spirit's guidance: not "holy men" (2 Peter 1:21), but "the inspiration of the community," so that "it is equally susceptible of investigation and description by the canons and techniques of the secular historian."[65]

What Happened

The New Orleans Convention

The next synodical convention, addressing the issues and individuals involved, was held in New Orleans, Louisiana, July 6–13, 1973. The concerns related to the seminary faculty's teaching concerning the historical-critical method again appeared. During the morning session on Thursday, July 12, the seminary's three official representatives, Edgar Krentz, Robert Bertram (1921–2003), and John S. Damm (1926–2019), addressed the convention. Then the Floor Committee on Seminary Issues called on Martin Scharlemann, who declared: "There is such a thing as a historical-critical method which undermines the authority of Scripture."[66]

Another floor committee had prepared a resolution specifically "To Repudiate the Historical-Critical Method of Interpreting Scripture."[67] The convention ran out of time before it could consider that resolution, but it did adopt Resolution 3-09, "To Declare Faculty Majority Position in Violation of Article II of the Constitution." This resolution clearly and boldly condemned

---

63 *Faithful* I and *Faithful* II.

64 *A Comparative Study of Varying Contemporary Approaches to Biblical Interpretation* (St. Louis: LCMS, 1973), 19.

65 *Comparative Study*, 4.

66 1973 *Proceedings*, 37–38.

67 Res. 2-38, 1973 *Proceedings*, 121–22.

elements of the teaching of the faculty majority related to the historical-critical method.[68] Specifically, it said that

> justification for the use of the historical-critical methodology is claimed on the basis of its use under what are termed "Lutheran presuppositions"—being baptized, ordained, professed subscribers to the Scriptures and the Lutheran Confessions. The history of Biblical studies has relentlessly borne out, however, that such "neutral" use is fiction.[69]

After New Orleans

At a fall 1973 forum on synodical issues, Martin Scharlemann gave a presentation to Concordia Seminary students entitled "Historical critical what?" He offered a critical evaluation of the historical-critical method. In contrast to the claims made by the seminary faculty majority, he maintained that there was "only one historical-critical method" with its own recognized presuppositions which questioned the very texts of Scripture.[70]

On January 20, 1974, the seminary Board of Control officially suspended President Tietjen. That evening, a student gathering was called, and on the following day students began a moratorium on classes. A month later, the majority of students and faculty dramatically walked off the seminary campus to form a seminary-in-exile. While the specific issue of historical-critical teaching may not have appeared on the surface of the Walkout, everyone with an interest at the time—those who left and we who stayed—knew of its importance in bringing matters to such a pass.

Near the end of 1974, Eugene Klug (1917–2003), a professor at Concordia Theological Seminary, Springfield, Illinois, and a member of the Seminary Issues floor committee at the New Orleans convention, reviewed in detail a book by German theologian Gerhard Maier, *The End of the Historical-Critical Method.*[71] The review highlighted how the book pointed out the failure of the historical-critical method among recent German scholars. The method self-destructed through its rejection of biblical authority, its acceptance of subjective conclusions, its failure to be accepted by the laity, and its failure to take Scripture's own authority on authorship. Yet this failure

---

68 1973 *Proceedings*, 133–39; see specifically 1973 *Proceedings*, 134 and 136–38.

69 1973 *Proceedings*, 136.

70 Martin Scharlemann, "Historical critical what?" Address presented before an open forum on synodical issues sponsored by the Task Force on Sem and Synod, Concordia Seminary, St. Louis, October 24, 1973, available at https://scholar.csl .edu/synodhistory/Synodical_History/Year/17/. Accessed 8/4/2021.

71 *Spr* 38 (October 1974): 289–302, review of *Das Ende der historisch-kritschen Methode* by Gerhard Maier (Wuppertal: Rolf Brockhaus, 1974).

Photograph by Paul Ockrassa

Two students stand in front of the boarded-up entrance to the Walther Arch on the east side of campus (February 19, 1974).

is not widely recognized. Although historical criticism was being laid to rest in official publications of the LCMS, the historical-critical method remains a dominant method in most other denominations and seminaries, to say nothing of public universities.

Continued Conversations

Early in 1974, President Preus appointed an Advisory Committee on Doctrine and Conciliation (ACDC) to delineate the issues and develop proposals to achieve doctrinal consensus. Unsurprisingly, the historical-critical method was among the topics. Moderate and conservative positions were articulated, and each responded to the other.

The moderate position admitted that "there are many definitions of the historical-critical method, but all of them presuppose the use of the principle of analogy in modern historical investigation." This "principle of analogy" was first asserted by the German scholar Ernst Troeltsch (1865–1923), who stated that an event from the past could only be accepted as historically credible if it also occurs in the present. This principle, as such, calls into question almost all biblical miracles. Not satisfied that the moderates had been adequately wary concerning this principle, conservatives rejected the "consistent application of the principle of analogy."[72]

Citing the faculty majority's *Faithful to Our Calling*, the moderate position reiterated the claim: "In and of itself so-called 'historical-critical' methodology is neutral."[73] This contrasts with a warning that former St. Louis professor Martin Franzmann (1907–76) had voiced to the faculty in the early 1960s. Franzmann began by saying:

> The historical-critical method cannot be considered as merely a theologically-neutral tool or technique of interpretation, comparable to textual criticism, grammar, or lexicography. None of these latter undertakes to pass a value judgment on the historical substance of revelation; the historical-critical method does.[74]

Dean Wenthe (1944–), who upon graduation from Concordia Seminary in 1971 was called as a professor of Old Testament at Concordia Theological Seminary, had written in December 1972:

> The historical-critical method is not a neutral tool, but rather a very special instrument that is inseparable from its own presuppositions, procedures, and results. As one surveys the anti-supernaturalistic presuppositions, the secular procedures and the far-reaching results, it becomes obvious that a wedding between the bride and "Lutheran presuppositions," is as impossible as the marriage of light and darkness.[75]

The assertion of historical criticism's neutrality is at best inaccurate and at worst a deceptive fraud perpetuated by its advocates.

The ACDC could not agree on a mutual understanding of the historical-critical method (HCM). While the moderates asserted that they could use historical criticism with Lutheran presuppositions, conservatives responded that "to use the method with presuppositions other than those implied in the HCM itself calls the whole process into question."[76] These inherent presuppositions of historical criticism diminish the divine inspiration of Scripture, and the method itself emphasizes the human dimensions of the biblical narratives. Such presuppositions also included an attitude of doubt about all things

---

72 *ACDC*, 67, 88.

73 *ACDC*, 70, quoting *Faithful* I, 41.

74 Martin Franzmann, *The Historical-Critical Method*, mimeographed copy in the author's files, dated "c. 1960 for Faculty Presentation."

75 Quoted in *Watershed*, 11. This publication offers much more evidence for the use of and advocacy for the historical-critical method at Concordia Seminary in the early 1970s.

76 *ACDC*, 89.

in the Bible, perhaps even excluding the possibility of supernatural events recorded in Scripture. Finally, by dissecting the biblical text into supposed "earlier parts," the method destroyed the unity and authority of the Bible.

The ACDC participants came to a stalemate. Many of the advocates of historical criticism departed the Missouri Synod for other fellowships.

The Difference This Makes

Seminary Biblical Studies Today

A half-century after these events occurred, it is a cause for rejoicing in the LCMS that the Holy Scriptures are being taught in accordance with the historical-grammatical approach. Certainly, historical study is necessary for a book about God's activities in the ancient world as well as in our world today. Criticism, in the sense of careful discrimination of the historical and grammatical data, is still practiced. Yet it is always under submission to the biblical text itself.

LCMS seminary graduates are well trained in biblical studies, doctrinal scholarship, and historical research, even as they also acquire practical skills. The current president of Concordia Seminary, Thomas Egger, and former president, Dale Meyer, are both exegetical scholars, representing solid biblical scholarship with confessional integrity. Concordia Theological Seminary president Lawrence Rast is an historian of American Christianity and especially of Lutheranism in North America. Both of these seminaries are recognized as top schools in the country to prepare pastors for congregational ministry, continuing to receive high scores from accrediting agencies the Association of Theological Schools and the Higher Learning Commission.

The Bible in the Life of the Christian

An important question remains: "How can I read the Bible for my own spiritual nurture?" The easy answer is: "Just do it!" While reading requires a certain degree of understanding, it is possible for most people beginning in early grade school to grasp the meaning of words, sentences, and paragraphs. The same is true for Bible study.

There are several good guides for Bible study, but here are a few principles drawn from reliable students of the Word:

1. *Choose a translation that you enjoy.* The English Standard Version is used extensively in the LCMS. Avoid paraphrases such as Eugene Peterson's *The Message* and Kenneth Taylor's *The Living Bible*, which give the author's paraphrasing of passages but do not accurately render the original biblical text.

2. *Read the section you wish to study.* Generally a chapter is sufficient.

3. *Look over the context of that section.* Depending on the section, a chapter or two before and after will provide helpful insights. Sometimes the whole book is worth skimming to give you a sense of how your section fits into the larger context.

4. *Look at footnotes and other guides that point to similar ideas in other passages of Scripture.* A concordance, which provides references to other places where a specific word is used, can also help you follow the biblical principle that Scripture interprets Scripture.

5. *Compare what you have read with your general understanding of the creeds and the catechism.* What teachings do you see in your reading?

6. *Luther held that Scripture should "bear or carry Christ."* Therefore it is good to ask, "Where is Christ in my reading?" And in a similar vein, determine whether the reading is strong in Law (rules or judgments or failures or indications of sin) or Gospel (promises or forgiveness or grace or pointing to salvation) themes.

7. *How does this passage apply to our (your) contemporary situation?* This is the practical use, putting a biblical section into practice in one's own life.

A simple reading of the biblical text is most beneficial, without recourse to historical-critical pretexts.

Sometimes a study Bible with notes can profitably guide your thinking or offer devotional ideas along the way. *The Lutheran Study Bible* does so, using the English Standard Version.[77] An earlier publication, *The Concordia Self-Study Bible*, used an earlier edition of the New International Version.[78] However, there are some study Bibles which have pronounced theological biases. These should be avoided, including the *Scofield Reference Bible* and the *Ryrie Study Bible*, because they are anti-sacramental and present dispensational pre-tribulationist premillennial views contrary to biblical truth.[79]

A plain reading of the Bible will allow the Holy Spirit, who caused these Scriptures to be written, to speak to your heart and affect your (spiritual) life. A useful approach is to read a section of Scripture (a chapter or less) and, after asking the Spirit to guide your reading, consider several questions: What

---

77 Edward A. Engelbrecht et al., eds., *The Lutheran Study Bible* (St. Louis: Concordia Publishing House, 2009).

78 Robert G. Hoerber et al., eds., *Concordia Self-Study Bible* (St. Louis: Concordia Publishing House, 1986).

79 See CTCR, *The End Times: A Study of Eschatology and Millennialism* (St. Louis: LCMS, 1989).

does this passage say about God? Where do I see myself in this passage? How does this passage speak to my contemporary world? Is there a lesson that I can use in my life today? Then pray that God would keep the reading in your thoughts throughout the day.

As St. Paul encourages in Colossians 3:16: "Let the Word of Christ dwell in you richly"!

The Church and the Bible

It seems obvious that the Bible is the book of the church. Yet with the historical-critical method, the Bible was wrested from the hands of the church and tendered to the grasp of academic elites. Thankfully, today, the Bible has been returned to God's people. Bible translation work throughout the world continues to place the living voice of the Gospel into the ears and hearts of people so that they can hear God's faith-creating and faith-sustaining Spirit in their heart language. Scripture study by laypeople is increasing, especially within conservative Christian denominations. The Good News of God's love and free forgiveness through Christ continues to be read and shared as people grow in faith and understanding until Christ returns. May you find this to be true in your own life.

"Amen. Come, Lord Jesus!" (Revelation 22:20).

For Discussion

1. Give a brief definition of the historical-critical method. What does this method assume?

2. What reasons for the 1974 Walkout are explained in this chapter?

3. Although many who advocated for the historical-critical method claimed that it was neutral, what dangerous conclusions did some St. Louis seminary professors draw in the early 1970s?

4. Why is historical study of the context of a Bible verse important?

5. What is the benefit of looking at the Bible using a traditional historical-grammatical approach?

6. How has this chapter helped you to recognize the blessing of having a trustworthy method of Bible study?

Digging Deeper

Burgland, Lane A. *How to Read the Bible with Understanding*. 2nd edition. St. Louis: Concordia Publishing House, 2016.

Engelbrecht, Edward A., ed. *Lutheran Bible Companion*. Volume 1: *Introduction and Old Testament*. Volume 2: *Intertestamental, New Testament, and Bible Dictionary*. St. Louis: Concordia Publishing House, 2014.

Engelbrecht, Edward A., Dawn Mirly Weinstock, Gail E. Pawlitz, and Sarah J. Steiner, eds. *Know the Bible Now: A Visual Overview*. St. Louis: Concordia Publishing House, 2016.

Lindsell, Harold. *The Battle for the Bible*. Grand Rapids: Zondervan, 1976.

Surburg, Raymond F. *How Dependable Is the Bible? An Evangelical Perspective*. A Holman Book. Philadelphia: J. B. Lippincott, 1972.

Voelz, James W. *What Does This Mean? Principles of Biblical Interpretation in the Post-Modern World*. St. Louis: Concordia Publishing House, 1995.

CHAPTER FOUR

CONFESSIONAL SUBSCRIPTION

Scott R. Murray

Christians have confessed the faith through summaries of
biblical teaching since the New Testament era (for example,
1 Corinthians 15:3–5). The Lutheran Church requires her
pastors and teachers to subscribe unequivocally to her
official confessions. What does this subscription mean?
To what does it obligate these servants? The faculty majority
at Concordia Seminary attempted to reduce the doctrinal
authority of the Lutheran Confessions by arguing that these
documents had to be interpreted historically or interpreted
according to the Gospel or by denying that the Bible was
a source capable of delivering a standard of teaching.
In the end, the Gospel itself was endangered.

Introduction

At ordination services, worshipers are often struck by the vow taken by
the man being ordained. Standing before God, the congregation, and his
brothers in the office of the ministry, he solemnly promises to carry out his
responsibilities as a pastor in conformity with Scripture and the Lutheran
Confessions.

Consider, though: What value would such a stated commitment to the
Lutheran Confessions have if these Confessions were to be regarded simply
as an historical artifact, that is, as only a testimony to what Lutherans used to
believe back in the sixteenth century? Or what if the Lutheran Confessions
were to be considered merely a witness to the Gospel, lacking specific binding
authority beyond a vaguely defined "Gospel"? If a pastor were to have such
understandings in mind while taking his ordination vow, how strong an

assurance would this man being ordained thereby offer to the church about the way he intends to conduct himself in the ministry?

The status of the Lutheran Confessions and their authority in the church amounts to no small matter. Yet about this important topic the faculty majority of Concordia Seminary proved ambivalent at best.

A Defense for Confessing and Confessions

Confessing Christ has deep significance. It results from the work of the Holy Spirit (1 Corinthians 12:3). Therefore the Lutheran Church is a confessing and confessional church. Jesus Himself encouraged His followers to confess Him: "Everyone who acknowledges Me before men, I also will acknowledge before My Father who is in heaven, but whoever denies Me before men, I also will deny before My Father who is in heaven" (Matthew 10:32–33). Our Lord tightly tied confession to our eternal status in the presence of God. For his part, the apostle Paul added: "Since we have the same spirit of faith according to what has been written, 'I believed, and so I spoke,' we also believe, and so we also speak" (2 Corinthians 4:13). We cannot help but express what we believe.

Confessional statements do not have a life of their own. Although they arise out of the church's desire to bear witness to the Lord's gifts to His Bride in the Word of God, they are not really the church's possession. They are, rather, God's gift *to* His possession, the church (1 Peter 2:9). They are not anyone's personal possession and never can be. A confessional statement is a corporate one to which every member pledges loyalty. It is *mine* precisely because it is *ours*.

A creed or confession serves as a standard for Christian congregations and their teachers. As the saying goes, "Good fences make good neighbors." So, for example, the Lutheran Confessions are a pattern of teaching and practice so that an agreed standard marks our lives together as we are committed to a single, dependable measure of God's truth. A confessional standard protects laypeople from teachers who desire to manipulate the divine revelation in favor of their own home-cooked version of what to teach. A confession or a creed objectively establishes a standard. The confessors who produced and collected the Lutheran Confessions clearly understood their content in precisely this way. As the Formula of Concord puts it:

> Fundamental, enduring unity in the church requires above all else a clear and binding summary and form in which a general summary of teaching is drawn together from God's Word, to which the churches that hold the true Christian religion confess their adherence. For this

same purpose the ancient church always had its reliable creeds. (FC SD Rule and Norm 1)[1]

Of course, the Bible is the church's doctrinal standard. Are we Lutherans elevating our Confessions over Scripture, the Word of God? May that never be! The Bible remains the standard that sets all others.

In the nineteenth century, an international commission established the exact official length of a meter. That meter is kept in Sèvres, just outside of Paris. Every meter must conform to the length of that "model" meter. It typically does not enter the minds of people to question whether the meter stick in their broom closet in fact measures a true meter. Still, that stick in the closet must be no longer or shorter than the meter kept in France. Similarly, the Bible is the measure of what is to be believed, taught, and confessed in the church. Our Lutheran Confessions, the doctrinal contents of which conform with the Bible's own teaching, have become a measurement of faithful teaching. This is so and can only be so because these Confessions are a correct exhibition and exposition of God's Word. The relationship between the two standards is that the Bible is a "norming norm" and the confession that depends on it is called a "normed norm."

The Bible is like the meter in Sèvres while the Lutheran Confessions are like the meter stick in your broom closet. When we say that we accept the Lutheran Confessions as a norm or standard, we mean that they, too, can be used to measure teachings and teachers, just as you can use that meter stick from your closet to make measurements. The Confessions tell us whether a particular teacher's teaching measures up to the divine truth, for the standard of the Lutheran Confessions has been set by the ultimate standard, the Bible.

In The Lutheran Church—Missouri Synod

The Lutheran Confessions are gathered in a single volume, the *Book of Concord*, first published in 1580. It contains the three ecumenical creeds: the Apostles', the Nicene, and the Athanasian Creeds. It also contains the Lutheran confessional writings composed in the sixteenth century: the Augsburg Confession and its Apology, the Small and Large Catechisms of Martin Luther, the Smalcald Articles, the Treatise on the Power and Primacy of the Pope, and the Formula of Concord.

To become a member of the ministerium of the Lutheran Church, a pastor unconditionally subscribes to this *Book of Concord*. He signs his name to the Lutheran Confessions, indicating that he makes them his own and promising

---

1   K-W, 526.

to be faithful to them.[2] The first president of the Missouri Synod, C. F. W. Walther, asked: "Why are the Symbolical Books of our Church [the Lutheran Confessions] to be subscribed to by ministers of the same not conditionally, but unconditionally?" Answering his own question, he wrote that "a merely conditional subscription contradicts both the purpose of the Symbols in general and also the purpose of the oath of subscription in particular."[3]

As is the case today, also at the time of the Walkout every Synod-rostered professor as well as all the pastors in the LCMS unconditionally subscribed to the *Book of Concord* "as a true and unadulterated statement and exposition of the Word of God."[4] So how did they find themselves to be at odds about the meaning of the Bible and the expression of biblical truth in the *Book of Concord*?

The faculty majority at Concordia Seminary began to use the approach to biblical interpretation that arose from the Enlightenment and came to be called the "historical-critical method." That method began with the presupposition that the Bible could err like all other human writings, and therefore it could not be the absolute touchstone of truth. As far as this method is concerned, the Bible is just as susceptible to error as the Quran. Further details on historical criticism and its assumptions about the Bible are provided elsewhere in the present book.[5] For present purposes, it suffices to note that the historical-critical method presumed that the Bible and the standard it offered would be basically like a meter in Sèvres that had been shortened.

If the Bible and its content comes to be regarded as bent or shortened, and in that way seems an uncertain and unreliable standard of teaching in the minds of interpreters, then any confessional statements derived from the original standard will end up being taken as even less certain than the original. Think of it this way: a corrupted computer code may lead to disaster when it is run. As programmers were saying in the 1970s, "garbage in, garbage out." The Bible is the "source code" of the church's confessions. If we presume that it has errors, then what kind of a standard could these confessions possibly be for the church's teaching and practice? These confessions would have a

---

2   *Lutheran Service Book: Agenda* (St. Louis: Concordia Publishing House, 2006), 166.

3   C. F. W. Walther, "Answer to the Question, 'Why Should Our Pastors, Teachers, and Professors Subscribe Unconditionally to the Symbolical Writings of Our Church?'" trans. Alex. Wm. C. Guebert and Matthew C. Harrison, in *Walther's Works: Church Fellowship* (St. Louis: Concordia Publishing House, 2015), 18.

4   Constitution of the LCMS, in *Handbook: Constitution, Bylaws, Articles of Incorporation* (LCMS, 2019), 11.

5   See especially above, chapters 2 and 3, pp. 39–82; and below, chapters 8 and 9, pp. 169–215.

dubious norming capacity. If the Bible could not offer the divine truth, then no confession based on the Bible could serve as a standard of truth or a norm for the teaching of the truth.

The Concordia Seminary Board of Control reported to the 1973 convention of the LCMS on efforts it had made to seek

> to determine how subscription to the Lutheran Confessions was understood by individual faculty members. It asked faculty members to explain their position on other issues which the board had isolated and listed in its Progress Report. The board concentrated especially on such matters as the relation between fact and faith, the interrelation between the Old and the New Testaments, creation, original sin, prophecy and fulfillment, Messianic prophecy, our Lord's virgin birth, miracles, the relation between the Scriptures and the Confessions, the meaning of inspiration, infallibility, and inerrancy . . . .[6]

The concerns mentioned in this partial listing included a number of paramount issues. We should not fail to note that the relationship between the Scriptures and the Confessions and confessional subscription were also included in the list.

Some members of the seminary's faculty majority had reimagined the standard of the Lutheran Confessions in a way that made it sound as if these Confessions were respected and honored, even though for them the Lutheran Confessions had actually become a standard that could in at least some respects be ignored or worked around. As a practical matter, professors recognized that they could not formally reject the Lutheran Confessions as a standard for their teaching without provoking an explosion among the rank-and-file members of the Synod. But well before the 1973 LCMS convention, President J. A. O. Preus had reported the FFC's finding that "all professors claim allegiance to the Lutheran Confessions. However this subscription is limited and circumscribed so that in practice it is something less than full subscription"—an understatement of significant magnitude.[7]

For the faculty majority, confessions could only be approximations of the truth—at best, a near miss—because no text could ever command the unconditional allegiance of any teacher.[8] It was typical of the philosophical scene at the time to reject out of hand any restriction on the content of teaching via an external, objective standard. Applying such thinking to the church, no

---

6   1973 *Convention Workbook*, 99.

7   Blue Book (Zimmerman, 230).

8   Robert D. Preus, "Confessional Subscription," in *Evangelical Directions for the Lutheran Church*, eds. Erich Kiehl and Waldo J. Werning (Chicago: Lutheran Congress, 1970), 44.

theological "cop" should be able to norm the teaching of the church's professors, and no theologian worth his salt would submit himself to such an authority. Consider this, however: if fourth-century or sixteenth-century confessions in the *Book of Concord* were being resisted, would St. Paul or even Jesus Himself be permitted to norm the content of teaching?[9]

Historicism

As just noted, professors in the faculty majority at Concordia Seminary did not outright reject the Lutheran Confessions. They actually spoke highly of these Confessions, even while chipping away at their authority. Perhaps the most common method for doing so was to intone solemnly that the Lutheran Confessions have to be understood historically.

On the surface, who could object to this? For it would be inexcusable to use the Lutheran Confessions without examining their historical context. For example, one cannot adequately understand the Augsburg Confession without a basic knowledge of late medieval politics within the Holy Roman Empire, the involvement of the papacy in broad swaths of daily life, the invasion of Europe by the Turks, the documents that served as preparatory studies for the Augsburg Confession, and a great deal more. Yet this is not all that was meant by the faculty majority and others when they spoke and wrote about treating the Lutheran Confessions historically.

What they meant also was that the Confessions were testimonies to what Lutherans believed in the sixteenth century. Just because sixteenth-century Lutherans taught and believed certain things, however, did not necessarily obligate twentieth-century people to anything. After all, someone might say, we have learned so much in the years since then! Did Lutherans of the past believe the content of the *Book of Concord*? Yes, it is a wonderful witness to a long dead world and its even deader faith. It should be well-noted that the compilers of the Lutheran Confessions stood far removed from any such thinking. They

> would not have conceded that their confession was historically conditioned in the sense that it contained theological viewpoints which would some day become outmoded. They were sure that their confession presented "divinely delivered truth," and that it was "a true norm and declaration of the pure truth."[10]

---

9 See Robert Preus, "Confessional Subscription," 44–45.

10 Harry A. Huth, "Confessional Subscription and Theological Pluralism," *Spr* 39 (March 1976): 198, quoting (and translating into English) from the Latin text of the Preface to the Book of Concord.

The fact is that one can subscribe to *any* literature of the past simply as an historical artifact. Shakespeare's plays reveal many interesting things about his time, his place, and what he thought of his time and place, yet it is not incumbent on me to share any of his views. Confessional subscription that is merely historical enables readers today to talk, even at learned length, about the content of the Lutheran Confessions. From this perspective, readers can even praise the confessors for their work, just as we might admire Shakespeare for his creative insights. However, such eulogies of the Lutheran Confessions can hide from an unwary observer the fact that they are being spoken over the corpse of the Confessions.[11] By contrast, in adopting *A Statement of Scriptural and Confessional Principles* at its 1973 convention, the Synod responded by rejecting

> the view that our confessional subscription means only that we regard the Confessions as a historically correct response to the problems encountered by the church when the Confessions were written.[12]

The attempt to relegate the Lutheran Confessions to the ash heap of history shows the chauvinism of modernity: we're so smart; bygone generations are so ignorant. The argument that historically bound texts cannot order and shape our theology and practice can be pushed to the point of absurdity, though, as follows: A document written just 10 years ago is also "history," so why should that artifact of history be more authoritative than another artifact written 500 years ago, 2,000 years ago, or perhaps 5 years ago? At issue here is not the age of the authority but rather authority itself. Members of the faculty majority did not want to be subject to any external standards.[13] When they said they wanted to understand the Lutheran Confessions historically, they meant that these Confessions were "just history," that is, irrelevant.

Gospel Reductionism

The faculty majority also argued that the Lutheran Confessions were authoritative only in their delivery of the Gospel. Professors reduced all confessional statements to be either *the Gospel* or *not-the-Gospel*. Anything that

---

11 See Scott R. Murray, "Confessional Loyalty or 'I Let That Subscription Lapse'?" *CTQ* 80 (January 2022): 34–36.

12 *A Statement*, part VI.3 (cf. below, p. 274).

13 Scott R. Murray, *Law, Life, and the Living God* (St. Louis: Concordia Publishing House, 2002), 216.

was *not-the-Gospel* was deemed nonbinding. President Preus reported to the Synod about the views of some professors:

> They state that they accept . . . [the Lutheran Confessions] because they are "a living witness to the fact that at that place in the church's life . . . these men confessed Christ in such a way that they maximized His benefits," or because "they bring out to me the evangelical thrust of the Gospel."

"Thus," Preus continued, "Gospel reductionism is applied to confessional commitment."[14]

Gospel reductionism leads to the conclusion that anything which is to be binding on the church's public teachers simply does not apply. Such restrictions or requirements would, by definition, be regarded as Law and therefore not binding.[15] As a result, professors and pastors would not have to be tied down to specific teachings about a range of biblical subjects from the fall of Adam to the virgin birth of our Lord. The Gospel-reductionistic Gospel turned out to be a Gospel with minimal content. It was "Gospel" in that it was good news for a bad situation.

In 1973 the Synod noted in Res. 3-09 that even careful statements by the faculty majority had not gone into such Gospel truths as vicarious satisfaction, substitutionary atonement, or the imputation of Christ's righteousness.[16]

Here is a specific case of Gospel reductionism with respect to the Lutheran Confessions: The *Book of Concord* echoes the biblical teaching that Adam and Eve really existed. The devil led them away from God's Word to their own thoughts (SA III VIII 5), and ever since they disobeyed the Lord all their offspring except Jesus have inherited the status of being children of wrath (FC SD I 9). Nonetheless, a Concordia Seminary professor told the FFC that it was unnecessary to hold that Adam and Eve were the first two human beings created by God.[17]

When the FFC questioned members of the faculty majority further about this matter, some intriguing theological wiggling resulted. One professor was

---

14 Blue Book (Zimmerman, 390). See above, chapter 1, pp. 15–37; and below, chapter 5, pp. 105–21.

15 See Murray, *Law, Life, and the Living God*, 216 *et passim*.

16 1973 *Proceedings*, 136–37.

17 Blue Book (Zimmerman, 390). On Adam and Eve, see especially below, chapter 8, pp. 169–93.

unable to say that Adam and Eve were specific historical persons. Instead, Adam typified what the professor faced:

> I see myself as a part of that Adam mess, my experience has, well, everything in my life that I laid out for you points in that direction, and it has a tremendous message for me completely apart from the character of Adam, and I suppose that it does because I see myself as a son of Adam as Paul laid out sons of Adam here.[18]

This statement is instructive. Rather than Adam's experience as recorded in God's Word telling us who we are as fallen creatures, the experience of the individual tells the professor who Adam is. In this way human experience, not a revelation from God, becomes the norm of theology. When human experience becomes the norm of theology, who will want to be bound to the Lutheran Confessions?

The interview with this particular professor went beyond registering his opinion about the question of Adam and Eve's simple existence. It also involved the fall into sin. As noted previously, the Lutheran Confessions teach that Adam and Eve had a real fall (AC II 1). Yet this professor suggested that the Confessions referred to Adam strictly for the sake of pointing to "the fallenness of all men," the need for a Savior. The fall may not be true in itself: "As I understand the Confessions, they talk about this in order to show one's need for Christ as Savior, and I use the Confessions precisely this way, just as I use the Scriptures in that way. . . ."[19]

Notice a couple of things about this statement by the professor. First, the Law-Gospel message of the need for a Savior and God's provision of a Savior in Christ is not only what the professor said that he himself was interested in ("I think I know what . . . [Paul's message in Romans 5] about God and God's action in response to the event in Adam and the event in Christ is, and that is his message to me"), but the professor also claimed that this was the extent of what *the Lutheran Confessions* were interested in. That is, the Confessions were not "discussing the historicity of Adam."[20] Second, just as through Gospel reductionism the professor reinterpreted the fall of Adam, reducing its meaning to a personal experience rather than a real occurrence happening to the first man, so he further used the same method to reinterpret the text of Scripture. When the divine Word is subject to such reinterpretation, any subsidiary authority such as the Lutheran Confessions becomes all the more prone to reinterpretation according to Enlightenment

---

18 Prof. K [Holland Jones], Blue Book (Zimmerman, 394).

19 Prof. K [Holland Jones], Blue Book (Zimmerman, 394).

20 Prof. K [Holland Jones], Blue Book (Zimmerman, 394).

standards and theological uncertainty.[21] This professor was asserting authority over the texts rather than recognizing the texts as having authority over him and his teaching.

A Statement responded to Gospel reductionism with respect to the Lutheran Confessions as follows:

> We recognize that the doctrinal content of the Confessions centers in Jesus Christ and the Gospel of our justification by grace through faith, but we reject the view that the doctrinal content of the Confessions includes only those confessional statements which explicitly and directly deal with the Gospel of Jesus Christ. Accordingly, we do not accept the idea that our subscription to the Lutheran Confessions permits us to reject such confessional positions as the existence of the devil and of angels or that Adam and Eve were real historical persons whose fall into sin was a real historical event.[22]

Weak Statements

Gospel reductionism produced weak statements of confessional fidelity. For example, in 1970 the self-styled Committee for Openness and Trust within the LCMS offered a statement, to which they (ironically!) subscribed, in which they made a perfunctory mention of the Confessions. This committee was identified by a St. Louis *Globe-Democrat* reporter as a "liberal faction" in the Missouri Synod that included several professors from Concordia Seminary.[23]

The statement said, "We identify too with the historic confessions of the Lutheran Church, understood, as all such statements must be, in the historical setting and terms of their time. We see these confessional statements as setting forth a life of Christian freedom in the Gospel."[24] Now, to "identify with" the Lutheran Confessions is to condemn them by faint praise. What

---

21 Luther's reply to the thinking of Erasmus remains absolutely correct: "The Holy Spirit is no Skeptic, and it is not doubts or mere opinions that he has written on our hearts, but assertions more sure and certain than life itself and all experience" (*Bondage of the Will* [1525], AE 33:24). Note also Hermann Sasse, "Quatenus or Quia," in *The Lonely Way*, trans. Matthew C. Harrison et al. (St. Louis: Concordia Publishing House, 2002), 1:460. Sasse pointed out that uncertainty about the theological content of the Confessions quickly spills over to uncertainty about the theological content of the Bible.

22 *A Statement*, part VI.4 (cf. below, p. 274).

23 John Durbin, "Lutheran Faction Here Urges More Freedom in Beliefs," *St. Louis Globe-Democrat*, February 2, 1970.

24 The Committee for Openness and Trust, "A Call to Openness and Trust" (1970), Introduction.

does it mean to "identify with" them? For example, I could talk about identifying with marriage. However, that is not the same as pledging my complete fidelity to my wife alone as long as we both shall live. Mere "identifying with" would be both meaningless and a mockery of marriage. We don't just "identify with" the Lutheran Confessions; we confess them in their full content and pledge ourselves to them as a faithful and correct exposition of God's Word, and we promise to be faithful to their content by not committing adultery with any other theology.

Evaluating this statement by the Committee, Robert Preus wrote that according to it "the confessions serve as a mere example for us today." He added: "Interestingly, this statement too feels free to break with the confessions on their insistence upon a definite doctrine of the presence of Christ's body and blood in the Lord's Supper."[25]

The Committee highlighted its theological ambivalence by further declaring: "We see an urgent need for Christian education to use the Scripture, creeds, and doctrinal propositions to help each Christian to develop his own theology and life-style."[26] Theologizing, then, is reduced to my own activity and effort (Law!), rather than being a faithful reception of the gifts that God has graciously handed down to His church (Gospel!) in the Lutheran Confessions. If every person is a liar and only God is true (Romans 3:4), then all calls to develop one's own "theology and life-style" end badly (and did!). Gospel reductionism always paves the way for a return to the Law. Freedom of action and theologizing ends up talking about our work rather than God's work—the exact opposite of what the Gospel reductionists advertise!

Rejecting the Biblical Interpretations of the Confessions

Even the most cursory reading of the Lutheran Confessions shows that the Bible and its content forms their structural center. Therefore to reject the content of the biblical interpretations in the Lutheran Confessions is like removing the structural steel from a high-rise office tower. That tower would collapse into a dusty heap in a second. Yet the faculty majority insisted that subscription to the Confessions does not obligate the confessor to the biblical interpretations in the confessional writings.

As a bald statement, this is correct. Confessional subscription has never been understood to bind one to the Confessions' detailed reading of every specific Bible passage they cite. However, more was at stake than the way some passages might have been interpreted in the Confessions. Doubt was being cast on the way the Bible was used throughout the Confessions.

---

25 Robert Preus, "Confessional Subscription," 45.

26 "Call to Openness and Trust," VI.2.

We saw earlier the assertion that even though the Confessions were simply reflecting Scripture when they spoke of Adam as a historical person, still it was not necessarily against the Confessions to regard Adam as a typical or conceptual character rather than a specific individual.[27] A related example: President Preus reported an FFC interview with a professor who grew up understanding Genesis 3:15 as a Messianic prophecy (as do Ap XII 55 and FC SD V 23). But the professor added: "It is an interpretation which at this moment I do not find satisfying to the Scriptural evidence as the other interpretation. . . ." The interviewer responded, "You're saying that you'd prefer not to accept this particular exegetical use of Genesis 3 which the Confessions use." The professor replied: "I'm saying that that is my personal preference and that I would regard that as one of those exegetical points on which there is an allowable degree of difference."[28]

The Confessions stand or fall on their reading of the Bible. Scripture remains "the only rule and guiding principle according to which all teachings and teachers are to be evaluated and judged" (FC Ep Rule and Norm 1).[29] When we subscribe to the Lutheran Confessions, we are saying that their doctrinal content is a true and correct explanation and summary of Scripture. Only because of this do we pledge our fidelity to their content.[30] Therefore *A Statement* rejected

> the notion that we are not bound by our confessional subscription to the exposition of Scripture contained in the Confessions or to the doctrinal content which the Confessions derive from individual Bible passages.[31]

It would be detrimental to the authority of the Lutheran Confessions to argue that the exposition of the biblical texts in the Confessions could be rejected. It would be like taking the structural steel out of a building.

We might perhaps disagree with the way some biblical texts were used in the Lutheran Confessions. Still, in subscribing to these Confessions, we conclude that they used these Bible passages in accordance with the analogy of the faith (Romans 12:6), that is, the summation of the articles of the Christian faith as drawn from Scripture. Walther's wonderful 1858 essay on confessional subscription agreed with the seventeenth-century Lutheran

---

27   Prof. K [Holland Jones], Blue Book (Zimmerman, 394).

28   Prof. M [Walther Wegner], Blue Book (Zimmerman, 397–98).

29   K-W, 486.

30   See Ralph A. Bohlmann, "Principles of Biblical Interpretation in the Lutheran Confessions," in *Crisis* 2:164.

31   *A Statement*, part VI.2 (cf. below, p. 274).

Photograph by Paul Ockrassa

Dr. Walter Brueggemann, dean of Eden Seminary, receives the Concordia Seminary exiles. Behind him is the Seminex banner, which takes its inspiration from Isaiah 11:1: "There shall come forth a shoot from the stump of Jesse, and a branch from his roots shall bear fruit." The banner was designed by terminated faculty member Robert Werberig (February 19, 1974).

theologian Johann Gerhard that biblical interpreters should never produce anything against the analogy of the faith.[32] Walther concluded:

> If, for instance, an exegete [interpreter] does not reach the specific sense of a Bible passage and yet interprets it in such a manner that his interpretation rests on other clear Bible passages, he is indeed mistaken in supposing that a certain teaching is contained in this specific Bible passage, but he is not erring in doctrine. In like manner, he who unconditionally subscribes to the Symbolical Books declares that the interpretations that are contained in the Symbols are "according to the analogy of faith."[33]

In any case, it should be recalled that the confessors who produced the Lutheran Confessions were highly skilled interpreters of Holy Scripture. We can expect any misreadings of the biblical text in the Confessions to be the exceptions, not the rule.

---

32 Johann Gerhard, *On the Nature of Theology and Scripture*, trans. Richard J. Dinda, *Theological Commonplaces* (St. Louis: Concordia Publishing House, 2006), 498.

33 Walther, "Answer to the Question," 13.

95

Conclusion

When we hear the vows a pastor takes at his ordination, we will know exactly what he is promising and how beneficial his promise of fidelity is to the church. Faithful confession of the truth of God's Word as it is delivered to us in the Lutheran Confessions imposes no burden, but instead becomes a joy and a privilege. Robert Preus wrote that "it is not only un-Lutheran but unevangelical *not* to subscribe the Lutheran Confessions. Confessionalism springs from a love of Christ, a love toward lost sinners, and a loyalty to the Gospel."[34]

To this we can only give a hearty Amen! Only a full and unequivocal subscription to the Lutheran Confessions will maintain Lutheran clergy as Lutheran and preserve a Lutheran Church in which they can serve.

For Discussion

1. What happens when we no longer adhere to agreed standards of teaching? What happened in the Missouri Synod?

2. Despite being written centuries after the time of Christ and the apostles and before modern scientific discoveries or historical research, why can we treat the Lutheran Confessions as a standard for teaching?

3. How should we respond to the idea that words are incapable of conveying the divine truth to us? If words cannot convey divine truth, what would Jesus mean in John 8:31–32?

4. What happens to the teaching of original sin if Adam is not a historical person? See FC Ep I.

5. Could we say that the use of the Bible in the Lutheran Confessions is not binding upon Lutheran pastors and congregations? In what way?

6. Is it legalistic to insist that our pastors and teachers subscribe unequivocally to the Lutheran Confessions? Why or why not?

7. Should public teachers of the church submit to external authorities? Why or why not?

8. What happens to the content of the Gospel when Gospel reductionism is used on our Confessions?

Digging Deeper

Bohlmann, Ralph A. *Principles of Biblical Interpretation in the Lutheran Confessions*. Revised edition. St. Louis: Concordia Publishing House, 1983.

---

34 Robert Preus, "Confessional Subscription," 50.

Murray, Scott R. "Confessional Loyalty or 'I Let That Subscription Lapse'?" *Concordia Theological Quarterly* 86 (January 2022): 25–42.

Preus, Robert D. "Confessional Subscription." Pages 43–52 in *Evangelical Directions for the Lutheran Church*. Edited by Erich Kiehl and Waldo J. Werning. Chicago: Lutheran Congress, 1970.

Walther, C. F. W. "Answer to the Question, 'Why Should Our Pastors, Teachers, and Professors Subscribe Unconditionally to the Symbolical Writings of Our Church?'" Translated by Alex. Wm. C. Guebert and Matthew C. Harrison. Pages 11–28 in *Church Fellowship*. Walther's Works. St. Louis: Concordia Publishing House, 2015.

DOCTRINAL RESOLUTIONS
AND STATEMENTS

Raymond L. Hartwig

Since earliest times, doctrinal resolutions and statements have been the church's response to doctrinal questions and challenges.

Earliest Doctrinal Resolutions and Statements

When questions arose concerning Gentile converts, the Jerusalem Council resolved the matter with what may have been the church's earliest doctrinal resolution (Acts 15:22–29). And when early Christians confessed their faith and identified one another with the outline of a fish, the five letters of the Greek word "fish" (ιχθυς) served as an acrostic for "*Jesus Christ God's Son Savior*," one of Christianity's earliest doctrinal statements.

As serious doctrinal challenges arose in the early church, simple doctrinal statements became formal creedal statements, that is, the Nicene, Athanasian, and Apostles' Creeds. And when, in the sixteenth century, Martin Luther and his followers recognized the need for targeted doctrinal statements to address serious errors in the church's teachings and practice, those statements became the content of the *Book of Concord* of 1580 by which the early Lutherans defended their teachings as being those of the Holy Scriptures and the historic catholic (universal, Christian) faith.

Early Missouri Synod Doctrinal Statements

In North America centuries later, when the recently formed Missouri Synod faced doctrinal challenges from other Lutherans, it adopted official doctrinal statements such as C. F. W. Walther's *Church and Ministry* (*Kirche und Amt*) and his thirteen theses on predestination. Well before Walther's death in 1887—in fact, already in 1866—doctrinal disputes among other Lutherans in the United States prompted the formation of the General Council of the Evangelical Lutheran Church in North America as a reaction against an Americanized Lutheranism, particularly in the wide-ranging General Synod. Ultimately, however, the General Council proved unable to solve differences in doctrine and practice. In 1918 it merged with the General Synod and others to form the ULCA.

The Missouri Synod never joined the General Council. Yet it remained well aware of the serious doctrinal challenges of the times, as evidenced in an address given by J. W. Behnken during the 1926 dedication of the new campus of Concordia Seminary in St. Louis:

> One of the cancerous diseases which have developed in many theological institutions today is that some professors have joined the ranks of Modernists, evolutionists, higher critics, etc. . . . By the grace of God this shall never happen at our new Concordia Seminary. . . . May He ever keep our seminary firm . . . that it may ever be a training camp to send forth battalion after battalion of stalwart warriors, who in the face of modern Bible-undermining, Christ-denying, faith-destroying attacks will valiantly contend for the faith which was once delivered unto the saints. . . .[1]

A Brief Statement

Shortly thereafter, the Synod's 1929 convention "specially resolved" that the president of the Synod appoint a committee "to formulate theses . . . to present the doctrine of the Scriptures and the Lutheran Confessions in the shortest, most simple manner"[2] to serve as a basis for discussions with other church bodies. This committee, headed by Concordia Seminary president Francis Pieper, authored *A Brief Statement*, following the form of Pieper's earlier "Ich Glaube, Darum Rede Ich" ("I Believe, Therefore I Speak," 1897). This statement was adopted by the 1932 convention.[3] It began to serve as the Missouri Synod's doctrinal norm "almost equal to that of the great Confessions of the Lutheran Church, . . . culminating in its reaffirmation

---

1   John W. Behnken, "1926 Dedication Sermon," *CJ* 15 (July 1989): 234–35.

2   1929 *Proceedings*, 112–13.

3   The 1932 convention's floor committee for Constitutional Matters, after accepting minor changes to the *Brief Statement*, recommended its adoption "as a brief Scriptural statement of the doctrinal position of the Missouri Synod." The minutes of the convention reported: "Synod *adopted* this report," which included making the English text the official text (1932 *Proceedings*, 154–55 [italics original]).

in 1947 and the stated expectation in 1959 that it even be used as a basis for determining orthodoxy."[4] However, when the Synod's Committee on Constitutional Matters opined that this essentially gave the document the same status as Scripture and the Lutheran Confessions, it found such use of the statement to conflict with Article II of the Synod's constitution.

This opinion was sustained by the 1962 LCMS convention.[5] But this opinion further fanned the flames of disagreement. In a subsequent "Opinion regarding Dissenting Groups and Activities within the Synod" the CCM drew attention to

> the organizing of groups, to the calling of meetings, secret or open, to attempted manipulation of existing groups, to circularizing, and to a wide scale of joint actions, all of which by their very nature tend to polarize or fragment the constituency of the Synod.[6]

To State or Not to State

Recently influenced by German theologians, the faculty of Concordia Seminary weighed in.[7] Arthur C. Repp, vice president for academic affairs and a spokesman for the faculty majority, argued that the Synod's doctrinal resolutions "cannot serve as confessional norms" and that "the principle that elevates them to normative status must be rejected" because it is "un-Lutheran, unconstitutional, contrary to the advisory nature of the Synod, and unaccept-able because it is too broad to be meaningful and valid."[8] In an article in the final *Lutheran Witness* issue before the Synod's 1973 convention, he added:

> What is indeed the Lutheran stance toward doctrinal resolutions? To begin with, we need to be reminded that in theological discussions and controversies the sole and final norm for a Lutheran is always Scripture. It's a cruel hoax to make it appear that those who are against making new synodical statements of a doctrinal nature do so because they do not want to accept the written Word of God as the only rule of faith. As a matter of fact, it is because they do not want to encroach on Scripture that they oppose additional binding resolutions. . . .

---

4   Carl S. Meyer, "The Role of *A Brief Statement* Since 1932," *CTM* 33 (April 1962): 199.

5   Res. 6-01, 1962 *Proceedings*, 122–23.

6   Minutes, Commission on Constitutional Matters, October 16, 1969.

7   See above, "Historical Introduction," pp. 1–11.

8   Arthur C. Repp. "The Binding Nature of Synodical Resolutions for a Pastor or Professor of The Lutheran Church—Missouri Synod," *CTM* 42 (March 1971): 153.

Should it happen that the Lutheran Church believes that the time has come that a new confession should be drawn up for new needs, that can indeed be done. But this is the task of all Lutherans, not of a single body of Lutherans, lest that synod or that church body become a splinter group from the body of Lutheranism. . . .

Not only is this tendency today to formulate binding doctrinal resolutions un-Lutheran; it is, I believe, unconstitutional because it would expand our confessional basis without following the proper channels. . . .

Therefore, we regard it as un-Lutheran, unconstitutional, and contrary to the advisory nature of the Synod. We must therefore emphatically reject the present tendency to make synodical resolutions of a doctrinal nature binding on the members of the Synod.

In a counterpoint piece, Harry A. Huth, a member of the CTCR, maintained that doctrinal resolutions are a time-honored tool for Lutherans:

When the Synod accepted Article II of the constitution as its confessional base, it adopted a resolution on doctrinal matters. It declared that it recognizes the Scriptures as the only rule and norm of faith and practice. This position is confirmed in Article VIII of the Constitution, which says: "All matters of doctrine and of conscience shall be decided only by the Word of God."

First of all, then, the Synod set up the principle that the Scriptures are the sole and final authority for all that it teaches and does in God's name. Secondly, however, the Synod declared that while it recognizes that the Scriptures alone establish articles of faith, it at the same time recognizes that the Lutheran symbols correctly confess these articles of faith. . . .

This is what the church of the Reformation did when in a period of grave controversies it composed and subscribed the Formula of Concord. . . .

The authors of the Formula of Concord did not prepare and adopt a new confession, but they did prepare and subscribe a new document which came to grips with the issues and stated which position Lutherans must hold on the basis of their old confession.

A synodical resolution is a legal expression of the Synod to which all who function in the Synod's name are bound. Heirs of the Reformation still have the right and the obligation to clarify and assert their doctrinal position on the basis of their confessional commitment whenever they see a need to do so. . . .

A synodical resolution is a legitimate way for our church body still today to declare its acceptance of and adherence to the Biblical doctrine. In fact this is the only way that Synod can officially express its position.[9]

A Statement of Scriptural and Confessional Principles

At the 1971 synodical convention in Milwaukee, Wisconsin, President J. A. O. Preus called attention to the history of the General Council in the nineteenth and early twentieth centuries to demonstrate what can happen when church bodies fail to state their positions and apply their theology when facing doctrinal challenges. Two years later, he pleaded with the 1973 convention to put its foot down and address the challenges facing the Synod from within and without. Preus had also prepared the way for the convention to do just that. On March 3, 1972, after consultation with the Synod's vice presidents, he issued *A Statement of Scriptural and Confessional Principles*, intending this document to serve as "a tool to identify theological and doctrinal issues which the Synod needs to consider and resolve."[10]

While a theological professor of the LCA, himself critical of *A Statement*, observed that it contained "nothing even slightly innovative" and only "traditional, and never retracted, solid Missourianism," the faculty majority at the St. Louis seminary strongly disagreed, insisting that the statement contained "a spirit alien to Lutheran confessional theology."[11] It answered with *Faithful to Our Calling, Faithful to Our Lord*, a document in two parts.[12] Part I was a joint statement by the faculty. Part II consisted of confessions of faith by individual faculty members.

Widespread discussion of the Preus and faculty documents followed throughout the Synod, cultivated by a study document prepared by a St. Louis professor on leave, Ralph Bohlmann, who was serving as CTCR executive secretary. At length, the 1973 convention adopted Resolution 2-12, "To Understand Article II of the Synod's Constitution as Requiring

---

9   Arthur C. Repp and Harry A. Huth, "Synodically Adopted Doctrinal Resolutions, Are They Binding?" *LW*, June 24, 1973, 11–13.

10 J. A. O. Preus, quoted in Ralph A. Bohlmann's preface to "Study Edition of 'A Statement of Scriptural and Confessional Principles'" (St. Louis, 1972), 5.

11 Editor's note: The former quotation is from Leigh Jordahl, "Review of Lutheranism in North America, 1914–70," *dialog* 11 (Autumn 1972): 320. The latter is from "Response of the Faculty of Concordia Seminary, St. Louis," *LW*, April 30, 1972, 30.

12 Published by Concordia Seminary's Office of Seminary Relations in late 1972. This present book refers to these parts as *Faithful* I and *Faithful* II.

the Formulation and Adoption of Synodical Doctrinal Statements," and Resolution 3-01, which adopted *A Statement of Scriptural and Confessional Principles* as one such doctrinal statement.[13]

Doctrinal Statements and Resolutions Going Forward

Two years later, in the 1975 Resolution 3-04, "To Reaffirm the Right of the Synod to Adopt Doctrinal Statements and Establish Procedures," the Synod noted that even the 1962 convention had asserted the Synod's right to adopt doctrinal statements.[14] The resolution adopted a recent opinion of the CCM that defended the Synod's "right to adopt doctrinal resolutions and to ask its members to uphold them. . . . Indeed, insofar as such resolutions are in accord with the Scriptures they are binding on those who accept Article II of the Synod's Constitution."[15] The resolution also provided for a special committee to be appointed to propose an addition to the Synod's *Handbook* clarifying the specific status of doctrinal statements and providing procedures for adopting such statements as well as for expressing dissent and possible revision.[16]

This Special Committee on Doctrinal Statements, reporting to the 1977 convention, introduced the distinction, adopted by the Synod then and still in the bylaws today, between doctrinal resolutions and doctrinal statements (1977 Res. 3-07).[17] Doctrinal resolutions are "adopted for the information, counsel, and guidance of the membership" (Bylaw 1.6.2 [a]). Doctrinal statements "set forth in greater detail the position of the Synod, especially in controverted matters" (Bylaw 1.6.2 [b]). This distinction does not alter the authority and status of those resolutions establishing the position of the Synod adopted prior to the 1977 convention.[18]

Which is again to say: "Since earliest times, doctrinal resolutions and statements have been the church's response to doctrinal questions and challenges." Across the LCMS, doctrinal resolutions and statements alike remain this church body's official responses to doctrinal questions and challenges.

---

13 1973 *Proceedings*, 111–15, 127–28.

14 1975 *Proceedings*, 94–95; see Res. 3-17, 1962 *Proceedings*, 105–6.

15 See 1975 *Convention Workbook*, 206.

16 1975 *Proceedings*, 95.

17 Res. 3-07, 1977 *Convention Proceedings*, 129–30.

18 "1.6 Confessional Position of the Synod, Doctrinal Resolutions and Statements," *Handbook: Constitution, Bylaws, Articles of Incorporation* (St. Louis: LCMS, 2019), 33–34.

CHAPTER FIVE

THE THIRD USE OF THE LAW

Scott R. Murray

Instead of recognizing that God's Law both informs and accuses
sinners, some Concordia Seminary professors and others
came to think of the Law as no longer applying to the believing
Christian to provide moral direction. Although this may seem
surprising, the Gospel then took on a norming role in their
theology—indeed, a legal role. Their supposed freedom from
the Law led the faculty majority to reject the authority of Synod
leaders over their teaching and practice. This rejection of the
Law, part of the faculty's "Gospel reductionism," effectively
confused Law and Gospel. Thereby it endangered the true
Gospel of God's grace and the comfort it brings to sinners.

Introduction

Suppose your pastor conducted a public extramarital affair. Suppose
further that when called to account for this, he simply claimed that biblical
Law no longer applied to him because he had been called into the freedom of
the Gospel. Would the freedom of the Gospel liberate him from the responsibility to shape his life according to the Ten Commandments? We would never
accept such a lackadaisical obedience to God's Law! We know the answer to
the question: Should clergy or seminary students—or, for that matter, any
Christian—ignore the Law of God?

Yet consider what happened in the days leading up to and following
February 19, 1974. Students and faculty members walked off the Concordia
Seminary campus in what was billed as a spontaneous march into exile. This
event had been brewing in the cauldron that was this seminary following the
1973 LCMS convention in New Orleans, Louisiana. On that memorable
February day, students and their wives planted little crosses in the quadrangle

105

of the seminary campus. Each cross was emblazoned with the name of a professor or student who would participate in the "march to exile." Students produced nicely constructed and well-painted plywood coverings to board up the Walther Arch under Luther Tower, emblazoned with the single word "Exiled." Television news cameras arrived to capture the exciting event of rebellion against what was characterized as the entrenched and retrograde theological thinking of the LCMS, thinking that had been seemingly enforced on the progressive faculty majority. Students and faculty waited for the news media's departure before they returned to the campus in time for lunch at the seminary dining hall. All of this was touted as a spontaneous protest, bubbling up from the grassroots, when in fact "the well-planned and carefully orchestrated walkout took place in full view of the public media, newspaper reporters, and radio and television newscasters. They had been informed in advance about the planned walkout and were present throughout the proceedings."[1] The claim of spontaneity now seems humorous.

In days following, it was discovered that many "files, student records, and other items disappeared from the seminary campus."[2] These items eventually included quite a number of volumes from the seminary's Fuerbringer Library, which eventually found their way into the library collection of Seminex.

How did those who aspired to be Lutheran pastors and those who trained them cook all this up while claiming spontaneity? How could such future clergy and their teachers ignore basic canons about truthfulness (Eighth Commandment) and the responsibility of Christians to care appropriately for the property of others (Seventh Commandment)?

While an answer to these questions may have many facets, one is that the students had been taught, and at least some of the faculty majority had been teaching, that God's Law no longer applied to Christians and should not be proclaimed to them after conversion to provide moral direction. Members of the majority of the Concordia Seminary faculty had not been consistent in their views on the third use of God's Law. President J. A. O. Preus's 1972 Blue Book report to the Synod, which detailed the position of the faculty majority, noted: "The findings range from confusion and ambiguity to a rejection of the third use of the Law as a positive ethical guide for Christians."[3] The Blue Book indicated that some professors believed "God's Law accuses man of his sin but does not function as guide and norm of Christian good works."[4]

---

1 *Exodus*, 124, 128.

2 *Exodus*, 129.

3 Blue Book (Zimmerman, 384).

4 Blue Book (Zimmerman, 237).

It is no wonder that people who hold such a position on God's Law felt both that they could put on a charade before the news media and that seminary property could be filched as they found these actions at that moment to be good, expedient, and to their benefit. The Law of God was no guide to their actions, a fact that showed. How did they arrive at this rejection of the Law as a guide?

The Law in Lutheran Theology

Lutheran theology teaches that God's Law is good and right. It is the eternal will of God. God's Law remains a guide for Christians to know what is God-pleasing. This is called the third use of the Law, one of the three uses or functions of the Law described by the Lutheran Confessions. See especially Article VI of the Formula of Concord. There are not "three laws," but God's single eternal will that can function in different ways, perhaps even at the same time in different people. When preachers proclaim the Law of God to sinful human beings, God uses this Law to fulfill His purposes. What are those purposes?

The first use of the Law curbs gross outbursts of sin by threatening Lawbreakers with the thunder of God's wrath and the threat of punishment, both temporal and eternal. Humans for whom the Law functions in its first use are like the proverbial donkey who needs to be beaten to stay the course and not stray from the path set before it. The threat of certain punishment, whether temporal or eternal, may restrain someone contemplating murder from actually committing that heinous crime. This is what Paul described:

> Now we know that the law is good, if one uses it lawfully, understanding this, that the law is not laid down for the just but for the lawless and disobedient, for the ungodly and sinners, for the unholy and profane, for those who strike their fathers and mothers, for murderers, the sexually immoral, men who practice homosexuality, enslavers, liars, perjurers, and whatever else is contrary to sound doctrine, in accordance with the gospel of the glory of the blessed God with which I have been entrusted. (1 Timothy 1:8–11)

The most important use of the Law is the second, which is also called the theological function of the Law. Here, God uses the Law to lead us poor sinners to repentance, that we might seek His abundant grace in the Gospel and the right use of the sacraments. The reason Lutherans think of this function of the Law as the most important is because it is the use of the Law that is most closely tied to the work of saving sinners. The Law points out the sinner's complete depravity, forcing us to confess that our righteousness must come from elsewhere. (Of course, it comes from Christ, Galatians 3:24.)

107

In writing to the Roman Christians, Paul prepared them for the manifesto of divine righteousness by showing every person under the deadly threat of God's Law:

> Now we know that whatever the law says it speaks to those who are under the law, so that every mouth may be stopped, and the whole world may be held accountable to God. For by works of the law no human being will be justified in His sight, since through the law comes knowledge of sin. (Romans 3:19–20)

The third use of the Law is simply that God makes clear to the forgiven Christian what good works are, so that the fruit of faith can be ordered and shaped by His explicit word rather than by our own faulty and fallen imagination. In this sense, the Law still applies to believers after they are converted and given faith in Christ. Indeed, the faithful will crave and welcome God's explicit instruction in His Word about what works are pleasing in His sight. Paul had his own sin clarified as he confessed: "For I would not have known what it is to covet if the law had not said, 'You shall not covet'" (Romans 7:7).

Many members of the faculty majority at Concordia Seminary denied that Christians were subject to the dictates of the Law.[5] This contention had negative results on their teaching and their response to proper church authority. Direction from the authority of the Synod or the seminary's Board of Control was labeled legalistic and anti-Gospel, and therefore to be rejected out of hand as un-Lutheran.[6] After they walked out, the faculty resisted questions about their teaching for this reason. They thought that any inquiry into their teaching was a clear indication of unfaith on the part of the questioners, who were hopelessly immersed in a legalistic attitude. Any word of Law was seen as a silencing of the Word of God itself. This fit very well into the theory that the Bible's only authority was in the Gospel.[7]

Historical Background

Where did this begin? Many of the members of the faculty majority were quite favorably struck by European theology after World War II. Several faculty members had been deeply influenced by Werner Elert and his theology. That influence started in part because of the participation of Missouri Synod professors in the Bad Boll conferences, so called because the first of the meetings were at Bad Boll, Germany, in 1948–49. Many of those LCMS participants returned from Germany deeply impressed by the breadth of learning

---

5   See Blue Book (Zimmerman, 230).

6   See *Exodus*, 134.

7   See above, chapter 1, pp. 15–37.

evidenced in these discussions. They grew eager to make use of the Germans' theology and method to overcome what they grew to think was a legalistic approach to theology that had overcome the Missouri Synod in the first half of the century. Edward H. Schroeder documented the increasing influence of Werner Elert within the Concordia Seminary faculty.[8]

Elert taught theology at the University of Erlangen in Germany. Although he brought salutary emphases in Lutheran theology to the forefront in his work, Elert also introduced a view of the Law's third use that did not comport with the Lutheran Confessions. He focused his approach on Law and Gospel to the point that Law-Gospel as an independent theological principle actually judges the content of Scripture.

Elert denied the third use of the Law. Why? Elert had been a pastor in the Breslau Synod, which labored heroically against the Prussian Union of 1817 in which the government attempted to enforce a union between the Lutheran churches and the Calvinist churches in Prussia. This was one of the indirect causes of the Saxon immigration that brought many of the Missouri Synod's founders to North America. Given this history, confessional Lutherans were deeply suspicious of the imposition and influence of Calvinism in the Lutheran Church. Elert's anti-Calvinist bias led him to denigrate the Law's instructive purpose.

There is no doubt that Calvin's doctrine of the third use of the Law is problematic. Whereas Lutheranism taught that the chief use of the Law is its accusing function, Calvin held that the chief use of the Law was the informative use.[9] For Calvinism, the Law functions primarily to make sinners better. Lutheranism teaches that the Law primarily exposes sin. Elert argued that because there was no *purely* informatory use of the Law, the third use of the Law was out of bounds, an abandonment of Luther's Gospel principle.[10]

It was incorrect for Elert to assume that the Formula of Concord simply cribbed Calvin's doctrine of the Law.[11] The Formula of Concord never asserted that the Law would have nothing but an informative function. The Law both informs and threatens Christians because they remain both just and sinner until they draw their last ragged breath. No confessional Lutheran

---

8   Edward H. Schroeder, "Law-Gospel Reductionism in the History of The Lutheran Church—Missouri Synod," *CTM* 43 (April 1972): 232–47.

9   John Calvin, *Institutes of the Christian Religion*, trans. Henry Beveridge (Grand Rapids: Eerdmans, 1975), 1:309 [2.7.12].

10   Werner Elert, *Law and Gospel*, trans. Edward H. Schroeder (Philadelphia: Fortress, 1967), 46.

11   See Scott R. Murray, *Law, Life, and the Living God* (St. Louis: Concordia Publishing House, 2002), 28.

Photograph by Paul Ockrassa

Concordia Seminary students and faculty walk north on DeMun Avenue into exile. Dr. Richard R. Caemmerer, who had joined the faculty in 1940 and had been serving as faculty secretary, is walking behind and to the left of the banners (wearing a dark coat and hat) (February 19, 1974).

claims that all God does for Christians through His Law is to inform them of His will. Elert had set up a straw man, only to knock it down. Still, his view became the default position held by many of the seminary faculty majority.

Gospel Reductionism

The Blue Book reported that "the St. Louis Seminary faculty and the synodical President at a meeting on May 17, 1972, agreed that the basic issue is the relationship between the Scriptures and the Gospel."[12] The faculty majority adhered to what at the time was called Gospel reductionism. When John Warwick Montgomery raised this issue in the mid-1960s, he referred to it as Law-Gospel reductionism.[13] By 1972, St. Louis Professor Edward Schroeder was calling it merely "Gospel Reductionism" and treating the Gospel as an essential interpretive standard for biblical exposition. The Bible does not tell us what the Gospel means, ran this thinking; instead, the Gospel tells us what the Bible means. Further, whatever is not Gospel had no authority for the

---

12 Blue Book (Zimmerman, 203).

13 *Crisis* 1:110–27, especially 120.

church, her teachers, or her children. Schroeder even claimed that this was the biblical interpretive method of C. F. W. Walther and Martin Luther.

Schroeder performed a sleight of hand in attributing to the Gospel an interpretive function for the Bible, as though the Gospel tells us what the Bible means, when in fact the Bible tells us what the Gospel means. God defines the Gospel in His Word. Notice that the Gospel was reduced to the status of a rule for biblical interpretation. Casting the Gospel as an interpretive rule turned Gospel not so subtly into Law—not the Law of God, though, but an independent principle above the Bible that ruled over the Word of God.

Classical Lutheran theology has used the Gospel as an indispensable theological criterion that orders and shapes what we say in our pulpits and devotional books, in formal confessions and other theological works. Yet even while the Gospel principle orders what we say in our theology, it does not determine the content of God's Word. The Good News as taught in Scripture tells us what God proclaims about Himself, His Son, and His precious promises. It is not a tool by which we can tell God what He means when He speaks in His Word. It is up to Him to tell us what we are to believe, teach, and confess, as well as to give us the faith that believes and responds.

The Gospel principle functions in this way throughout our Lutheran Confessions. For example, when Luther sought to cleanse the Mass of its legalistic elements, he emphasized that the Gospel forbade the works-righteous practices that had crept into the medieval "sacrifice" of the Mass. (See SA II II.) This and similar church teachings and practices were declared out of bounds, for they "buried Christ" (Ap IV 18, 81). The Gospel principle functioned to overrule the false belief that good works justified sinners in the sight of God, a belief that was false because it contradicts what God says when in His Word He tells the Good News about Jesus. The Gospel principle, drawn from Scripture, kept and keeps churches and Christians from having legalistic practices imposed on them as ways of satisfying God. Among confessional Lutherans, it still safeguards Christians from a reimposition of the Law in church teaching and rites.

If the Gospel principle rules over teaching, it also rules over teachers, who work in service to the Gospel. It was a grave mix-up when the faculty majority claimed that the Gospel principle was an interpretive principle to tell us what the Bible means. This principle then kept the Word of God from being used to judge teachers and their teaching and left faculty members free to develop their own theological opinions without any possible interference from an external authority such as the Bible. They became judges over the Bible and its content. Oversight by the Synod or the Board of Control was

111

instantly considered legalistic and anti-Gospel.[14] This unbounded freedom had tragic consequences, as noted above.

The oddity here is that "Gospel reductionism" eventually led to treating the Gospel as a principle that ruled over the Word of God. Ironically, it turned the Gospel into Law, even though it claimed to free the church from Law. When Law is kicked out the front door, however, it ends up making its way through the back door and being injected into the content of the Gospel. The resulting Law-Gospel mélange leaves consciences uncertain about their status in God's sight. As soon as the Gospel is used to order Christian life, then its content as free and completely gratuitous forgiveness of sin for Christ's sake is called into question. If the Gospel in the strict sense also carries with it a legal function, it begins to obligate Christians to certain acts, words, or thoughts. This is what Luther called cooking Law and Gospel together in the same pot of porridge.[15] The Gospel then ceases to be what it is. Christians are left wondering whether salvation is free or not. This uncertainty is monstrous. In simple and pointed words in a sermon, Luther emphasized this aspect of the Good News: "The Gospel is sheer gift, giving, and salvation, which tells us only to hold out the sack and let the gift be given to us."[16] By cooking the Law into the porridge we no longer have the Gospel.

Law and "Exhortation"

As noted, when the Law is no longer preached to Christians, the Law will worm its way into the Gospel. For example, members of the faculty majority had to account for the epistles of St. Paul. These biblical letters typically conclude with sections of ethical instruction, answering the question: "Since we have so great a salvation, how shall we live?" This very Paul, the apostle who so clearly articulated the doctrine of justification without works of the Law, was quite willing to tell Christians what to do and what not to do, recurring to the Law to inform them and to shape and order their lives in the world. He proclaimed the Law in his epistles after delivering the forgiving Gospel. This is a classic case of the third use of the Law. To be clear, the same Law accused as well as informed. God still used it in what we call the second use as well.

In coming to grips with such ethical sections in New Testament epistles, opponents of the Law's third use engaged in some strange linguistic gyrations. Let me back up a bit to explain.

---

14 See the letter of the Seminex faculty in *Exodus*, 134.

15 See Luther's 1532 sermon for New Year's Day on Gal. 3:23–29 [*How Law and Gospel. Are to Be Thoroughly Distinguished*], AE 57:61–76.

16 Sermon for New Year's Day on Gal. 3:23–29 [*How Law and Gospel. Are to Be Thoroughly Distinguished*] (1532), AE 57:69.

Edward Schroeder talked about "evangelical alternatives" to the third use of the Law. Since he thought the Law cannot be used as the standard or norm for the actions of Christians, the alternative must be that the Gospel becomes the source of ethical action for the Christian life. For if the Law only accuses, it cannot be the Law that directs the Christian concerning proper ethical actions. However, we should note well that there is a wide difference between the Law *always* accusing (which the Lutheran Confessions teach; e.g., Ap IV 38) and the Law *only* accusing. If it *only* accuses, then it can have no informing function at all.

In the article of justification, it can truly be said that the Law only accuses. But the Law also exists outside the article of justification. There it can be said always to accuse even as it gives direction about what is and is not right and God-pleasing. For example, in the Large Catechism Luther wrote of the Law in this way when he distinguished the blessings of domestic service from the self-appointed righteous works done, for example, by monks.

> For when a priest stands in a golden chasuble, or a layperson spends a whole day in the church on his or her knees, that is considered a precious work that cannot be sufficiently extolled. But when a poor servant girl takes care of a little child or faithfully does what she is told, this is regarded as nothing. (LC I 314)[17]

What is the standard for knowing that monastic and churchly works are not God-pleasing while the simple piety of a faithful girl caring for a small child is very precious in the Lord's sight? The Ten Commandments.

> Just think, is it not a devilish presumption on the part of those desperate saints to dare to find a higher and better way of life and status than the Ten Commandments teach? They pretend, as we have said, that this is a simple life for an ordinary person, whereas theirs is for the saints and those who are perfect. They fail to see, these miserable, blind fools, that no one is able to keep even one of the Ten Commandments as it ought to be kept. (LC I 315–16)[18]

The standard that distinguishes false piety from a God-pleasing one is none other than the Ten Commandments. These commandments from God rescue us from being burdened by the commandments of men. (See Matthew 15:9.) They also tie us to a specific standard of piety. As homey and tied to our daily work as it is, this standard provides the right definition of what it means to embark on the quest for holiness as a Christian. The Law of God is good and wise. It provides a pattern for good works.

---

17   K-W, 428.
18   K-W, 428.

However, if you have rejected the Law as a pattern for righteousness for the Christian, then what would you call the ethical instruction that is unquestionably in the Bible—quite evident, for example, in the latter portions of Paul's epistles? You would be unable to refer to it as "Law," third use or otherwise! Here is where the monstrous gyrations came in. Members of the faculty majority made an effort to salvage ethics even as they were rejecting the Law's third use. Sooner or later the question arose: What guides action, if not the Law?

Those who denied the third use of the Law found such guidance in the Gospel. They saw the Gospel as providing exhortation for the Christian ethical life. They made it a norm, or standard, for behavior.[19] The Blue Book reported that some St. Louis professors jumbled the Good News of Christ together with the fruits of faith, that is, good works: "The teachings concerning the fruits of the Gospel (such as good works or social action) are on occasion confused with the Gospel itself (God's proclamation of grace in Jesus Christ)."[20]

St. Louis professor Walter J. Bartling, like many New Testament scholars, called the ethical instruction "parenesis," from the Greek word that means "to exhort." To Bartling this exhortation was not binding, because anything binding is Law. Still, there undeniably was ethical exhortation in the epistles of Paul. How was it to be understood if, in Bartling's words, "parenesis is not an ungainly addition, but is central to the cross itself"?[21] Bartling's answer was, in sum, that the Gospel becomes the way to understand this material. He contended that "the Gospel is the norm for every interpretation of parenesis and for any contemporary translation."[22] Then he added: "*Parenesis* is . . . the *usus practicus evangelii.*"[23] This means that "exhortation is the practical use of the Gospel." Bartling turned out to be so allergic to the third use of the Law that he had to define exhortation (commands, Law) as a use of the Gospel! In so doing, he completely confused Law and Gospel. Bartling's "Gospel" ultimately became Law because it told Christians, even in a mild way, what they should do.

---

19   See Murray, *Law, Life, and the Living God*, 108.

20   Blue Book (Zimmerman, 226).

21   Walter J. Bartling, "Hermeneutics and Pauline Parenesis," in *A Project in Biblical Hermeneutics*, ed. Richard Jungkuntz (St. Louis: LCMS [CTCR], 1969), 63.

22   Bartling, "Hermeneutics and Pauline Parenesis," 74.

23   Bartling, "Hermeneutics and Pauline Parenesis," 75.

Wherever the Law is diminished through a rejection of its third use, the Gospel inevitably becomes infected by Law elements, such as parenesis or exhortation. Law remains Law, though, even if someone calls it Gospel.

The muddled mélange of Gospel and exhortation is nothing other than a blatant confusion of Law and Gospel. It robs consciences of certainty in the Good News. It also leaves the Christian unable to describe good works in specific terms. When that happens, believers are easily roped into man-made forms of righteousness that God has not commanded. "Parenesis" becomes a way of describing the Law as a form of the Gospel.

The Catechisms

Concordia Teachers College, River Forest, Illinois, education professor Stephen Schmidt had accepted the St. Louis faculty majority's view on the third use of the Law. He asserted that the biblical Ten Commandments were not a guide for morality. The Law could only accuse, he explained, so it could not carry out the benign function of informing Christians about good works.[24] Here again we see the old bugaboo of the Law *only* accusing. As noted earlier, the Lutheran Confessions did say that the Law always accuses. In fact, the Confessions made this assertion no less than eight times. However, opponents of the third use mistakenly understand this to mean that the Law could *only* accuse, and therefore it could not also inform. Yet accusation and information are not mutually exclusive. In fact, they require each other. How could the Law accuse if we remained unaware of its content (see Romans 7:7)? What Word of God does not at least inform?

The St. Louis faculty majority and others had made sure that their various talking points were widely available. *A Statement of Scriptural and Confessional Principles* rejected such talking points, such as the contention that "Christians, as men who have been freed from the curse of the Law, no longer need the instruction of the Law to know what God's will is for their life and conduct."[25] Radical freedom stood out as paramount for the faculty majority, even to the extent that in ethical endeavors God had no say; the Law just didn't apply, so it could not provide a divine standard for action. Once more, the question arose: so what would direct moral behavior for Christians?

Ominously, Stephen Schmidt made morality a function of the Gospel instead of the Law. A rejection of the third use of the Law again results in turning the Gospel into Law! This runs counter to the content of the Small Catechism, as taught to every Lutheran child by parents and pastors. A quick

---

24   Stephen Schmidt, "Toward a Model of Moral Education," *Religious Education* 65 (November–December, 1970): 478.

25   *A Statement*, part II.4 (cf. below, p. 266).

review of the Table of Duties shows that our vocations are governed by specific biblical statements of Law. For that matter, the explanations to the Ten Commandments at the beginning of the catechism certainly give Christians ethical instruction. It would be absurd to think that the first chief part of Christian doctrine in the Small Catechism would be used only with non-Christians or only in order to threaten. The Small Catechism was written by Luther for the use of Christians, even as he himself used it daily.

Luther almost always explained the Ten Commandments as not only forbidding some things ("We are to fear and love God, so that we do not curse, swear, practice magic, lie, or deceive using God's name . . .") but also as exhorting Christians to do other things ("but instead use that very name in every time of need to call on, pray to, praise, and give thanks to God").[26] He never thought of the Ten Commandments as separable from the entire teaching of the faith, even though he consistently set the catechetical order as Commandments, Creed, Lord's Prayer. These chief parts of Christian doctrine may appear to be silos of theology, but Luther understood that they feed into and inform one another. Albrecht Peters writes: "As God's unchanging command, it [i.e., the Ten Commandments] remains normative for the entire way of the Christian."[27] Luther's catechisms present the Law to Christians, not only to accuse but also to give specific shape to the works of the Christian life.

In a sermon that he preached at St. Mary's Church in Wittenberg for her absent pastor, Johann Bugenhagen, Luther made it clear that the Ten Commandments still applied to Christians and that the prophets' and apostles' exhortations to obedience throughout Scripture were fine and useful expositions of the Ten Commandments.

> The Ten Commandments, which deal with holy life and conduct toward God and man, cease too, in the sense that they cannot damn us believers in Christ. He became subject to the Law in order to redeem us who were under the Law (Gal. 4:5); yes, He became a curse for us to save us from the curse of the Law (Gal. 3:13). However, the Ten Commandments are still in force and do concern us Christians so far as obedience to them is concerned. For the righteousness demanded by the Law is fulfilled in the believers through the grace and the assistance of the Holy Spirit, whom they receive. Thus all the admonitions of the prophets in the Old Testament, as well as of Christ and the apostles in the New Testament,

---

26 SC I 4 (K-W, 352).

27 Albrecht Peters, *Commentary on Luther's Catechisms: Ten Commandments*, trans. Holger K. Sonntag (St. Louis: Concordia Publishing House, 2009), 43.

concerning a godly life, are excellent sermons on, and expositions of, the Ten Commandments.[28]

The Law remains God's eternal will for Christians, rejecting some works as out of bounds and exhorting us to do others. The text of the Ten Commandments in Exodus is prefaced by a statement of God's saving activity when He rescued Israel from Egypt: "I am the LORD your God, who brought you out of the land of Egypt, out of the house of slavery" (Exodus 20:2). God gave the Law to people He had saved. Through the catechism, God does similarly today as the head of a Christian household teaches the Ten Commandments to the members of that household. Practically, then, in the catechisms the Law is taught to believers. In the 1970s, we might say, the laypeople of the LCMS who had been steeped in the Small Catechism knew that any rejection of the Law for Christians did not square with the instruction that they had received. Clearly, Luther wanted the Law to be taught to Christian youth and adults through the catechisms. The dearth of traditional catechism instruction today may leave the church in the lurch should a similar crisis arise again.

Church Authority and Law

Where the third use of the Law is junked and where Gospel Reductionism is used as an interpretive tool poised over God's Word to impose meaning upon it, correct teaching or pure doctrine becomes unimportant. Perhaps it is even thought to be dangerous. Where the Law's third use is rejected, the Bible cannot provide a clear and objective witness to inform Christians of its truth. Edward Schroeder remarked that the purpose of catechism instruction "is not that they will have the right answer for the great and final examination but rather that they can have that answer happening in their own lives."[29]

This language of the "happening-ness" of the Word of God comes from the *existentialist* approach to truth that gained ascendancy in the latter half of the twentieth century. In this approach, experience was portrayed as everything; judgment of what was happening was rejected. In theology, experience assumed priority over the content of God's Word. Priority in the life of the church was to go to experience and moral action untethered to the Word of God. Regarded as sacrosanct, experience could never undergo evaluation by God's unchanging and eternal will in Holy Scripture. The CTCR report

---

28   *Sermons on John 1–2* (1537–38), AE 22:38–39.

29   Edward H. Schroeder, "Is There a Lutheran Hermeneutics?" in *The Lively Function of the Gospel: Essays in Honor of Richard R. Caemmerer on Completion of 25 Years as Professor of Practical Theology at Concordia Seminary, St. Louis*, ed. Robert W. Bertram (St. Louis: Concordia Publishing House, 1966), 96.

Gospel and Scripture wisely warned against the prioritization of contemporary experience. It noted that such a focus on experience would be detrimental to both the Gospel and the proper preaching of the Law. It observed that "the Lord's directives for his children's individual and community life" are

> incompatible with a "gospel" that speaks of redemption in terms of what God is doing now in the sociopolitical structures, instead of inviting us to trust in what He did once for all on Calvary. When such a "gospel" supplants the Scriptures as norm of doctrine and life, then it is awkward to call anything wrong, since whatever is going on is somehow what God is doing now.[30]

This thinking clearly disconnects us from the scriptural Gospel. In so doing, it removes from sight the historic work of Christ in offering His life as a ransom for many (Matthew 20:28) and His sacrifice as a "once for all" redemption (Hebrews 9:12). It attacks the very heart of the faith, the Good News of salvation in Christ.

The existentialist approach to theology came from European sources, especially for Luther historians who gave birth to the Luther Renaissance of the early twentieth century. This Luther Renaissance arose when aggressive Roman Catholic biographies of Luther challenged Protestant hero-worship of the reformer. Such literature tarred and feathered Luther as a sexual deviant intent upon the destruction of the Roman Catholic Church. This attack drove Luther scholars to delve much more deeply into the literature of Luther, giving birth to a renewed interest in understanding his work.[31] This effort produced a much more sympathetic portrait of Luther.

But the portrait of Luther that emerged was not left untouched by prevailing philosophical fads, which included existentialism. The now all-but-forgotten French philosopher Jean-Paul Sartre was the leading proponent of the existentialist approach after 1945. This approach rejected categories of substance or essence in favor of lived experience. Doctrinal content was deemed less important than the experience of the Gospel in the life of the Christian. Experience trumped truth every time. Existentialism colored many scholars' view of Luther's faith and teaching. Unhappily, Lutheran theologians who viewed Luther's faith through this lens did not seem to notice that existentialism was itself a philosophical point of view like any other, complete with its own weaknesses and misapplied emphases. The danger was that Luther would become understood as more like some twentieth-century existentialist than the sixteenth-century reformer he was.

---

30   CTCR, *Gospel and Scripture*, 8.

31   See Murray, *Law, Life, and the Living God*, 42–45.

The Luther Renaissance also overemphasized the contrast between Luther and his colleague Philip Melanchthon. (This tendency eventually marked the work of Concordia Seminary professor Richard Caemmerer, who repeatedly told students that he wanted to "de-Melanchthonize" them.[32]) Ultimately, such an extreme contrast between Luther and Melanchthon drove a wedge between Luther and the Lutheran Confessions. Theologians wanting to be Lutheran found it very easy to characterize Melanchthon as more Calvinist than Lutheran regarding, for example, the Law's third use. This in turn led them either to raise questions about the Formula of Concord or to engage in rather creative readings of it.[33]

In the twentieth century, existentialistic Lutheranism characterized the Law as whatever produces anxiety and which is quelled by the Gospel. Anxiety might be quelled with an antidepressant or a cup of tea in a quiet spot. But are these things the Gospel? Without reference to the person of Christ working the forgiveness of sins, the existentialistic approach fails to offer a Christ-centered response to the human problem. Such a subjective approach was loath to permit an informing and directing use of the Law.

We must not separate the power of the Word of God to make the Gospel present among humans from its ability to inform us of the will of God, whether Law or Gospel. I am amazed by the number of times when Jesus equated trust in His person with trust in the content of His Word (Mark 8:38; Luke 6:47; 9:26; John 5:24; 12:48; 14:23; etc.). Yet the faculty majority took to describing the divine promises as a personal relationship *as opposed to* the delivery of information or the proclamation of the substitutionary atonement. In fact, however, each depends mutually on the other. The content of the Gospel and the Person who confers the Gospel on the church must not be separated. Either they hang together, or, to borrow a phrase from Benjamin Franklin, they shall surely hang separately.

---

32   Editor's note: Personal conversation, Dr. Walter Rosin with the editor in 1997. See Ken Schurb, "Twentieth-Century Melanchthon Scholarship in the Missouri Synod: With Particular Reference to Richard Caemmerer's 'The Melanchthonian Blight,'" *CTQ* 62 (October 1998): 287–307.

33   Editor's note: German Lutheran Free Church Professor Wilhelm Oesch, who grew up in the Missouri Synod and studied at Concordia Seminary in the late 1910s and early 1920s, observed that Werner Elert opposed not only the Formula of Concord's position on the third use but also its entire teaching on God's Law (Wilhelm Oesch, "De tertio usu legis," *Lutherischer Rundblick* 4 [1956]: 21–23 *et passim*). See Ken Schurb, "Philip Melanchthon, the Formula of Concord, and the Third Use of the Law" (PhD, diss. The Ohio State University, 2001), 30–31, archived at https://etd .ohiolink.edu/apexprod/rws_etd/send_file/send?accession=osu14882053185094 05&disposition=inline. Accessed 2/12/2023.

119

If Jesus' Word is distinguished from Jesus' person, then doctrinal standards of any kind come to be considered as invalid and inauthentic. People then think lightly or even contemptuously of the church's effort, under the mandate of the Lord, to guard the truthful Word and to say and teach only that which agrees with the divine speech in the Bible (1 Corinthians 1:10; Jude 3). For the faculty majority, there could be no church authority apart from the existential character of the Gospel—which is a very slippery notion! An existentialist Gospel cannot be codified in doctrinal standards. Doctrinal orthodoxy is seen not as a piety to be pursued in faithful service to the Lord of the church, but rather as an evil to be avoided. Enforcement of doctrinal standards by church authorities or overseers becomes laughable at best.

When the Gospel was set forth by the faculty majority only as a vague promise (instead of as the proclamation of historically specified divine acts worked by Christ, such as His suffering and death), the doctrinal content of the Bible and the biblically faithful Confessions of the church could not be used to forbid the use of the historical-critical method of biblical interpretation. Whatever did not contradict the Gospel, defined quite minimally, seemed just fine. The Law could no longer be used to hold anyone to a standard, especially for faithful and sound teaching in the church. Instead, teachers thought themselves free to experiment with methods of biblical interpretation that came not from Jesus and the prophets and apostles but from non-biblical or even anti-biblical sources. Criticism of the methods or results of theological inquiry undertaken by the faculty majority was seen as just more Law. This majority remorselessly accused the Synod and her leaders of being hopelessly legalistic and anti-Gospel. As it turned out, many of the people who insisted that they were for the Gospel alone often themselves ended up being quite legalistic and accusatory. At least the church authorities desired to make discriminations based on the text of Scripture and the Lutheran Confessions instead of rallying around a poorly defined Gospel.

When the students and faculty majority walked off the Concordia Seminary campus on February 19, 1974, their actions were consistent with their theology, the theology taught by the faculty and learned by the students. They accepted no external control on their behavior and no boundaries on their freedom to teach and act as they saw fit. They held that the Law simply did not apply to them as they lived out what they thought of as the Christian life.

120

For Discussion

1. What could happen to the need for the proclamation of the forgiveness of sins if the Law is no longer proclaimed to Christians from our pulpits?

2. If the Law no longer applies to them, should Christians still say, "I, a poor miserable sinner . . ."?

3. Is the Gospel a principle by which to interpret the Bible? Why or why not?

4. How did the Concordia Seminary faculty majority answer the previous question? Explain how your answer to question 3 may differ from that of the faculty majority.

5. Why do Christians still need to have the Law proclaimed to them?

6. When the Law no longer defines what is God-pleasing, who decides what is good and right? What problems can arise?

7. How does the third use of the Law protect the Gospel?

8. Why should the Gospel have predominance in Lutheran preaching?

Digging Deeper

Cooper, Jordan. *Lex Aeterna: A Defense of the Orthodox Lutheran Doctrine of God's Law and Critique of Gerhard Forde*. Eugene, OR: Wipf & Stock, 2017.

Montgomery, John Warwick, editor. *Crisis in Lutheran Theology: The Validity and Relevance of Historic Lutheranism vs. Its Contemporary Rivals*. 2 volumes. 2nd edition. Minneapolis: Bethany Fellowship, 1973. Reprint, Irvine, CA: New Reformation Publications, 2017. Volume 3. Irvine, CA: New Reformation Publications, 2017.

Murray, Scott R. *Law, Life and the Living God: The Third Use of the Law in Modern American Lutheranism*. St. Louis: Concordia Publishing House, 2002.

Silcock, Jeffrey G., trans. and ed. *The Antinomian Disputations (1537–40)*. Pages 1–238 in volume 73 of Luther's Works. Edited by Christopher Boyd Brown. St. Louis: Concordia Publishing House, 2020.

Sonntag, Holger, ed. and trans. *Only the Decalogue Is Eternal: Martin Luther's Complete Antinomian Theses and Disputations*. Minneapolis: Lutheran Press, 2008.

CHAPTER SIX

THE MISSION STAFF WALKOUT

Roy S. Askins

The church's work cannot be separated from her understanding
of God's Word. As the LCMS worked through the tumultuous
issues at Concordia Seminary regarding the interpretation
of Scripture, the Synod was also working through a
tremendous upheaval in the theology of missions, one that grew
out of the Mission Affirmations adopted by the LCMS
at its 1965 convention. This upheaval resulted in the
resignations of the majority of the Synod's mission staff
in 1974 and their entrenchment in the AELC.

Introduction

As the faculty of Concordia Seminary prepared to walk off the campus
and form "Concordia Seminary in Exile," another storm was brewing. This
one would swirl about the LCMS missions department and bring about what
might be called a "Missionex."

The storm concerning biblical theology brewing on the seminary campus
also clouded the theology of the church at large. It fostered doubt regarding
the authenticity of Scripture. It shook faith in the biblical foundations upon
which pastors were trained to care for God's people. In so doing, this storm
even threatened the parishes of the LCMS with an erosion in confidence in
the atoning work of Christ.

As recognition of biblical foundations collapsed, questions also arose
concerning the fundamental task of the church. Uncertainty regarding
the Word of God caused people to wonder about the church's mission and
work. If the church could not know what God's Word says, for example, then
should full agreement with other church bodies in the doctrine drawn from
the Bible be required before joining with them to work together in mission?

123

What would be the criteria for full ecumenical fellowship with other church bodies? How could a church that lacked certainty in her doctrine and teaching go on to proclaim and teach a distinctly "Lutheran" message in her mission to the world?

In other words, the storm at Concordia Seminary spun off another storm in missions. The two storms were intimately related: one undermined confidence in scriptural truths; the other altered the LCMS's expression of biblical theology in her mission to the world.

While the seminary Walkout occurred on a single day, February 19, 1974, the mission staff "Walkout" took longer. It began on April 10, 1974, and continued into October. While the students and faculty walked off the seminary campus in protest of the "heavy-handed" tactics of LCMS president J. A. O. Preus and the FFC, the LCMS missions staff walked out because of the "heavy-handed" tactics of Board for Missions chairman Waldo Werning, who was attempting to shift the trajectory of LCMS missions away from that set by the 1965 Mission Affirmations. The Rev. William Kohn, executive secretary for the Synod's mission board, stated in his letter of resignation:

> I shall at this time use this means to protest the legalism of the Board for Missions in its dealing with people, against the spirit of isolationism and separatism as it has developed in the Board's outlook on missions and against its arbitrary use of power to achieve greater centralization.[1]

The immediate event that precipitated Kohn's threefold complaint was the board's refusal to renew the contract for the Rev. James W. Mayer, secretary of the Asia region of LCMS missions. But this refusal was the fruit of blossoming troubles elsewhere in the relationship between the mission staff and the board. Werning and the conservative mission board majority that served with him had chosen a path that diverged in significant ways from what moderates had established in the Mission Affirmations conceived by the Rev. Dr. Martin L. Kretzmann and adopted by the 1965 LCMS convention.

The "battle for the Bible," as the controversy surrounding the seminary Walkout and the formation of Seminex is often called, centered on the struggle to curb historical-critical interpretation of the Bible by members of the Concordia Seminary faculty and others. However, discussions about Seminex often lack an accounting of the issues that the Mission Affirmations injected into LCMS theology and practice in the realms of missiology and ecumenical involvement. These two struggles should not be regarded as distinct. Moderates in the Missouri Synod regarded them as two sides of the same

---

1   Kohn to Board for Missions, 1974, ELCA Archives, Kretzmann Papers, 2002-0243 b23 f4. (Martin Kretzmann's papers, at the ELCA Archives, will hereafter be identified simply as the Kretzmann Papers.)

coin.[2] The 1970s saw not only a "battle for the Bible" but also a full-fledged war for the heart and soul of LCMS missions, both foreign and domestic.

Werning had not been the first to spot problems in the Mission Affirmations, nor would he be the last. The CTCR "clarified" those affirmations in 1974.[3] The LCMS still struggles today, as some would put mission at the center of the church's message, even at the expense of other biblical teachings. In practice, a division has opened up between those who are concerned with mission and those who want to see to the church's faithful confession. Such a division should not exist. For in fact, the mission and evangelism of the church and the faithful confession of the church in the proclamation of the Word and administration of the Sacraments are one and the same. Faithful preaching and teaching sit side by side with faithful mission and witness. This chapter will show part of the history of how this unhappy and false division became ingrained in the LCMS.

Historical Background

The historical background for Missionex begins with a short study of the "Statement of the 44." Next, and also by way of background, we will explore how the Mission Affirmations fundamentally altered the trajectory of LCMS missions. Then we will be ready to grasp why in 1974 the missions staff reacted so negatively to the critique and ignoring of, if not quite full rejection of, the Mission Affirmations by the Board for Missions.

The "Statement of the 44"

In 1945, a group of forty-four prominent LCMS pastors and theologians gathered in Chicago, Illinois, to discuss and sign what many at the time called "A Statement." (This document is not to be confused with President J. A. O. Preus's 1972 *A Statement of Scriptural and Confessional Principles*, which the LCMS adopted in 1973.[4])

The Chicago meeting occurred in September 1945, as World War II was ending. Even for the church, this was a time of rebuilding and consolidation. Previous consolidation among Lutherans had left three major Lutheran

---

2   Editor's note: The St. Louis seminary journal paid editorial tribute to Martin Kretzmann and the Mission Affirmations in Herbert T. Mayer, "Structure and Mission," *CTM* 43 (November 1972): 643–44.

3   CTCR, *The Mission of the Christian Church in the World: A Review of the 1965 Mission Affirmations* (St. Louis: LCMS, 1974).

4   The present book usually refers to the latter document as *A Statement*. See below, pp. 265–77.

church bodies in North America: the United Lutheran Church in America (ULCA), which tended to be the most flexible regarding participation with other church bodies and in its interpretation of Scripture; the American Lutheran Church (ALC), which attempted to take a middle position; and the LCMS, which took a more conservative approach toward fellowship and Scripture. Beyond American Lutheranism, the greater church was moving toward union. Church bodies were merging, and the groundwork was being laid for vast parachurch organizations such as the Lutheran World Federation (1947) and the World Council of Churches (1948).

The forty-four men who signed the statement in Chicago were concerned with the topics of their day. They sought ecumenical engagement. They saw restraints or expressions of concern about ecumenical conversations with other church bodies as "legalistic" attempts to stymie one of the fundamental tasks of the church.[5] With respect to extra-biblical or extra-confessional documents such as synodical constitutions and bylaws, they suspected that such documents ended up substituting man's authority for the authority of Scripture. The forty-four wanted to move the LCMS to broader interaction and participation with other church bodies, particularly in relation to fellowship and joint prayer. The issue of biblical interpretation that plagued Concordia Seminary in the 1960s and 1970s was not their issue. They affirmed the inerrancy of Scripture: "We affirm our faith in the great Lutheran principle of the inerrancy, certainty, and all-sufficiency of Holy Writ."[6] They were concerned with questions of fellowship between the LCMS and other Lutheran church bodies.

Their statement was released against the desires of then-LCMS president John Behnken. It created a firestorm in the Synod. It proved memorable, too, bearing ongoing influence within the LCMS not only through the Mission Affirmations but also in the public consciousness of LCMS leaders. For example, the December 14, 1970, meeting of the Synod mission staff opened with a devotion in which W. F. Bulle, the secretary for medical missions, read "the 12 points of 'A Statement' [that is, the "Statement of the 44"]," written a quarter of a century earlier.[7]

---

5   "Statement of the 44," Thesis 1, 3 (*Moving Frontiers*, 422–23); online at http://www.projectwittenberg.org/etext/lcms/ST44/ST44.htm).

6   "Statement of the 44," Thesis 2 (*Moving Frontiers*, 422).

7   Mission Staff Minutes, December 14, 1970, CHI, LCMS Board for Missions, box 2 of 9.

The Mission Affirmations

The next significant document to carry the torch of LCMS participation in ecumenical endeavors and to advocate for a broad mission theology was the Mission Affirmations, adopted at the 1965 LCMS convention in Detroit, Michigan. The mission staff eventually walked out in 1974 largely because it differed with the Board for Missions over the affirmations. For a full appreciation of this story, it becomes necessary to examine these affirmations in some detail.

The Affirmations on Mission (or "Mission Affirmations") were the brainchild of Martin Luther Kretzmann, who had been a thirty-year missionary to India. In 1963, the LCMS recalled him from Concordia Theological Seminary, Nagercoil, India, to serve as the director of a study of missions requested by the 1962 convention.

The resulting Mission Study provided the basic wording and theological foundation for what became the Mission Affirmations. Kretzmann based his study on questionnaires sent to LCMS foreign missionaries, numerous consultations with domestic church workers, and discussions concerning missions with various organizations such as the LWF. His report's two main sections established a theological foundation for missions, then set out practical suggestions for reorganizing the missions program of the LCMS. The latter, operational portion suggested consolidating the six focused mission boards into one.[8] But the most important change came with the theological foundations in the first portion. The changes here sought to send the LCMS on a new theological and ecumenical trajectory.

The missions floor committee at the Detroit convention reorganized the five headings in Kretzmann's Mission Study and added one more. Thus the Synod adopted six Mission Affirmations:

- Res. 1-01A "The Church Is God's Mission"
- Res. 1-01B "The Church Is Christ's Mission to the Whole World"
- Res. 1-01C "The Church Is Christ's Mission to the Church"
- Res. 1-01D "The Church Is Christ's Mission to the Whole Society"
- Res. 1-01E "The Church Is Christ's Mission to the Whole Man"
- Res. 1-01F "The Whole Church Is Christ's Mission"[9]

---

8   1965 *Convention Workbook*, 130.

9   Res. 1-01 A–F, 1965 *Proceedings*, 79–81. The Mission Affirmations also included extensive rationales and resolveds not included here.

Photograph by Paul Ockrassa

Faculty and students walk off of Concordia Seminary property (February 19, 1974).

The LCMS reaffirmed these affirmations at its conventions in New Orleans, Louisiana, in 1973 and also in Anaheim, California, in 1975.[10] They were still understood as a guide to direct the Board for Missions in its work. At the time when the mission staff walked out in 1974, the Mission Affirmations, though they raised concerns for many people, were still largely understood by others as the driving theology for LCMS mission work.

At first glance, these affirmations appear remarkably benign. No one disagrees that "The Church Is God's Mission" nor that the church seeks to care for "the Whole Man" or the "Whole World." Such vague language became common among the "moderates," those who advocated for a more liberal approach to the interpretation of Scripture and in the ecumenical endeavors of the LCMS.[11] Vague language allowed significant latitude in the interpretation of these affirmations. In 1973 the board reported that while the Mission Affirmations "eloquently show a deep compassion for men in their spiritual and physical condition," it went on to state that at times "they [the affirmations] have been regarded as sanctioning many types of missions and ecumenical policies which are beyond the Scriptures, the Confessions,

---

10   Res. 1-06, 1973 *Proceedings*, 102–3; Res. 2-01A,1975 *Proceedings*, 85–86.

11   On the use of vague language in reference to Scripture and inerrancy, see Armand J. Boehme, "The Smokescreen Vocabulary," *CTQ* 41 (April 1977): 25–40.

and other synodical resolutions."[12] For Kretzmann and the moderates in the mission department, the vagueness of the Mission Affirmations enabled them to promote and encourage ecumenical policies and missionary activities that stood at variance with traditional LCMS practice. This included encouraging the development of ecumenical seminaries for LCMS partner churches and the participation of LCMS daughter churches in ecumenical organizations, among other practices.

If the various affirmations themselves appeared vague, the rationales— the *Whereas* and *Resolved* statements—were less so. While there was much in these statements worth commending, in a few key points the Mission Affirmations subverted those helpful passages in dangerous ways. For the sake of space, we will focus on the problematic portions.

Affirmation I states: "The church's ministries of worship, service, fellowship, and nurture all have a missionary dimension."[13] Therefore any doctrine or practice of the church that did not have an immediate missionary application would be suspect at best. The minutes of the first meeting of the Commission on Mission and Ministry in the Church (CMMC), a commission established to implement the Mission Affirmations throughout the LCMS, record this statement: "All of theology should have a missionary dimension."[14] Affirmation I, with this kind of implication, moved justification from its central place in theology and put missiology there instead. The results of such a change for Lutheran theology are profound. The doctrine upon which the church stands or falls is the justification of the sinner by Christ's atoning work on the cross. It is the center, like the hub of a wheel. If justification is replaced or a particular spoke is emphasized instead, the entire wheel becomes unbalanced.

In the second affirmation, the missions floor committee, drawing on Kretzmann, wrote: "That we recognize our sister mission churches in other lands have been placed by God into other circumstances and are subservient not to us but to the Lord, who makes His church His mission to the whole world."[15] The sentiment sounds appropriate: a daughter church, when fully formed, becomes a sister church and is no longer subservient to the mother church. The context, however, tells a different story. During his time in India, Kretzmann became deeply involved in ecumenical dialogues with other church bodies, such as the Church of South India, a pan-denominational

---

12   "Report of Board for Missions," 1973 *Convention Workbook*, 11.

13   Res. 1-01A, 1965 *Proceedings*, 80.

14   CHI, CMMC Archives, 1965, "Minutes for Meeting 1 of the CMMC," 13.

15   Res. 1-01B, 1965 *Proceedings*, 80.

union church. He had encouraged the fledgling India Evangelical Lutheran Church (IELC) to participate in the pan-Lutheran organization, the Federation of Evangelical Lutheran Churches (FELC). The IELC joined the FELC, but not until after Kretzmann left.[16] However, he was ultimately not concerned with daughter church autonomy, but rather with preventing the LCMS from warning a daughter church against or hindering it from entering into fellowship with a heterodox church body.

Affirmation III started by noting the "real and living unity" of every Christian "with every other member of Christ's holy body, the church." Its second *Resolved* stated: "We affirm as Lutheran Christians that the Evangelical Lutheran Church is chiefly a confessional movement within the total body of Christ rather than a denomination emphasizing institutional barriers of separation."[17] This affirmation created significant confusion regarding what the LCMS allowed or did not allow with regard to faithful ecumenical dialogue. By Kretzmann's own admission, the affirmations lacked any clear definition of the church.[18] This lack of clarity also prevented any distinction between orthodox and heterodox church bodies. The Lutheran Confessions define the church as "the assembly of saints in which the gospel is taught purely and the sacraments are administered rightly" (AC VII 1).[19] But treating the Lutheran Church as merely one confessing movement among others reduces any concern for pure doctrine to theological nit-picking. It removes the theological boundaries necessary for discussions of church fellowship and unity and thereby obscures the endeavor for unity.

While the moderates believed that the Lutheran Confessions were true for their time, they thought that these documents could not bind the modern church. In 1957, Kretzmann wrote: "The Confessions state the truth of the Scriptures for their day, even as we must state it for ours." In the same article, he also wrote: "Luther did not, and could not, speak the Gospel to the atomic scientist of the 20th century, no more than we can speak the Gospel to the peasant living in the feudalism of the 16th century."[20] More than a decade later, soon-to-be Concordia Seminary president John Tietjen expressed

---

16   See "Church of South India—Lutheran Conversations," 1966, 2010-0109, box 5 folder 3, Kretzmann Papers, 2.

17   Res. 1-01C, 1965 *Proceedings*, 80.

18   See his "Notes for Mid-West Regional Professional Conference, English District, May 27–28, 1975," 5. Kretzmann Papers, 2002-0243, box 9, folder 1.

19   K-W, 43.

20   Martin L. Kretzmann, "India Seminary President Takes Issue with Dr. Sasse," *The Lutheran Layman*, August 1, 1957, 7. Used by permission from International Lutheran Laymen's League, all rights reserved.

much the same idea in his 1969 article "The Gospel and the Theological Task." The Gospel is enduringly true and valid, Tietjen indicated, but the Gospel can only be expressed in a theology that is inherently formed by the time and place in which it is expressed. This makes each expression of the Gospel unique: "For theology to be relevant, the theological task has to begin not with the gospel but with the situation to which it is addressed. ... [The gospel] cannot be formulated in terms enduringly valid for every age and condition. Each formulation of the gospel is conditioned by the situation to which it is addressed."[21] For the moderates, the Lutheran Confessions could not be an enduring expression of the Gospel since the confessors spoke to the sixteenth century, not the twentieth. The dangers of this theology will become more evident later in this chapter.

Affirmations IV and V are related: "The Church Is Christ's Mission to the Whole Society" and "The Church Is Christ's Mission to the Whole Man" both suffer from a confusion of God's right-hand and left-hand governance. In His right-hand governance, God works through the church by the proclamation of the Word and the distribution of the Sacraments to proclaim the Gospel to the people of God and to the world. In His left-hand governance, God works through the rule of law, through government, political office, and commerce. Affirmations IV and V emphasize the church's social involvement and interaction, whether in political discourse (Affirmation IV) or caring for the individual needs of people around the world (Affirmation V), at the expense of God's work in the means of grace. In these two affirmations, social action for the temporal well-being of the neighbor trumps the oral proclamation of the Word and distribution of the Sacraments as the primary means by which God saves sinners, His proper and primary work. In fact, the Mission Affirmations never once mention the means of grace as the tools by which Christ builds and sustains His church.

Finally, Affirmation VI drives the LCMS toward broader ecumenical involvement by deploring "anything that seeks to divide what God has joined together." Of course, no Christian would disagree with such a statement. Division in the body of Christ does not please God and should not please the Christian. However, the ecumenical movement of the first half of the twentieth century used this language to encourage uncritical participation and external unity among churches that held fundamentally different doctrine and teachings. A "pretend" unity is no unity. The vague and "smokescreen" language of the Mission Affirmations allowed the mission staff to use Affirmation VI, along with Affirmation III, to sanction "many types

---

21 John H. Tietjen, "The Gospel and the Theological Task," *CTM* 40 (June, July–August 1969): 119.

of missions and ecumenical policies which are beyond the Scriptures, the Confessions, and other synodical resolutions."[22]

The Mission Affirmations built on the foundation laid by the "Statement of the 44." The latter sought to overcome "narrow legalism" and "man-made traditions."[23] So did the former, even if not using that exact language. The forty-four deplored "man-made walls and barriers and all ecclesiastical traditions which would hinder the free course of the Gospel in the world."[24] The Mission Affirmations declared that the Lutheran Confessions were "not intended to be a kind of Berlin Wall."[25] The two documents advanced similar goals within the LCMS.

In the early 1970s, LCMS president J. A. O. Preus referred the Mission Affirmations to the CTCR for clarification. The theological issues in the Mission Affirmations put the CTCR in a difficult position. The LCMS in convention had not only adopted the Mission Affirmations in 1965 but had also regularly recommitted to them at subsequent conventions (e.g., in New York, 1967; Denver, 1969; and New Orleans, 1973).[26] To reject the affirmations outright might call into question the wisdom of numerous synodical resolutions. On the other hand, the Mission Affirmations could not be left open to the worst possible interpretations. So in September 1974, the CTCR took a middle road in its document *The Mission of the Christian Church in the World: A Review of the 1965 Mission Affirmations*. It attempted to close various interpretive loopholes. But in so doing, Martin Kretzmann lamented, the CTCR interpreted the Mission Affirmations in a manner "that the truths they express are effectually negated."[27]

What Happened

This reinterpretation of the Mission Affirmations was occurring as a conservative majority, headed by Waldo Werning, was taking over the Board for Missions. These two events, with the Walkout at the seminary as a catalyst, set up the reaction that led to "Missionex." (To be clear, the staff members of the

---

22 "Report of the Board for Missions," 1973 *Workbook*, 11.

23 "Statement of the 44," Thesis 1 (*Moving Frontiers*, 422).

24 "Statement of the 44," Thesis 3 (*Moving Frontiers*, 423).

25 Res. 1-01C, 1965 *Proceedings*, 80.

26 From "Mandate and Mission: Report of the Mission Study Commission of the LCMS," quoted in Martin Kretzmann, "Mission Affirmations Revisited: The Doctrine of the Church," Mid-West Regional Professional Conference, English District, May 27–28, 1975, 11. Kretzmann Papers, 2002-0243 box 9, folder 1.

27 Kretzmann, "Mission Affirmations Revisited," 6.

mission department who resigned from their positions in 1974 never referred to themselves as "Mission in Exile" or "Missionex," but they did share with Seminex professors significant theological concerns and frustrations with Synod president J. A. O. Preus's administration.)

Unlike Seminex, the mission staff did not walk out on a single day. The staff resignations began in April 1974 and lasted to the following October. Here is the list of staff members, their positions, and the days on which they resigned:

- Dr. William H. Kohn, executive secretary, April 10
- James W. Mayer, secretary for South Asia, April 19
- W. F. Bulle, secretary for medical missions, April 19
- Marion Kretzschmar, administrative assistant, April 19
- Walter H. Meyer, secretary for North America, April 19
- William Reinking, secretary for Africa and Middle East, May 15
- Paul H. Strege, secretary for East Asia, May 15
- Doris Lamb, administrative assistant, July 15
- James Cross, secretary for North America, July 31
- Phyllis Kersten, administrative assistant, August 15
- William T. Seeber, assistant to the executive secretary, September 30
- Reuben J. Schmidt, associate executive secretary for North America, October 30

Of the twelve staff members who resigned, eight had been assigned in 1966–67 to the single mission board created by the Synod per the recommendation of Kretzmann's 1965 Mission Study. They were assigned to this staff specifically to implement the Mission Affirmations in the Synod's foreign and domestic mission efforts.

After Kohn resigned as executive secretary, Herman H. Koppelmann served as acting executive secretary until the Rev. Alvin L. Barry was appointed and filled the position on March 1, 1975. Koppelmann had served on the mission staff for the Board for World Missions from 1948 to 1966. Barry eventually became president of the LCMS from 1992 to 2001.

A New Board and the Mission Affirmations

The immediate precipitating issue leading to the resignation of the mission staff was the board's refusal to renew the employment contract for James Mayer at the end of 1973. The roots of that refusal, however, grew out of an ongoing conflict between the board and the mission staff that began

133

much earlier. At its 1965 convention, the Synod had elected Werning to the Board for European Affairs.[28] When the boards were merged in 1966 per convention mandate, Werning was chosen as secretary of the combined mission board.[29] Over the course of time, he took issue not only with the Mission Affirmations but also with other writings of Martin Kretzmann. This conflict framed the issues between the board and the various members of the mission staff leading up to the staff departures in 1974.

In a March 29, 1974, letter distributed by the mission staff to the LCMS District mission executives, mission conference chairmen, and sister church presidents, William Kohn, James Mayer, and William T. Seeber, on behalf of the mission staff, offered a chronology of events along with a statement titled "The Immediate Issue in the Synodical Mission Crisis."[30] "Immediate Issue" charged the majority members of the Board for Missions with acting in a "legalistic and loveless behavior" that began as far back as September 1970, when Werning presented a paper on "Confessional Practice" that included a fourteen-point "blueprint for winning the Confessional battle."[31] The staff spokesmen did not identify the particular issues with Werning's paper, instead continuing in "Immediate Issue" with identifying the next milestone: the "Minority Report" to the 1971 LCMS convention. This document had been written in large part by Werning and signed by conservatives (then in the board minority) Henry J. Andreas, Otto Hintze, Walter Kayser, and Herman R. Mayer. The board majority prevented it from being included in the Synod's 1971 *Convention Workbook*. Much to the consternation of the moderate board majority, though, President Preus published the report and sent it in a separate mailing to all convention delegates.[32] The mission staff and the executive committee of the Board for Missions responded with a mailing of their own, after which the minority wrote and distributed a "Supplement to the Minority Report" that was given to the 1971 convention delegates.

The "Minority Report" compiled Werning's concerns regarding Kretzmann, the interpretation of the Mission Affirmations by the mission staff, and the consequences of these issues in LCMS missions up to 1971.

---

28   1965 *Proceedings*, 75.

29   Waldo J. Werning, *Making the Missouri Synod Functional Again* (Fort Wayne, IN: Biblical Renewal Publications, 1992), 138.

30   Public Mission Staff letter (hereafter "Immediate Issue"), March 29, 1974. Kretzmann Papers, 2002-0243, box 24, folder 1.

31   "Immediate Issue," 1. See Waldo J. Werning, "Confessional Practice," in *Evangelical Directions for the Lutheran Church*, eds. Erich Kiehl and Waldo J. Werning (Chicago: Lutheran Congress, 1970), 71–81, esp. 79–80.

32   "Immediate Issue," 1.

Werning pointed to three articles by Kretzmann that raised theological concerns. The first of these was "Where Is the Church Going in World Missions?"[33] The "Minority Report" raised questions of universalist teaching in Kretzmann's writing. It identified several issues with respect to the second of these articles, "What on Earth Does the Gospel Change?"[34] The minority said that this article expressed an unbiblical view of fellowship, "[that we d]eclare ourselves in fellowship with all who bear the name of Christ, of whatever branch of the church they may be"; that it questioned the historicity of Christ's descent into hell and ascension into heaven, seeking to reinterpret these events "in light of what man has learned about the world"; and that it glossed over (at best) a bevy of Christian doctrines such as a male-only clergy, Christ's presence in the Sacrament, and the inspiration of Scripture because "they have no essential connection with the Gospel." (This was *Gospel* in the "Gospel Reductionist" sense.)[35] The last of the three Kretzmann articles was on theological education, a piece offered to the LCA Board of World Missions. This paper presented problems of an ecumenical nature. It set forth the "immediate goal of carrying out these ministerial training programs in cooperation with other Protestant bodies, and stated as our policy that we will no longer support a denominational training program."[36]

Responding to the "Minority Report," the Board for Missions majority concluded that the minority was loveless and that it was violating "the spirit of the Mission Affirmations."[37] As if the flurry of documents being mailed to delegates in preparation for the convention were not enough, the board minority then wrote a supplement to the original "Minority Report" and distributed it to delegates too. By the time they arrived in Milwaukee for the convention, delegates had seen the infighting. One side was upholding the Mission Affirmations and Kretzmann while the other was raising concerns.

The Synod's 1971 convention in Milwaukee, Wisconsin, became the transition point between the moderate majority and the conservative minority on the Board for Missions. The floor committee refused to accept either

---

33   Martin Kretzmann, "Where Is the Church Going in World Missions?" in *Where Is the Church Going? Papers and Proceedings, Workshop on Church and Ministry, July 29–31, 1969* (St. Louis: Concordia Seminary Print Shop, 1970).

34   Martin Kretzmann, "What on Earth Does the Gospel Change," *Lutheran World* 16 (October 1969): 307–21.

35   "Minority Report," 1971 *Convention Workbook*, 2. On Gospel Reductionism, see above, chapter 1, pp. 15–37.

36   "Minority Report," 1971 *Convention Workbook*, 3.

37   "An Analysis and Evaluation of Board for Missions 'Minority Report' to Milwaukee Convention," 12. Kretzmann Papers, 2002-0243, box 21, folder 7.

the majority or minority report, leaving the issues unresolved. Elections at the convention left the board evenly split between moderates and conservatives. There was one swing voter, who eventually sided with conservatives. At the board's next meeting, Werning was elected chairman.[38] After additional conservative gains at the New Orleans convention in 1973, the Board for Missions was composed of ten conservatives and three moderates.[39] According to moderates on the staff, the perceived goal of the new conservative majority was fourfold:

- to implement isolationism by forcing mission units at home and abroad into a separatism from other Lutherans and Christians;

- to centralize all decision-making in the hands of the [Board for Missions];

- to neutralize all called staff through the use of political power and deliberate undercutting of staff and mission units;

- to negate the intent and the thrust of the Mission Affirmations.[40]

While the precipitating cause of the mission staff walkout might have been the refusal of the board to renew James Mayer's contract, that refusal amounted to evidence of a deep and ongoing disagreement over the Mission Affirmations. Looking at the four points above, it seems clear that the charges of isolationism, centralization of power, and neutralizing the mission staff were all different ways of saying that the board was attempting to "negate the intent and thrust of the Mission Affirmations." Those affirmations encouraged uncritical engagement with other church bodies, including hiring non-Lutherans to assist in mission work abroad, encouraging the joint education of missionary pastors in ecumenical seminaries, and so on. Under Werning, the board was attempting to redirect the mission staff in a direction that was more faithful to the Scriptures and the Lutheran Confessions, but the staff wanted none of it.

James Mayer

After the "Minority Report" of the conservatives in 1971, moderates on the Board for Missions submitted minority reports to the 1973 and 1975 LCMS conventions. The "Minority Report" to the 1975 convention in Anaheim, California, offered additional details regarding the board's refusal

---

38   "Immediate Issue," 1.

39   Walter Meyer, "Chronology of the 'Missions Problem,'" 3. Kretzmann Papers, 2002-0243 box 5, folder 2.

40   Meyer, "Chronology of the 'Mission Problems,'" 4.

to renew James Mayer's contract as area secretary for Asia. Toward the end of 1973, a visitation team had toured the Asia region of LCMS mission work. The team's report, "largely negative in tone and," the "Minority Report" added, "without sufficient feedback from the churches and missions visited," gave the board reason not to renew Mayer's contract.[41]

The fallout from the board's decision not to renew Mayer's contract was immediate and intense. Not only were there protests from the entire mission staff and a majority of all the staff members at synodical headquarters but also from missionaries and church leaders around the world. Local church leaders from Papua New Guinea and India traveled to the United States to ask the board to reconsider its actions. Missionaries were mobilized in the effort to support Mayer. On February 8, 1974, Arnold J. Lutz sent resolutions adopted by LCMS missionaries in India to the Board for Missions, asking the board to reconsider the appointment of Mayer. Missionaries from Taiwan, South Korea, and the Philippines did likewise.[42]

The mission staff linked this "mission crisis" with the "seminary crisis" that was then underway. In a February 13, 1974, letter written to the "pastors, teachers and lay membership of The Lutheran Church—Missouri Synod," the mission staff stated that this " 'mission crisis' is just as serious and can have even more far-reaching implications" than the crisis at the St. Louis seminary. (Note that this letter was dated less than a week before the seminary Walkout.) The staff wanted to "alert the church to the inextricable nature of the 'mission crisis' and the 'seminary crisis.' "[43] The letter also included a "Statement Re 'The Seminary Issue' and the 'Mission Issue' in the LCMS made on Jan. 24, 1974," in which William H. Kohn, executive secretary of the mission staff, demanded that the Concordia Seminary Board of Control reconsider its decisions. Kohn drew parallels between the seminary board's actions and the decision by the mission board not to renew James Mayer.[44]

1975 Synod Convention

The effect on the mission department of losing twelve of its seventeen staff members cannot be underestimated. Not only did the mission department lose hands to do the work but also the historical and institutional knowledge upon which this type of work so often depends. The loss was so

41   1975 *Convention Workbook*, 21.

42   Letters to the Board for Missions in Waldo J. Werning papers, CHI, Box 3 of 11, Mission, 2004-07-04.

43   LCMS Mission Staff, "Report to the Synod on Problems in Mission," dated February 13, 1974, CHI.

44   William Kohn, "Statement Re 'The Seminary Issue' and the 'Mission Issue,' " CHI.

immense that the Board for Missions publicly acknowledged its own mistakes in dealing with the staff. Its report to the 1975 synodical convention said in part:

> We have grieved our Lord by not always exercising the best judgment in board-staff-field relationships, also in our dealings with sister churches. . . . There have been differing views within the board, within the staff, as well as between the board and staff, as to what the Word of God says about mission. . . . These differences have led to poor communication, a lack of frankness, and confusion in the exercise of authority and the proper role for board and staff members. Board and staff members were hurt deeply, and finally a majority of the staff resigned.[45]

The sharp division between those who wanted to continue promoting the Mission Affirmations and the board, which wanted to curtail the unscriptural interpretations of the affirmations, was evident. The report, while acknowledging failures, discussed the board's work almost without reference to the Mission Affirmations. It mentioned them in reference only to attempted meetings between the board and staff to discuss the Mission Affirmations in light of the CTCR report with which the moderates vehemently disagreed.

The division between these two perspectives carried into the convention as well. Overture 2-06A, "To Support the Synod's Board for Missions," commended the board for its work despite criticism from many sources, including "former members of executive staff who at times failed to cooperate in implementing directives from the Board for Missions." Overture 2-10, "To Maintain Confessional Integrity on the Mission Fields and Commend and Support Present Mission Board Chairman," named Werning specifically as worthy of commendation.[46] On the other hand, Overture 2-11, "To Ask Mission Board to Resign," asked the members of the board to resign and added that "the board be instructed to return to the use of the Mission Affirmations."[47] In short, the division within the Synod surrounding the "mission crisis" was publicly evident, just as in the "seminary crisis," and fundamental to the moderates' concerns over the "mission crisis" were the Mission Affirmations.

---

45 1975 *Workbook*, 15.

46 1975 *Workbook*, 31–32. Overtures 2-07A, 2-08, 2-09A and 2-09B all offered similar support to the mission board.

47 1975 *Workbook*, 33. Overtures 2-12, 2-13A, 2-13B, 2-13C, and 2-14 all requested either a change in the Board for Missions or some measure of chastisement. Overtures 2-11, 2-12, and 2-13A all reference the failure of the board to implement the Mission Affirmations.

The convention did not reelect Werning to the Board for Missions, but it did decide to affirm his sentiments. In Resolution 2-01A, the Synod expressed sadness over the theological division that had plagued the mission staff and the board, yet it expressed appreciation for the board's "spirit of humility and commitment which permeates its report," a report submitted over Werning's name and that of Executive Secretary A. L. Barry.[48] Resolution 2-01A also acknowledged and affirmed Werning's concerns with the Mission Affirmations. It reaffirmed "the Scriptural truth that in the proclamation of the Gospel the verbal and/or written witness is indispensable" and that partnership in mission "is possible only as we uncompromisingly remain faithful to the Scriptures and the Lutheran Confessions."[49] The former quote addressed Werning's concerns about the focus on social action to the exclusion of oral proclamation of the Word while the latter quote spoke to his concerns regarding the ecumenical nature of the Mission Affirmations.

The remaining missions resolutions adopted by the 1975 convention returned to business as normal. If Werning accomplished anything during his tenure with the Board for Missions, he managed to expunge—at least outwardly—this set of theological assumptions from the public guidance of LCMS mission work. At the Synod's next convention in Dallas, Texas (1977), the three overtures concerned with the Mission Affirmations were directed, by a general "Reference Resolution," to the CTCR for further consideration.[50]

Partners and a New Synod

Most of the mission staff members who resigned from the LCMS did not abandon mission work. They left in protest over what they saw as the failures of the LCMS to execute the mission of the church properly. Four former LCMS mission staff members became founders of a new, independent mission agency called Partners in Mission (PIM). This organization originally functioned as a division of Evangelical Lutherans in Mission (ELIM), the moderate "confessing movement" within the LCMS that started shortly after the 1973 LCMS convention. ELIM hired the Rev. Walter Meyer, the Rev. Paul Strege, Mrs. Marion Kretzschmar, and the Rev. James Mayer to serve as interim staff for the new organization, which was founded on May 10–11, 1974.[51] PIM enshrined the Mission Affirmations into the very heart of its existence. One of its primary objectives was to

---

48   1975 *Proceedings*, 85.

49   1975 *Proceedings*, 86.

50   Resolution A, 1977 *Proceedings*, 219.

51   "Mission in Hope," Kretzmann Papers, 2002-0243 box 22 folder 1.

"stimulate an aggressive mission program which is strategically sound, in accordance with Scripture and the Lutheran Confessions, and in accordance with the Mission Affirmations."[52]

Although ELIM brought PIM into existence, the new mission agency would find its fullest expression when a new synod was formed, the AELC. ELIM had intended to continue as a confessing movement within the LCMS, but it also had been developing structures necessary for starting a new church body, as it reported in its assembly book in 1975.[53] After the contentious events of the 1975 LCMS convention, these structures were put in place and the AELC was formed. It held its founding convention December 3–4, 1976, in Chicago, Illinois.

"Missionex" was very much in evidence within the new church body. Former LCMS executive secretary for missions, the Rev. William Kohn, served as interim president, then the founding convention elected him to the presidency.[54] That convention promptly dedicated itself to mission work in accord with the Mission Affirmations. The first resolution to pass the convention was Resolution 76-2, "To Declare Our Commitment to Be a Church in Mission." It explicitly stated: "That we recognize and affirm the Mission Affirmations (1965) as a faithful and forthright exposition of the mission of God to which we are called." It proceeded to urge AELC members to faithfully study and implement them, with particular focus on encouraging partnership with other church bodies around the world.[55] Later the same day, the convention passed Resolution 76-7, "To Enter into Partnership with Partners in Mission," and the following day passed Resolution 76-8, "To Enter into Partnership with Seminex."[56] The AELC firmly committed itself to the theology of the Mission Affirmations and implemented this theology through its new mission agency, PIM.

The AELC continued to function as an independent church body for eleven years before it joined with two much larger Lutheran church bodies in the United States on January 1, 1988, to become the ELCA.

---

52 "The New Synodical Mission Agency," *Missouri in Perspective*, May 20, 1974, 8.

53 Evangelical Lutherans In Mission, *Third Annual Assembly, Chicago, Illinois, August 13–15, 1975*, eds. Elwyn Ewald and Steve Hitchcock (St. Louis: ELIM, 1975), 20.

54 "Minutes of the Founding Convention," The Association of Evangelical Lutheran Churches (AELC), 2. Kretzmann Papers, 2002-0243, box 5, folder 2.

55 "Minutes of the Founding Convention," AELC, Appendix C, 1–2.

56 "Minutes of the Founding Convention," AELC, 2, 4.

The Difference This Makes

The controversy that boiled over in the LCMS in 1974 included more than a battle for the Bible. The conflict also raged over the heart and soul of the church's mission and work. In 1965, at the high point of the moderates' control within the LCMS, they brought a new theology to the church. This theology did not center on the justification of the sinner before God, but placed the church's mission at the heart and center of everything the church must do. Furthermore, this mission did not focus on Christ's work through Word and Sacrament, but upon works of social activism.

Yet as Waldo Werning and others pointed out, the Gospel must be preached. St. Paul declared that "faith comes from hearing, and hearing through the word of Christ" (Romans 10:17). The church does not exist for the primary purpose of conducting social welfare projects; if the church fails to proclaim the Word of the Gospel, then she has become nothing more than a humanitarian organization. When St. Paul exhorted the Galatians to do good to all, he added: "especially to those who are of the household of faith" (Galatians 6:10). When Jesus pointed to the good deeds of the sheep in His parable of the end times, He praised what the sheep did for "one of the least of these My brothers" (Matthew 25:40). This does not mean the church should not do acts of mercy for unbelievers, but rather, even in acts of mercy, the church cares first for her own.

The primary work of the church, her fundamental task, is the proclamation of the Good News through the means of grace. Through these gifts Christ blesses the world with forgiveness, life, and salvation. In *A Statement of Scriptural and Confessional Principles*, which the LCMS adopted at its 1973 convention, the Synod affirmed that

> the primary mission of the church is to make disciples of every nation by bearing witness to Jesus Christ through the preaching of the Gospel and the administration of the sacraments. Other necessary activities of the church, such as ministering to men's physical needs, are to serve the church's primary mission and its goal that men will believe and confess Jesus Christ as their Lord and Savior.[57]

The other significant goal of the moderates in the mission department finds expression in the notion that Lutheranism is a confessing movement within broader Christianity. This perspective was deeply ingrained in the AELC. Kretzmann thought it was one of the primary gifts that the AELC

---

57   *A Statement*, part III (cf. below, p. 266).

141

bequeathed to the ELCA.[58] In this perspective, no one particular confession can claim to understand the truth of God's Word. This is one of the most significant and insidious teachings of the Mission Affirmations. As a well-respected Lutheran theologian of the twentieth century noted, the Lutheran Confessions were not simply intended as a confession of a particular church at a particular time. Rather, the Lutheran confessors believed they were confessing the truth of the church of all time and space, the truth confessed by the "one, holy, catholic, and apostolic church."[59] The Lutheran Church is not merely a confessing movement, but a church that boldly proclaims the full truth of God's Word. And this happens not only as she declares that God's Word is inspired and therefore inerrant but also as she takes the biblical Gospel of Christ to the world. These two realities are of the same piece of cloth: the only way the church can proclaim the Good News to the nations is if she believes that she speaks the Word of God in all its truth and purity and power.

For Discussion

1. According to this chapter, which aspect of the crisis in the LCMS is often overlooked? What connection did it have with the events at Concordia Seminary?

2. What goals did the "Statement of the 44" attempt to advance?

3. When were the Mission Affirmations adopted? What were their main emphases?

4. In what ways did the Mission Affirmations become a point of controversy between the LCMS Board for Missions and its staff?

5. Where did matters stand within the LCMS after the 1975 convention with respect to missions?

6. Why is the Lutheran Church not simply a confessing movement within Christianity? Why is this a dangerous idea?

7. What are the primary means by which the church does the mission given her by Christ? How does the church highlight these means in her mission work?

---

58 "Ecumenism in the Association of Evangelical Lutheran Churches," 10–11. Kretzmann Papers, 2002-0243 box 6 folder 7.

59 See Hermann Sasse, "The Confessional Problem in Today's World Lutheranism," in *Letters to Lutheran Pastors*, Volume 2: *1951–1956*, ed. Matthew C. Harrison (St. Louis: Concordia Publishing House, 2014), 475–501.

Digging Deeper

CTCR. *The Mission of the Christian Church in the World: A Review of the 1965 Mission Affirmations.* St. Louis: LCMS, 1974 (includes the full text of the Mission Affirmations).

Rast, Lawrence. "A 1945 Statement from Lutheran Leaders Called 'The Statement of the 44.'" By Todd Wilken. *Issues Etc.* September 20, 2019, https://issuesetc.org/2019/09/20/2632-a-1945-statement-from-lutheran-leaders-called-the-statement-of-the-44-d-larry-rast-9-20-1. Accessed 9/25/2022.

Sasse, Hermann. "The Confessional Problem in Today's World Lutheranism." Pages 475–501 in *1951–1956*, volume 2 of *Letters to Lutheran Pastors*. Edited by Matthew C. Harrison. St. Louis: Concordia Publishing House, 2014.

CHAPTER SEVEN

CHURCH FELLOWSHIP

Cameron A. MacKenzie

Early on, the Missouri Synod's founders reserved its pulpits and altars for those who believed, taught, and confessed what they themselves did from Scripture and the Lutheran Confessions. During the twentieth century, that commitment began to fray. Tensions arose. The debates within the Synod regarding church fellowship contributed significantly to the polarization that culminated in the seminary Walkout and the formation of Seminex.

Introduction

Does it matter who preaches in your church? Does it matter who receives Communion there?

The founders of the LCMS certainly thought so. Several of them had left church bodies they found lacking in Lutheran commitment. In the Missouri Synod, they understood themselves to be establishing a church body for Lutheran congregations, pastors, and teachers who stood united in doctrine and practice. Such unity was the essence of church fellowship.

We often use the term "fellowship" for activities that bring Christians together, from potlucks to summer softball. But *church* fellowship means cooperation in activities that only the church does—principally, preaching God's Word and administering the Sacraments, but also closely related activities such as publishing devotional materials or training church workers. Such activities are uniquely Christian, for God uses His Word and Sacraments to bring us *really* together as the Body of Christ through faith in Him. When we are "in fellowship" with others, we do these things together. When we are not in fellowship, we do not.

The Missouri Synod's founders showed their doctrinal unity by requiring a commitment to the Scriptures and the Lutheran Confessions.[1] (The requirement remains.[2]) This theological commitment was to be more than lip service. At that time in North America, besides German Lutherans, there were many German *Reformed*. The latter were committed to the theology of men such as John Calvin instead of Martin Luther. They did not accept the Lutheran Confessions. In many places, Lutherans and Reformed shared facilities. Sometimes they also shared pastors, who ended up administering Communion to some who believed and others who did not believe that Christ's body and blood are in, with, and under the bread and wine.[3] The Missouri Synod's founders considered such arrangements a betrayal of God's Word. The Bible did not permit a church both to agree with God's Word and to deny it, yet such practices amounted to just that. In addition to unity in doctrine, the Missouri Synod also recognized unity in practice as a condition for membership.

In the twentieth century, things started to change. "Church fellowship" occasioned debate and division within the Missouri Synod, though Seminex was not a direct result of this controversy. When the 1973 LCMS convention condemned the doctrinal position of the St. Louis seminary faculty majority, it did not identify fellowship per se as an area of false teaching.[4] Nonetheless, the controversy over church fellowship was a major cause of the synodical polarization that culminated in the faculty and student Walkout at Concordia Seminary in 1974 and all that followed. By then it was clear that the Synod was no longer united on the conditions to be met before churches preach the Gospel and administer the Sacraments together. In fact, it was itself no longer united in doctrine and practice.

Historical Background

Throughout the first several decades of the Missouri Synod's history, its leaders recognized unity in doctrine and practice as the standard for church

---

1   "Our First Synodical Constitution," *CHIQ* 16 (April 1943): 3.

2   *Handbook: Constitution, Bylaws, Articles of Incorporation* (St. Louis: LCMS, 2019), 11, 13.

3   See E. Clifford Nelson, ed., *The Lutherans in North America*, rev. ed. (Philadelphia: Fortress Press, 1980), 35, 60–61, 75, 131–32; and Horace S. Sills, "The Union Church: A Case of Lutheran and Reformed Cooperation," on the website of the United Church of Christ. https://www.ucc.org/about-us_hidden-histories-2_the -union-church-a-case-of/. Accessed 10/20/2022.

4   Res. 3-09, 1973 *Proceedings*, 133–39.

fellowship. In 1872, they formed a national Lutheran church organization, the Synodical Conference, that united their synod with several others. Agreed on doctrine and practice, they decided to do church work together, such as sending out missionaries and training church workers.[5] However, within a few years the Synodical Conference was split by a controversy over predestination.[6] This dispute and others left Lutheran church bodies in America divided not only by ethnicity and geography but also over doctrine and practice. But did such divisions have to last?

The Ecumenical Movement

Through the first several decades of the twentieth century, Christian churches of all sorts grew discontented with previous denominational disarray and took steps to rectify it. One step was the creation of large cooperative organizations within denominations (such as the Lutheran World Federation [LWF]) and across denominational lines (such as the World Council of Churches [WCC]). Another was the formation of "united" churches (for instance, the United Church of Christ) that brought together various strains of Protestantism into new denominations.

Still another was consolidation of churches within denominational families. By 1968, 98 percent of American Methodists belonged to the United Methodist Church,[7] and by 1983, 95 percent of American Presbyterians belonged to the Presbyterian Church (U.S.A.).[8] Neither of these church bodies had existed in 1900. They developed through mergers over many years. As for Lutherans in the United States, they kept consolidating until

---

5   Walter A. Baepler, *A Century of Grace: A History of the Missouri Synod, 1847–1947* (St. Louis: Concordia Publishing House, 1947), 137–48, 155–65; and Armin Schuetze, *The Synodical Conference: Ecumenical Endeavor* (Milwaukee: Northwestern Publishing House, 2000), 31–33, 41–50, 51–58, 60.

6   For the Predestination Controversy, see Schuetze, *Synodical Conference*, 91–112; and Hans Robert Haug, "The Predestination Controversy in the Lutheran Church in North America" (PhD diss., Temple University, 1968).

7   These figures are based on those available for Methodist denominations in "Religious Bodies in the United States Arranged by Families," in Constant H. Jacquet Jr., ed., *Yearbook of American Churches [1970]* (New York: National Council of Churches, 1970), 94. They do not include the historic African-American Methodist church bodies that have a distinct denominational tradition.

8   These figures are based on those available for Presbyterian denominations in "U.S. Religious Bodies in the United States Arranged by Families," in Constant H. Jacquet Jr., ed., *Yearbook of American Churches 1985* (New York: National Council of Churches, 1985), 112.

1988 when about 63 percent of them formed the ELCA.[9] This percentage was far less than the Methodists or Presbyterians because the Missouri Synod did not join. The movement to merge came to a halt in the LCMS during the 1970s.

In the Missouri Synod

The Missouri Synod had not remained aloof from the ecumenical movement. It engaged in numerous efforts to overcome denominational differences through the course of the twentieth century. Over time, differences of an ethnic or linguistic nature either became less acute or disappeared as immigrant populations assimilated to American culture. The English Missouri Synod joined the German Missouri Synod in 1911 as the English District. In 1964 the Finnish National Evangelical Church merged with Missouri, and in 1971 the Slovak Evangelical Lutheran Church joined the Synod as the SELC District. Each of these synods was already in fellowship with Missouri at the time of the merger.[10]

When the differences were doctrinal, the situation became more complicated. Still, many Lutherans in North America found ways to overcome even differences of this sort. In 1917, 92 percent of the Norwegian Lutherans joined together in the Norwegian Lutheran Church of America despite previous disagreements over the doctrine of predestination. They simply agreed to disagree.[11] Another merger followed the next year when three synods, based largely in the eastern United States, formed the ULCA. Their compromise consisted of agreeing to adopt the entire *Book of Concord* but not insisting on exclusively Lutheran Communion and preaching in their churches [12] But neither the approach of the ULCA nor that of the Norwegians would work in the Missouri Synod, where unity of doctrine and practice remained the standard for church fellowship. How could Missouri proceed?

It determined to engage other Lutherans in talks to determine whether, after many years had passed since the doctrinal differences surfaced, the synods might actually be in agreement. Beginning in 1917, the Missouri,

---

9   These figures are based on those available for Lutheran denominations in "U.S. Religious Bodies in the United States Arranged by Families," in Constant H. Jacquet Jr., ed., *Yearbook of American and Canadian Churches 1990* (New York: National Council of Churches, 1990), 125.

10   *Christian Cyclopedia*, s.v. "Missouri and Other States, The English Evangelical Lutheran Synod of"; "Finnish Lutherans in America, 3"; and "Synod of Evangelical Lutheran Churches." http://cyclopedia.lcms.org/default.asp. Accessed 11/26/21.

11   Nelson, *Lutherans in North America*, 371–72.

12   Nelson, *Lutherans in North America*, 373–76.

Wisconsin, Iowa, and Ohio Synods each appointed a committee to work with their counterparts on doctrinal issues that had separated them. The synodical representatives, known collectively as the Intersynodical Committee, worked several years and agreed in 1928 to doctrinal statements about previously divisive issues in the "Intersynodical Theses." Missouri appointed a special review committee that found these theses woefully inadequate, and the Synod's 1929 convention rejected them.[13] The seeds of polarization were developing in Missouri over church fellowship: the Missouri appointees to the Intersynodical Committee thought the theses were good enough for consideration, but the review committee members assessed the theses harshly.

Yet Missouri refused to take no for an answer. It kept trying one approach after another to establish fellowship with these other Lutherans. This became the Synod's *modus operandi* until finally in 1969 it declared fellowship with the ALC.[14] But by then Missouri had virtually surrendered its principle that church fellowship depended on unity in doctrine and practice.

John Tietjen and Confessional Minimalism

Also in 1969, John Tietjen became president of Concordia Seminary. He would later become a central figure in the synodical upheaval that led to Seminex.[15] In 1969, that was all in Tietjen's future.

What lay in his past was an historical book he wrote on church fellowship, *Which Way to Lutheran Unity?* Tietjen rejected the Missouri Synod's original insistence on unity in doctrine and practice. He preferred instead what he called *confessional subscription*. That is, church bodies could be in fellowship as long as they affirmed the Bible as the rule and standard for doctrine and the confessional writings in the *Book of Concord* as a correct exposition of the

---

13 Nelson, *Lutherans in North America*, 445–47; Mark E. Braun, *A Tale of Two Synods: Events that Led to the Split between Wisconsin and Missouri* (Milwaukee: Northwestern Publishing House, 2003), 127–30; Charles F. Bunzel, "The Missouri Synod and the Chicago (Intersynodical) Theses," (STM thesis, Concordia Seminary [St. Louis], 1964), https://core.ac.uk/download/pdf/304930985.pdf. Accessed 11/26/21. See also John C. Wohlrabe, "The Missouri Synod's Unity Attempts during the Pfotenhauer Presidency, 1911–1935" (STM thesis, Concordia Seminary [St. Louis], 1982), 111–36, https://scholar.csl.edu/cgi/viewcontent .cgi?article=1058&context=stm. Accessed 11/26/21. For the theses themselves, see *Doctrinal Declarations* (St. Louis: Concordia Publishing House, 1936), 24–41.

14 See Braun, *Tale of Two Synods*, 130–32, 138–42, 294–301; Schuetze, *Synodical Conference*, 271–82, 293–318; and John H. Tietjen, *Which Way to Lutheran Unity: A History of Efforts to Unite the Lutherans of America* (St. Louis: Concordia Publishing House, 1966), 125–35.

15 For those events, see the accounts in Zimmerman and *Memoirs*.

Bible. Period. For Tietjen, this was all that church bodies needed to agree upon in order to establish fellowship with each other.[16]

It may look like unity when everyone says they accept Scripture and the Confessions, but is it? By 1966, when Tietjen's book appeared, American Lutherans were not only still divided by issues such as predestination, they were also at odds regarding the trustworthiness of the Bible.[17] They hardly agreed on what it meant for the Bible to be a standard for teaching, even if they all said that it was. They also disagreed on the nature of confessional subscription.[18] By 1969, however, Missouri seemed ready to follow Tietjen's minimalistic prescription for church fellowship, especially since the Synodical Conference was now history.

The Synodical Conference

The troubles in the Missouri Synod had spilled over into the Synodical Conference. The Wisconsin and Evangelical Lutheran Synods left the conference and brought about its effective end in 1963, but they had been concerned about Missouri for decades. During the 1930s, Missouri had come very close to declaring fellowship with the first version of the ALC. In 1938, it adopted its own *Brief Statement* (1932) and the ALC's *Sandusky Declaration* "as the doctrinal basis for *future church-fellowship*" between the two synods.[19] The Wisconsin Synod objected. More criticism came throughout the following decade when Missouri tried again and again to reach agreement with the ALC.[20]

The Wisconsin and Evangelical Lutheran Synods also raised other concerns, such as the sponsoring of Boy Scout troops by congregations, participation in the military chaplaincy program, and prayer with members of church bodies with which the synod was not in fellowship.[21] These issues

---

16 Tietjen, *Which Way to Lutheran Unity*, 55, 56, 151. Contrast *Anatomy*, 72–82.

17 See Zimmerman, 52–60, 84–89; Braun, *Tale of Two Synods*, 277–320; *Anatomy*, 107–45. See also above, chapters 1–3, pp. 15–82.

18 See Zimmerman, 50–51, 89–90; and above, chapter 4, pp. 83–97.

19 1938 *Proceedings*, 231 (italics original). Extensive excerpts from both of these documents are in Richard C. Wolf, ed., *Documents of Lutheran Unity in America* (Philadelphia: Fortress Press, 1966), 381–92 (*Brief Statement*) and 394–98 (*Sandusky Declaration*).

20 See Tietjen, *Which Way to Lutheran Unity*, 133; Braun, *Tale of Two Synods*, 294–301; and Schuetze, *Synodical Conference*, 271–332.

21 Braun, *Tale of Two Synods*, 83–102, 102–22, 175–77, 189–90, 198–206; and Schuetze, *Synodical Conference*, 241–69.

proved controversial *within* the Missouri Synod, too, especially the question of prayer.[22]

Joint Prayer or Prayer Fellowship

Should a person pray with someone who belongs to a church with which his or her own church is not in fellowship? Should a Lutheran pray with a Presbyterian? A Missouri Synod Lutheran with an ELCA Lutheran? Today, the Wisconsin Synod answers no. Praying together, the Wisconsin Synod says, is like going to Communion together. One should pray only with those with whom one is united in doctrine and practice.[23] The Missouri Synod places no such restriction on prayer with fellow Christians. But at the beginning of the twentieth century, the Missouri Synod sounded like the Wisconsin Synod.

For example, in 1905, just as the movement to unite Lutherans in North America was gathering steam, an important article appeared by Friedrich Bente, a respected professor at Concordia Seminary.[24] It was entitled "Why can't we establish and maintain common worship services with the members of the Ohio and Iowa synods?"[25] Bente maintained that those who were not united in doctrine should not pray with each other.

Theodore Graebner was another longtime seminary professor.[26] He wrote similarly in the Synod's magazine for preachers:

> It ought to be clear to anyone who gives sincere thought to the matter that any prayer in which we are asked to join those who speak not from the same faith as we, or in which we are asked to withhold an expression of conviction, or by the participation in and utterance of which we appear to treat as immaterial those articles of faith in which we differ, cannot be pleasing to God. For if joint prayer signifies anything, it signifies the spiritual unity of those who pray.[27]

---

22 Braun, *Tale of Two Synods*, 159–74.

23 See "Theses on Fellowship." https://wels.net/about-wels/what-we-believe/doctrinal -statements/church-fellowship/. Accessed 8/23/21.

24 *Christian Cyclopedia*, s.v. "Bente, Gerhard Friedrich." http://cyclopedia.lcms.org /display.asp?t1=b&word=Bente.GerhardFriedrich. Accessed 8/19/21.

25 Gerhard Friedrich Bente, "Warum können wir keine gemeinsame Gottesdienste mit Ohioern und Iowaern varanstalten und abhalten?" *Lehre und Wehre* 51 (February 1905): 49–53, and (March 1905): 97–115.

26 *Christian Cyclopedia*, s.v. "Graebner, Theodore Conrad." http://cyclopedia.lcms .org/display.asp?t1=G&t2=r. Accessed 8/19/21.

27 Theodore Graebner, "Letters to a Young Preacher: Joint Prayers," *Magazin für evang.-Luth. Homiletik und Pastoraltheologie* 44 (May 1920): 231–33.

The Synod's leading theologian after Walther's death was Francis Pieper.[28] In 1924, he equated prayer fellowship with Communion fellowship: "To pray with them [false teachers] or to partake of the Lord's Supper with them would mean to consent to, and to become 'partakers of their evil works.'"[29]

Finally, the 1927 *Concordia Cyclopedia*, edited by three more seminary professors, stated that "all joint ecclesiastical efforts for religious work (missionary, educational, etc.) and particularly joint worship and *mixed (promiscuous) prayer* among those who profess the truth and those who deny any part of it, is *sinful* unionism."[30]

The Adolph Brux Case

Yet not everyone in the Missouri Synod agreed with this position. One example was Adolph Brux, a missionary to India.[31] In 1924, while traveling to his station in India, Brux attended an evening prayer service at the Presbyterian hospice where he was staying. Two of his fellow LCMS missionaries did not. In response to criticism, Brux wrote an essay in defense of his behavior. Several years later the Synod's missions board took up his case. Finally, the synodical conventions of 1935 and 1938 resolved to send him back to the mission field only if he would admit his guilt. He refused and resigned from the Synod in 1940.

The Brux case coincided with other discussions within Missouri regarding prayer, and not just discussions. In January 1941, the Synod's president attended a meeting with Lutherans of all stripes about coordinating relief

---

28 *Christian Cyclopedia*, s.v. "Pieper, Franz August Otto." http://cyclopedia.lcms.org /display.asp?t1=P&t2=i. Accessed 8/19/21.

29 *Siebzehnter Synodal-Bericht des Oregon- und Washington-Distrikts der Ev.- Lutherischen Synode von Missouri, Ohio und andern Staaten, Spokane, Washington, July 9–15, 1924* (St. Louis: Concordia Publishing House, 1924), 8.

30 L. Fuerbringer, Th. Engelder, and P. E. Kretzmann, eds., *The Concordia Cyclopedia* (St. Louis: Concordia Publishing House, 1927), s.v. "Unionism" (italics added).

31 For the Brux Case, see Braun, *Tale of Two Synods*, 133–38; Christopher Vossler, "Missions in Missouri: The Story of Frederick Brand (I)," and "The Story of Frederick Brand (II)," *CHIQ* 87 (Spring 2014): 58–65, and (Summer 2014): 9–12, 19–20; and Jack Treon Robinson, "The Spirit of Triumphalism in the Lutheran Church—Missouri Synod: The Role of 'A Statement' of 1945 in the Missouri Synod" (PhD diss., Vanderbilt University, 1972), 127–51, as well as a briefer treatment by Robinson, "The Brux Case," *Currents in Theology and Mission* 4 (June 1977): 143–50.

efforts for Europe. The meeting opened and closed with prayer.[32] Then, in 1944, the Synod formally approved of joint prayer "at intersynodical conferences asking God for His guidance and blessing . . . provided that such prayer does not imply denial of truth or support of error."[33] Clearly, some prayers with outsiders now seemed okay, but not all. This distinction was ratified by subsequent conventions in 1947 and 1953.[34] Henceforth, circumstances would determine whether or not the Missouri Synod Lutheran was going to pray with others.[35]

The "Statement of the 44"

The 1944 resolution was addressing especially prayers at meetings being held with representatives of other Lutheran church bodies. This question, as well as general relations with other North American Lutherans, provoked a major assault on the Missouri Synod's practice of requiring unity of doctrine and practice for church fellowship. The assault came in a document then called "A Statement," which was signed by forty-four of the Synod's most prominent leaders and sent out to all the Synod's pastors in September 1945. The polarization that began in the 1920s now became evident to all.[36]

The document took issue with the Synod's understanding of church fellowship. Regarding prayer, it maintained that Christians who differed in doctrine could certainly "pray together to the Triune God in the name of Jesus Christ if the purpose for which they meet and pray is right according to the Word of God." Prayer was not regarded as a matter of church fellowship.[37]

---

32 Braun, *Tale of Two Synods*, 176; Schuetze, *Synodical Conference*, 287; and Edward E. Busch, "Another Turning Point," *Currents in Theology and Mission* 2 (April 1975): 80.

33 1944 *Proceedings*, 251–52.

34 1947 *Proceedings*, 517–18; 1953 *Proceedings*, 552.

35 Braun, *Tale of Two Synods*, 177; and Schuetze, *Synodical Conference*, 286–89.

36 Robinson's dissertation, "Spirit of Triumphalism in the Lutheran Church—Missouri Synod" (above, p. 152 n. 31), is the most complete account of the controversy but, as its title indicates, offers a rather negative interpretation. See also Braun, *Tale of Two Synods*, 177–85; and A. T. Kretzmann, "A Statement of the 44, 1945–1979," *CHIQ* 55 (Summer 1982): 69–81. *CHIQ* devoted almost all of the November 1970 issue to articles and reminiscences upon the twenty-fifth anniversary of "Statement of the 44." The "Statement of the 44," as it is being termed here, is available online at http://www.projectwittenberg.org/etext/lcms/ST44/ST44.htm. Accessed 10/22/2022. See also *Moving Frontiers*, 422–24.

37 "Statement of the 44," Thesis 8 (*Moving Frontiers*, 423).

Photograph by Paul Ockrassa

Led by banners, former students and faculty (some in academic regalia) of Concordia Seminary walk off the campus. Gerald Miller, student body president, is to the right of the banners (February 19, 1974).

The signers rejected the Synod's biblical basis for insisting on doctrinal unity. Beginning with C. F. W. Walther himself, the Synod had relied on Romans 16:17 to justify its insistence on complete doctrinal unity for fellowship with other church bodies.[38] But the forty-four argued that the passage was misapplied to other Christians, especially to other Lutherans: "We therefore deplore the fact that Romans 16:17–18 has been applied to all Christians who differ from us in certain points of doctrine." They also maintained that "[church] fellowship is possible without complete agreement in details of doctrine and practice which have never been considered divisive in the Lutheran Church."[39]

The "Statement of the 44" was charting a new direction for the Missouri Synod in the matter of church fellowship. Although the Synod's president was at first deeply upset by what the forty-four had done, he eventually decided to be content if they would "withdraw" their document as a basis for discussion.

---

38   Romans 16:17: "I appeal to you, brothers, to watch out for those who cause divisions and create obstacles contrary to the doctrine that you have been taught; avoid them." See C. F. W. Walther, *Church Fellowship* (St. Louis: Concordia Publishing House, 2015), 84, 156, 159, 239, 264, 373.

39   "Statement of the 44," Theses 5 and 11 (*Moving Frontiers*, 423, 424).

This they did in 1947.[40] But now the Synod had two approaches to church fellowship: the traditional one, insisting on unity of doctrine and practice, and a new one that said, in effect: not unity, but proximity. That second position evolved into John Tietjen's minimalist approach, a commitment in words only to the Bible and the Confessions.

Once the Synodical Conference had been relegated to the dustbin of history, the Missouri Synod could more freely engage with other North American Lutheran church bodies.[41] In 1965, it invited three of them to form the Inter-Lutheran Commission on Worship (ILCW) and jointly to prepare a new hymnal.[42] Since churches use hymnals to present the Gospel, the Missouri Synod had produced *The Lutheran Hymnal* (1941) with the other synods of the Synodical Conference, Lutheran churches in fellowship.[43] By 1965, such fellowship was no longer a requisite.

Similarly, in 1966, Missouri participated in founding the Lutheran Council in the United States of America (LCUSA), an intersynodical body that would do at least some church work together, e.g., mission planning, campus ministry, and military chaplains. This cooperation was occurring without unity in doctrine and practice.[44]

---

40 Robinson, "Spirit of Triumphalism in the Lutheran Church—Missouri Synod," 304–6.

41 The Wisconsin and Evangelical Lutheran Synods withdrew from the Synodical Conference in 1963. It was formally dissolved in 1967. *Concordia Cyclopedia*, s.v. "Synodical Conference." http://cyclopedia.lcms.org/display.asp?t1=S&t2=y. Accessed 8/25/21.

42 The ILCW consisted of the LCMS, the ALC, the LCA, and the Evangelical Lutheran Church of Canada. The LCMS entered into fellowship with the ALC in 1969 but never did so with the other church bodies. The four church bodies produced the *Lutheran Book of Worship* (1978). https://www.cuchicago .edu/academics/centers-of-excellence/center-for-church-music/hymnal-collection -index/inter-lutheran-commission-on-worship/. Accessed 11/21/21.

43 Carl Schalk, "A Brief History of LCMS Hymnals (before LSB)," 3. https://files.lcms .org/api/file/preview/DF374947-56E2-4C9E-8C2B-CD49E4CE3AF4. Accessed 11/21/21.

44 *Encyclopedia Britannica*, online ed., s.v. "Lutheran Council in the United States of America." https://www.britannica.com/topic/Lutheran-Council-in-the-United -States-of-America. Accessed 11/21/21. Also the Social Networks and Archival Context. https://snaccooperative.org/ark:/99166/w65q9m9h. Accessed 11/21/21.

Theology of Fellowship

In 1967, the LCMS adopted *Theology of Fellowship*, a document presented by the CTCR.[45] It helped to erode Missouri's traditional approach to establishing church fellowship. For one thing, it distinguished sharply between those who were outside of the church, for example, heretics, and those who were within, that is, erring Christians.[46] Then it dealt with Bible passages that "command Christians to separate themselves from certain persons, teachings, and practices."[47] In each case, the document concluded that the passage at hand ought not be applied to erring Christians but only against those who "either by false teaching or separatistic, schismatic, factious activities attack the Gospel and the faith of Christians."[48] One could come away from these conclusions thinking that the Synod had no *biblical* basis for refusing church fellowship with erring *Christian* churches.

A good example of this is the document's treatment of Romans 16:17–18. It maintained that St. Paul demanded separation "because these trouble-makers are not erring Christians, who need to be taught, but people who attack the church's very foundation, namely, the Gospel." The CTCR concluded that the Romans passage and all the rest must not be used when the church "attempts to heal the schisms in the church and to foster the unity of Spirit in the bond of peace," that is, dealing with erring Christians. Such "attempts" remained unspecified.[49]

In a concluding section, the document offered guidelines for the practice of fellowship. Far from repudiating joint prayer at inter-church meetings for doctrinal unity, it insisted that participants "*should* join in fervent prayer." Regarding prayers in other situations, the document instructed Christians to follow their consciences and refrain from judging others. The guidelines also urged cooperation with "churches of various denominations" to the extent that the "Word of God and conscience" would permit.[50] However, an appeal

---

45 *Theology of Fellowship* (St. Louis: LCMS, [1967]). According to its "Preamble," the origins of this document went back to 1956. See Res. 2-13, 1967 *Proceedings*, 91.

46 *Theology of Fellowship* found this distinction in Augustine (14), Luther (15), the Lutheran Confessions (17–18), Gerhard and Walther (22 n. 24), and the Bible (25, 1 Corinthians 3:12).

47 *Theology of Fellowship*, 23–24. The document went on to treat Matthew 7:15, 16; Galatians 1:6–9; Acts 19:8–10; 2 John 9–11; Romans 16:17–18; Titus 3:10; and 2 Corinthians 6:14–18.

48 *Theology of Fellowship*, 26.

49 *Theology of Fellowship*, 26.

50 *Theology of Fellowship*, 28 (italics original).

156

to the Word of God (or just "Word") in this document is vague. It could mean the Scriptures, but it could also mean the Gospel.[51]

By the 1960s, new approaches to the Scriptures, such as higher criticism and "Gospel reductionism," were making their way into the LCMS.[52] New ways of interpreting the Bible acted as a solvent to the doctrinal concerns that had previously separated the Missouri Synod from other Lutherans. After all, if the Bible contains mistakes and errors, why should we argue about what it asserts regarding predestination? Those assertions themselves might be wrong or contradictory. If the only thing that matters from the Bible is the Gospel, narrowly defined as, say, John 3:16, no other teaching should prevent Christians from worshiping or doing church work together. That, in turn, could open the door for church fellowship with non-Lutherans so long as there was agreement in the "Gospel."

Theology of Fellowship did *not* take such a minimalist position regarding the Gospel. It explicitly said that the Gospel is multifaceted and includes many articles: "The doctrine of the Gospel is not here to be understood as one doctrine among many, or as a bare recital of John 3:16, but rather as a doctrine composed of a number of articles of faith."[53]

However, it is noteworthy that the document appealed to the "Gospel" as the standard for establishing and maintaining church fellowship rather than the Bible. In a section on "guarding the fellowship," it advocated, first, "remaining steadfastly under the power of the Gospel in Word and Sacrament." Then, for those situations in which errors appear in teaching and preaching, it counseled "applying the corrective measures of the Law and the healing powers of the Gospel." Although numerous Bible passages were quoted, nowhere in this section did the document advocate using faithfulness to the Scriptures as a rule for church fellowship.[54]

At points the document advocated conformity to the Bible, yet the Gospel remained the ultimate test. A guideline that began by approving ecclesiastical *practice* as a consideration for church fellowship went on to say that when a practice is "in harmony with Scripture and the Lutheran Confessions,

---

51 For the "Word" as the Scriptures, see *Theology of Fellowship*, 21, 24, 15 (quoting Luther), 18 (quoting *Book of Concord*), 21 (quoting George Stoeckhardt), and 27 (probably, quoting the *Brief Statement*). For "Word" as Gospel, see *Theology of Fellowship*, 6, 8, 11, and 17. In other instances, as here in the appeal to "Word of God and conscience," it is not clear which is meant.

52 On the former, see above, chapters 2 and 3, pp. 39–82. On the latter, see above, chapter 1, pp. 15–37.

53 *Theology of Fellowship*, 18.

54 *Theology of Fellowship*, 19.

the church is edified." What kind of practice would contradict this principle? "When ecclesiastical practice constitutes a demonstrable denial of the gospel, the work of the church is undermined."[55] What about a practice that contradicts the Scriptures?

By maintaining that the Gospel can and does coexist with error in various churches, and by rejecting the application of Scripture passages traditionally used to refuse fellowship with such erring churches, *Theology of Fellowship* demonstrated a significant departure from the previous Missouri Synod emphasis on unity in doctrine and practice as the criterion for church fellowship. It's no surprise that Missouri entered into pulpit and altar fellowship with the ALC (which resulted from a 1960 merger involving the "old" ALC) just a couple of years later.

ALC Fellowship

On July 17, 1969, the LCMS "formally declare(d) itself to be in altar and pulpit fellowship with The American Lutheran Church" by a vote of 522 to 438.[56] This formed the climax of repeated efforts to achieve fellowship with fellow Lutherans originally represented in the Intersynodical Committee of the 1920s (but now without the Wisconsin Synod). The vote in favor of fellowship was hardly unanimous, but it was enough.

The new approach to church fellowship described in *Theology of Fellowship* was at work. In the Joint Statement and Declaration (1967) between representatives of the ALC and the LCMS that paved the way for the 1969 decision, the Gospel was now the standard: "All teaching in the church must be tested to determine whether it conforms to the pure teaching of the Gospel. . . . Likewise practices in the church that militate against the Gospel impair the true unity the church." [57] A fine statement, for sure, but what happened to the Holy Scriptures as "the only rule and guiding principle according to which all teachings and teachers are to be evaluated and judged" (FC Ep Rule and Norm 1)?[58] Biblical authority had been redefined in terms of the Gospel.

The Joint Statement avoided calling the Bible God's Word because God inspired it. Instead, it described the Scriptures as "the Word or address of

---

55 *Theology of Fellowship*, 28.

56 1969 *Proceedings*, 98; see 1969 *Proceedings*, 32–33, 96–99.

57 The American Lutheran Church and Lutheran Church—Missouri Synod, *Joint Statement and Declaration of the Representatives of the American Lutheran Church, the Lutheran Church—Missouri Synod and the Synod of Evangelical Lutheran Churches* (N.p: n.p, 1967).

58 K-W, 486.

God to man for the purpose of revealing His grace in His Son, Jesus Christ." Apparently, what made the Bible God's Word was not its source but its evangelical purpose. Only from this perspective were the Scriptures normative: "The Scriptures *as the Word of God* are the sole authority in the church both as the source of the church's message and the norm of its content."[59] The only question now was how far "Gospel"-based fellowship would extend.

Subsequent Developments

Between 1969 and 1973, the issue of church fellowship was not the major issue that it had been previously. Under the leadership of President J. A. O. Preus, the Synod turned its attention to doctrinal problems at the St. Louis seminary. During those years, it neither revoked fellowship with the ALC nor did it declare fellowship with any additional churches. Nonetheless, efforts both by liberals to do even more and by traditionalists to reverse the Synod's course became evident in the memorials submitted to Synod prior to its conventions in Milwaukee, Wisconsin (1971),[60] and New Orleans, Louisiana (1973).[61] Clearly, the LCMS could no longer claim a consensus regarding church fellowship.

Furthermore, when President Preus reported on what his FFC had discovered regarding doctrinal aberrations at St. Louis, he identified church fellowship as one of them. He described the new attitude:

> Complete agreement in doctrine is not necessary for the practice of church fellowship, so long as there is agreement in the essential aspects of the Gospel. Because the Eucharist is a means for the achievement of the unity of faith, non-Lutherans may be communed at our altars if they profess faith in Christ and recognize His presence in the Lord's Supper.[62]

Nonetheless, *A Statement of Scriptural and Confessional Principles* offered by Preus to address false doctrine at the St. Louis seminary did not include a section on church fellowship. The New Orleans convention did not approve any resolutions dealing with fellowship, though several had been formulated, for example, Res. 2-11, "To Decline Lutheran World Federation Membership," and Res. 2-31, "To Declare Altar and Pulpit Fellowship with the Independent

---

59 *Joint Statement and Declaration* (italics added).

60 1971 *Convention Workbook*, 130–45, 148–97.

61 1973 *Convention Workbook*.

62 Blue Book (Zimmerman, 237).

Evangelical Lutheran Church of Germany."[63] Obviously, that convention had more than enough to do without addressing church fellowship.

Scripture and the Lutheran Confessions

Unity in the Means of Grace

God creates fellowship among His people only by means of the Gospel and the Sacraments.[64] These are the instruments that the Holy Spirit uses to create and maintain the faith that is the bond between us. Without them, there are no believers, no church, and, obviously, no church fellowship.[65]

The founders of the LCMS insisted that church fellowship depended on doctrinal unity. They were following the convictions of the first Lutherans. Article VII of the Augsburg Confession states that "it is enough for the true unity of the church to agree concerning the teaching of the gospel and the administration of the sacraments." Unity does not come from observing the same "human traditions, rites, or ceremonies instituted by human beings."[66]

Over against those who argue that the Augsburg Confession permits fellowship on a minimal basis—say, the Gospel as expressed in John 3:16—the Formula of Concord explains that no church should condemn another on account of outward ceremonies not commanded by God so long as "there is unity ... in *teaching and all the articles of faith* and in the proper use of the holy sacraments" (FC Ep X 7).[67] To insist on anything less than complete agreement in doctrine is a violation of the Synod's commitment to the Lutheran Confessions.

Is this position biblical?

Our Lord Himself said, "If you abide in My word, you are truly My disciples, and you will know the truth, and the truth will set you free" (John 8:31–32). When He sent the disciples out to "make disciples of all nations," He told them to do so by baptizing and by "teaching them to observe

---

63 1973 *Proceedings*, 111–19.

64 "I am not ashamed of the gospel, for it is the power of God for salvation to everyone who believes" (Romans 1:16); "He saved us ... by the washing of regeneration and renewal of the Holy Spirit" (Titus 3:5); and "The cup of blessing that we bless, is it not a participation in the blood of Christ? The bread that we break, is it not a participation in the body of Christ?" (1 Corinthians 10:16).

65 In the present section, I have incorporated some of the material from my synodical convention essay from 2001, "Church Fellowship and the Gospel." See 2001 *Proceedings*, 87–91.

66 K-W, 43.

67 K-W 516 (italics added).

all that I have commanded you" (Matthew 28:19–20). Not just some things, but *all* of it!

But where is it that we find "all" these things? In the Bible, of course. St. Paul noted not only that the Scriptures make us "wise for salvation" but also that "all Scripture is breathed out by God and profitable for teaching, for reproof, for correction, and for training in righteousness, that the man of God may be complete, equipped for every good work" (2 Timothy 3:15–17).

God has given us the Bible to equip us for Christian faith and life. It is God's Word, not ours. We are not free to pick and choose from the Scriptures what we want to believe or how we want to behave. Christian doctrine belongs to God, not us.

There can be a lot of variety in the church regarding "human traditions, rites, or ceremonies instituted by human beings" (AC VII 3). Differences like these do not divide us. Doctrine is different, though. It is God's truth. That matters, because God uses this truth to save people from their sins. Therefore Christians must be united in doctrine.

Pulpit Fellowship

Of course, doctrine is to be preached and taught. People need to learn about sin and salvation. They need to hear about Jesus. That is the church's task, to tell them. But they need to hear *the truth* about Jesus—not speculation, mistakes, or errors, not false doctrine. Jesus Himself said, "In vain do they worship Me, teaching as doctrines the commandments of men" (Matthew 15:9). We are not free to mix in a little falsehood with the truth, to teach correctly about one thing but not another. Salvation lies at risk when we do not proclaim God's truth.

Teaching the truth also involves condemning falsehood. Think of how often St. Paul did this, and not only in Romans 16:17. He warned, for example, "See to it that no one takes you captive by philosophy and empty deceit, according to human tradition, according to the elemental spirits of the world, and not according to Christ" (Colossians 2:8). Again: "If anyone is preaching to you a gospel contrary to the one you received, let him be accursed" (Galatians 1:9).

Our Lord Himself warned against "false prophets, who come to you in sheep's clothing but inwardly are ravenous wolves" (Matthew 7:15). What is "sheep's clothing"? Through the prophet Jeremiah, God explained: "Behold, I am against the prophets, declares the LORD, who use their tongues and declare, 'declares the LORD'" (Jeremiah 23:31). False doctrine tells people "This is the Word of the Lord" when it is really someone's own idea, not God's.

Nowhere in the Bible do we read that erroneous teaching is okay so long as it does not contradict the "Gospel." False doctrine does not save anyone. It

161

misleads everyone. Members of the Missouri Synod have committed themselves to the truth and only the truth in carrying out their work together. Like their synodical fathers, today's members have also pledged themselves to the Scriptures as the "only rule and norm of faith and of practice" and to the Lutheran Confessions as "a true and unadulterated statement and exposition of the Word of God."[68] When pastors enter the pulpits of our churches, congregations should hear this truth come out of their mouths and nothing else.

What is true for these pulpits must be true also for all activities that include the proclamation of God's Word. When this Word is not involved, we can work with others who do not belong to our fellowship. Activities such as maintaining a food bank or demonstrating a concern for the unborn do not involve the means of grace. Doctrine is not at stake. But when an activity includes some form of Gospel proclamation, we must make sure that there is agreement in the Gospel in the first place, i.e., "in teaching and all the articles of faith" (FC Ep X 7).

Whenever and however the church goes about the Christ-given mission to "make disciples," it must do so in faithfulness to God's Word. Evangelizing the unchurched, sending missionaries abroad, publishing hymnals and Bible studies, and maintaining Christian schools are all specific ways to make disciples. If we do these things without agreement in doctrine, we open the door for error to enter the proclamation. Yet God saves people not through falsehood, but through the truth.

Communion Fellowship

Besides the pure preaching of the Word, church fellowship also involves the right administration of the Sacraments (AC VII). Administering the Sacraments according to the Scriptures requires unity in doctrine among those who commune together. We call this requirement "closed" or "close" Communion.[69]

Lutherans confess that in the Sacrament of the Altar God gives "forgiveness of sin, life, and salvation" to all who believe what our Lord says about the Supper, that it is His body and blood, "given for you" and "shed for you for the forgiveness of sins" (SC Sacrament of the Altar 6).[70] The main purpose of the Lord's Supper is to apply God's forgiveness of sins in Christ to the sinner.

Yet while forgiveness is this sacrament's *main* purpose, that is not its *only* purpose. The Lord's Supper is also a confession of faith. "As often as you eat this bread and drink the cup, you proclaim the Lord's death until He comes"

---

68   2019 LCMS *Handbook*, 11.

69   https://www.lcms.org/about/beliefs/faqs/doctrine#lords-supper. Accessed 12/3/21.

70   K-W, 362.

(1 Corinthians 11:26). Communing together demonstrates the faith in the crucified and risen Christ that communicants believe and share, faith that unites them in the church as the Body of Christ. By receiving the body of Christ together orally with our mouths, we show that we are the mystical Body of Christ. As St. Paul put it: "You are the body of Christ and individually members of it" (1 Corinthians 12:27). Going to Communion together shows God's relationship to us and our relationship to each other.

The Lord's Supper is different from preaching. Preaching proclaims a message from God to sinners about their sin and their salvation in Christ. All people are sinners. Therefore preaching is directed to all, unbelievers as well as believers. We want everyone to hear God's Word, for through the Word, the Holy Spirit works faith in the heart. By faith, believers become one with God and with each other. Believers are children of God and, therefore, brothers and sisters in the Lord.

Like the Word, the Lord's Supper nurtures and sustains both of these relationships—relations between God and man and relations between believers. Unlike the Word, though, it also reveals the relationships. Hearing the Word is passive and belief is invisible. We cannot see the Word at work, but we can see people kneeling before an altar to eat and drink the Lord's body and blood. The Sacrament is visible and external as well as invisible and internal. It marks us as belonging to God and to one another. It says that we belong to the church.

St. Paul explained: "Because there is one bread, we who are many are one body, for we all partake of the one bread" (1 Corinthians 10:17). When Christians eat together the bread that is the body of Christ, we ourselves are one body—not just symbolically but really, mystically and spiritually, the Body of Christ. All of us are one in Christ and through Communion are brought together in Him most intimately. One God dwells in us; one Spirit rules in us; and one Lord Jesus Christ saves us.

But false doctrine undermines the unity of faith that the Lord's Supper demonstrates. That is why our churches do not commune anyone who does not confess the truth to which we have committed ourselves in the Scriptures and the Lutheran Confessions. In practice, this means restricting Communion to those who belong to churches with whom we are united in doctrine and practice.

Different churches teach different things about God, man, sin, morality, salvation, and the Savior. These differences are important. But to commune people who belong to churches that teach doctrinal errors means just the opposite, that such errors are *un*important—that it doesn't matter, for example, if you think that it is wrong to baptize babies or if you believe that good works are necessary for salvation or if you insist that it is all right for

Christians to live sexually dissolute lives. Teachings like these mislead people, undermine the consolation of the Gospel, and may even rob them of their faith altogether. The errors that other churches hold are unacceptable to those who remain faithful to God's Word.

This does not mean that there are no believers in Christ within other churches. In any church where there is still some saving Gospel by which the Holy Spirit creates faith, people will be brought to saving faith. Still, belonging to a church that teaches or tolerates false doctrine is dangerous. It matters whether people hear that they are saved through faith in Jesus alone without the works of the Law; it matters whether they believe that God has clothed them with Christ in Baptism; it matters whether they are taught that the Christian life entails sexual purity in word and deed. These things matter greatly, and people risk their salvation by going to a church that mingles errors with the truth.

The concern for doctrinal unity in administering the Lord's Supper is important also for those who already belong to LCMS congregations. If churches commune those who reject what they teach, why do these churches teach it in the first place? If unity of doctrine is not a requirement for communing, for what else is it a requirement? Membership in the Ladies Aid? Receiving a packet of offering envelopes? Communion fellowship is divinely instituted, but these other things are not. If doctrinal errors do not matter for Communion, they can hardly matter anywhere else. If we ignore them at Communion, we will at best confuse people and suggest to them that true doctrine is not so important. At worst, we will undermine their faith.

Since doctrinal error endangers one's salvation, we have to take measures that lead people away from such error. Practicing closed Communion is one of these measures. So, too, is insisting that Gospel proclamation in all its forms be carried out by those who are truly agreed in doctrine as confessed by our church on the basis of the Bible and the Lutheran Confessions.

What Happened

Those Who Left

The issue of church fellowship did not disappear after the Missouri Synod declared fellowship with the ALC. The members of the Synod who left after their failure to retain control of the St. Louis seminary formed the AELC in 1976. It ended up numbering about 250 congregations with 100,000 members and 675 clergy.[71] From its beginning, the AELC committed itself

---

71   Association of Religious Data Archives. https://www.thearda.com/Denoms/D
    _1299.asp. Accessed 8/28/21.

to fellowship with other Lutherans in the United States and throughout the world. To that end it quickly joined the LCUSA, the LWF, Lutheran World Ministries, and Lutheran World Relief. At its 1978 convention, the AELC issued an invitation to the ALC and the LCA to take steps toward "organic union."[72] Subsequently the three church bodies came together to form the ELCA.[73]

At its first convention in 1988,[74] the ELCA joined the National Council of Churches[75] and the WCC[76] as well as the LWF.[77] According to the ELCA's website,[78] it entered into full fellowship with the Reformed in 1997,[79] with the Episcopalians and the Moravians in 1999,[80] and with the Methodists in 2009.[81] Clearly, whatever the liberals in the LCMS had accomplished during the 1960s by using confessional minimalism as a basis for membership in the ILCW and the LCUSA and for altar and pulpit fellowship with the ALC, none of that formed the end of the story. The ELCA has not let the Lutheran Confessions get in the way of church fellowship with non-Lutherans.

Those Who Stayed

What about the LCMS in the wake of the 1974 Walkout controversy and the founding of Seminex? Did it reaffirm its original position regarding church fellowship, that it depended on unity in doctrine and practice? It did, but it restricted church fellowship to altar and pulpit fellowship, not prayer.

In subsequent treatments of fellowship by the CTCR, prayer is hardly mentioned. In 1974, 1981, and 2000 the CTCR issued documents dealing

---

72   Nelson, *Lutherans in North America*, 560.

73   For the story of the merger, see Edgar R. Trexler, *Anatomy of a Merger: People, Dynamics, and Decisions that Shaped the ELCA* (Minneapolis: Augsburg Fortress, 1991).

74   Trexler, *Anatomy of a Merger*, 240.

75   https://nationalcouncilofchurches.us/member-communions/. Accessed 8/28/21.

76   https://www.oikoumene.org/member-churches?search_api_fulltext=&location_filter_2=1872&field_wcc_n_church_family_single=All&glossaryaz_title=. Accessed 8/28/21.

77   https://www.lutheranworld.org/country/united-states. Accessed 8/28/21.

78   https://www.elca.org/Faith/Ecumenical-and-Inter-Religious-Relations/Full-Communion/History. Accessed 8/28/21.

79   Presbyterian Church (U.S.A.), Reformed Church in America, and United Church of Christ.

80   The Episcopal Church and the Moravian Church.

81   United Methodist Church.

with altar and pulpit fellowship without saying much about prayer at all.[82] In 1991, the CTCR almost explicitly rejected prayer from considerations of church fellowship. It acknowledged that "some individuals in the Synod" had formerly expanded unionism to include "joint public prayer with other Christians," but went on to argue that unionism did not include "every joint Christian activity." The Synod's strictures against unionism applied only to churches and rostered members of the Synod (not individual lay members of churches). In fact, such strictures did not preclude "occasional attendance" at the service of heterodox denominations.[83] Ten years later, the CTCR categorized such attendance as "generally a matter of personal judgment and individual conscience."[84] CTCR statements do not automatically determine LCMS doctrinal positions. Still, there is no evidence that on the question of "prayer fellowship" the Missouri Synod today restricts prayer to those with whom it has complete agreement in doctrine and practice.

Omitting prayer from church fellowship, however, did not prevent the Missouri Synod after 1973 from reasserting the need for agreement in doctrine and practice for determining altar and pulpit fellowship. In 1981, the Synod declared that fellowship with the ALC did not exist because of *doctrinal* differences, for example, the ALC's 1970 decision to ordain women.[85] However, subsequent LCMS conventions have recognized church fellowship with other Lutheran churches, for example, with the Association of American Lutheran Churches in 2007[86] and several Lutheran church bodies around the world in 2016 and 2019, but always on the basis of

---

82 *A Lutheran Stance toward Ecumenism: With Application for the Lutheran Church— Missouri Synod* (St. Louis: LCMS, 1974), 12, 15–16; *The Nature and Implications of the Concept of Fellowship: A Report of the Commission on Theology and Church Relations of the Lutheran Church, Missouri Synod* (St. Louis: LCMS, 1981), 6, 12; and Office of the President and CTCR, *The Lutheran Understanding of Church Fellowship: Study Materials* (St. Louis: LCMS, 2000), 4 and 27 n. 61.

83 *Inter-Christian Relationships: An Instrument for Study* (St. Louis: LCMS, 1991), 27–28.

84 CTCR, "The Lutheran Understanding of Church Fellowship: A Report on Synodical Discussions," 2001 *Convention Workbook*, 50.

85 Res. 3-01, 1981 *Proceedings*, 153–55, https://files.lcms.org/file/preview/3C18DC16 -72BC-4671-AC69-A4EE5E45D385 Accessed 11/21/21. See the underlying report in 1981 *Convention Workbook*, 397–402.

86 Res. 3-01, 2007 *Proceedings*, 120. https://files.lcms.org/file/preview/CB49ED42 -E601-473E-93DC-2528F52B27C4 Accessed 11/21/21.

agreement in doctrine and practice (as routinely stated in the resolutions declaring such fellowship).[87]

The Difference This Makes

Does truth matter anymore? We live at a time when "tolerance" regarding religion and sexual immorality has become commonplace. Nobody is supposed to be "judgmental" regarding anyone else's beliefs or behavior. People seem practically at each other's throats regarding politics, yet everyone is supposed to be "nice" about religion.

But is "nice" really appropriate when eternity is at stake? Since our Lord promises eternal life to those who believe in Him and threatens condemnation to those who do not, much more lies at stake in religion than there ever could be in winning the next election. Not only life here and now but also the life to come depends on knowing and believing the truth about God and His relationship to us. And once knowing and believing it, we are to teach and confess it!

That's what church fellowship has been and continues to be about: God's truth. This truth saves people and directs lives. Knowing, believing, teaching, and confessing that truth matters because it is directly relevant to both how we live and how we die.

To many, the LCMS must seem mean and nasty—that is, *intolerant*, if you will—for refusing to participate with non-Lutherans and non-Christians in ecumenical worship services, or for restricting Communion to those who belong to our fellowship. But we are taking our cue from God's spokesmen of old for whom "Thus saith the Lord!" was the sole concern. Being mealy-mouthed with respect to sin does no good for sinners who need to repent. Being wishy-washy about the Savior does no good for people who need to believe in Him for their salvation.

Truth matters. As long as it does, Christians need to confess it and live according to it. That includes church fellowship based on unity of doctrine and practice.

For Discussion

1. Why would it be wrong to have a Baptist preach in your church? A Roman Catholic? An ELCA Lutheran?

---

87 In 2016, with confessional Lutheran churches in Norway and Uruguay (Res. 5-01 and 5-02, 2016 *Proceedings*, 150–53) and in 2019 with churches in Belgium, Portugal, South Africa, and Denmark (Res. 5-01 to 5-04, 2019 *Proceedings,* 147–51).

2. Besides preaching, what other activities require doctrinal agreement? Why?

3. If you go to Communion with someone, what are you saying about your relationship with that person? If you are estranged from someone, what should you do before you commune with him or her? Would that also be true if you had doctrinal differences?

4. What kind of differences do *not* matter in determining church fellowship? What kind of differences do matter?

5. Do your answers to question 4 differ from the answers given by the those who participated in the Walkout and the founding of Seminex? If so, how and why?

6. What is the lesson of history when churches no longer require unity in doctrine for church fellowship?

Digging Deeper

Braun, Mark E. *A Tale of Two Synods: Events that Led to the Split between Wisconsin and Missouri*. Milwaukee: Northwestern Publishing House, 2003.

Marquart, Kurt E. *Anatomy of an Explosion: Missouri in Lutheran Perspective*. Concordia Seminary Monograph Series 3. Edited by David P. Scaer and Douglas Judisch. Fort Wayne, IN: Concordia Theological Seminary Press, 1977; 4th printing, 2017.

———. *The Church and Her Fellowship, Ministry, and Governance*. Volume 9 of *Confessional Lutheran Dogmatics*. Edited by Robert D. Preus and John R. Stephenson. Fort Wayne, IN: International Foundation for Lutheran Confessional Research, 1990.

Walther, C. F. W. "Communion Fellowship." Pages 145–92 in *Church Fellowship*. Walther's Works. St. Louis: Concordia Publishing House, 2015.

CHAPTER EIGHT

CREATION AND THE FALL

Armand J. Boehme

One of the issues in the LCMS controversy was the understanding of how the world came into being. From its inception, the Missouri Synod taught a literal six-day creation. But different views that came into existence in the wake of the Enlightenment—a critical view of the Bible and evolution—led some within the Synod to view Scripture through the eyes of historical criticism and to favor theistic evolution in their interpretation of Genesis 1–3. Therefore the controversy included debates about how the world came into existence and whether Genesis 1–11 recount true history.

Introduction: Lutheranism's Historic View of the Creation of the World

Where you came from is important. People sense this, so they look extensively into their family trees, even their DNA. The *story* of where you came from is also a gift. Therefore people embrace their family histories.

Where you came from in the largest sense stands out as of towering importance, for it relates to where you are going. Of each person it may truly be said, "You are a creature created by God." God desires that each human being He has created come by faith in Christ to an eternal home.

Martin Luther understood and believed that he was a human being created by God. Luther held that the entire world was created by God in six normal days, as the biblical Book of Genesis says.

> Moses writes that God created heaven and earth and whatever is in them in six days. . . . But if you cannot understand how this could have been

done in six days, then grant the Holy Spirit the honor of being more learned than you are. For you are to deal with Scripture in such a way that you bear in mind that God Himself says what is written. But since God is speaking, it is not fitting for you wantonly to turn His Word in the direction you wish to go.[1]

Based on Holy Scripture, Luther taught that Moses was recounting history when he wrote the "accounts of the creation."[2]

The doctrine of creation formed an integral part of Luther's theology. One Lutheran theologian wrote: "Creation looms large with Luther." The reformer described the doctrine of creation as "the highest article of faith" because creation reveals both God's sovereignty and His love. God created everything good. When creation was spoiled by the fall into sin, God recreated and redeemed. For Luther, "creation and redemption hang together, and God the Creator is never divorced from God the Redeemer."[3]

This connection between creation and redemption is reflected in the Lutheran Confessions. The *Book of Concord* states that Adam and Eve were created in sinless perfection. They were tempted to sin by the devil disguised as a snake. As a result of the fall into sin, all human beings born after Adam and Eve, except One, are born with original sin.[4]

These Confessions not only teach a literal understanding of creation and the fall but also about the first promise of the Messiah. The "promise of grace given in Christ" was "first ... given to Adam," later to the patriarchs and prophets, and has now been given to the world (Ap XII 53–54).[5] Genesis 3:15 has been termed the *Protevangelium*, the "first Gospel." For

---

1   Ewald M. Plass, comp., *What Luther Says: A Practical In-Home Anthology for the Active Christian* (St. Louis: Concordia Publishing House, 1959), p. 1523, no. 4935. See also *What Luther Says*, p. 1495, no. 4836; and pp. 1523–24, no. 4937.

2   *Lectures on Genesis* (1535–45), AE 1:19. See also AE 1:42, 44, 69, 74, 75.

3   Herman A. Preus, *A Theology to Live By: The Practical Luther for the Practicing Christian* (St. Louis: Concordia Publishing House, 1977; updated edition, 2005), 61. See also Julius Köstlin, *The Theology of Luther in Its Historical Development and Inner Harmony*, vol. 2, trans. Charles R. Hay (Philadelphia: Lutheran Publishing Society, 1897), 321–74. Also *Lectures on Genesis* (1535–45), AE 1:3–236.

4   AC II; Ap II; XII 53–55; LC II 9–24; SA III I; III VIII 5, 9; FC Ep I; FC SD I; XI 90. See also Robert D. Preus, "Guiding Theological Principles: A Lutheran Confessional Approach to the Doctrine of Creation," in *Rock Strata and the Bible Record*, ed. Paul A. Zimmerman (St. Louis: Concordia Publishing House, 1970), 11–23; and William John Hausmann, *Science and the Bible in Lutheran Theology: From Luther to the Missouri Synod* (Washington, DC: University Press of America, 1978), 71.

5   K-W, 195. See also Ap II 46–50; FC SD V 23.

centuries its words were the Good News that held the promised Deliverer before the patriarchs so they could believe in Him.[6] The prophesied Seed of the woman, Jesus Christ, is the Second Adam who came to redeem lost sinners from their sins. By the fall of the first Adam, sin and death entered the world. But the Second Adam, Christ, brings righteousness and life. He is life-giving (Romans 5:15–21; 1 Corinthians 15:20–28, 45). Luther wrote that "Christ had to come as a second Adam bequeathing his righteousness to us through a new spiritual birth in faith, just as the first Adam bequeathed sin to us through the old fleshly birth."[7] Christ is able to give grace, righteousness, and justification because, as prophesied, His heel was bruised. He died on Calvary's cross, then rose on Easter (Genesis 3:15; Matthew 27:29–28:20).

Luther's understanding of creation was later confessed by other Lutherans. As one seventeenth-century theologian put it: "Creation is an external action of the triune God, whereby . . . in the space of six days . . . He omnipotently and wisely produced from nothing all things visible and invisible."[8] Lutherans historically have taken the position that God's creation of the world happened

---

6   Martin Naumann, *Messianic Mountaintops*, Concordia Theological Seminary Monograph 2, in *Spr* 39 (September 1975): 9. See also Franz Delitzsch, *Old Testament History of Redemption*, trans. Samuel Ives Curtis (Edinburgh: T&T Clark, 1881; repr., Peabody, MA: Hendrickson, 1988), 21–28; Ken Schurb, "Sixteenth-Century Lutheran-Calvinist Conflict on the *Protevangelium*," *CTQ* 54 (January 1990): 25–47; Hausmann, *Science and the Bible in Lutheran Theology*, 70–71.

7   *Preface to Romans* (1522, 1546), AE 35:375. See also AE 1:187–88; 25:45–49, 298–307, 513. Lutherans are not alone in regarding Genesis 3:15 as the first promise of the Gospel of Christ. See, for example, Josh McDowell, *Evidence that Demands a Verdict: Historical Evidences for the Christian Faith* (San Bernardino, CA: Campus Crusade for Christ, 1972), 151; Alfred Edersheim, *The Life and Times of Jesus the Messiah* (McLean, VA: Macdonald Publishing Company, n.d.), 1:164–66.

8   John Andrew Quenstedt, quoted in Heinrich Schmid, comp., *Doctrinal Theology of the Evangelical Lutheran Church*, trans. Charles A. Hay and Henry E. Jacobs, 4th ed. (Philadelphia: Lutheran Publishing Society, 1899), 169. See also Robert D. Preus, *The Theology of Post-Reformation Lutheranism* (St. Louis: Concordia Publishing House, 1972), 2:167–258.

in relatively recent time. Some call this a young earth view.[9] It was primarily the view of Christendom at large prior to the Enlightenment.[10]

From its beginning, the LCMS walked in the footsteps of previous Lutherans and other Christians. The Synod taught (1) that Genesis 1–3 was factual history; (2) that the world was created out of nothing (Latin: *ex nihilo*) by the spoken Word of God (Genesis 1:1–31; Psalm 33:6 and 9; Hebrews 11:3); (3) that Adam and Eve were real historical people (Genesis 5:1–5; 1 Chronicles 1:1; Romans 5:14–15; 1 Timothy 2:13–14; Mark 10:6); (4) that the world was created in six days (Genesis 1:31; Exodus 20:8–11); (5) that it was created in perfection (Genesis 1:31; Romans 5:12); (6) that the perfection of creation was destroyed by a real, literal fall into sin (Genesis 3:1–24; Romans 5:12); (7) that Adam and Eve's fall gave all human beings born after them, with One exception, original sin (Genesis 5:3; Psalm 51:5; Romans 5:12; Ephesians 2:1–3);[11] and (8) that the fall into sin was followed by the promise of a Savior, the Seed of the woman, who is Christ (Genesis 3:15).[12]

For a number of years after 1932, the Synod's doctrinal position concerning creation and evolution was set forth in the *Brief Statement*.[13] Moreover, a number of Missouri Synod authors wrote books and articles defending the above-listed teachings, notably Theodore Graebner.[14] He not only wrote but also became involved with various creationist movements and organizations

---

9   The phrase "recent time" was influenced by an essay by David Adams and Charles P. Arand, "A Few Reflections on Creation in Genesis 1," https://concordiatheo logy.org/2018/03/a-few-reflections-on-creation-in-genesis-1/. Accessed 9/6/2022. See also Charles Arand, "A Travel Guide to the Evangelical Creation Debates: What Is Young Earth Creationism?" https://concordiatheology.org/2018/02/a -travel-guide-to-the-evangelical-creation-debates-what-is-young-earth-creationism/. Accessed 9/6/2022.

10 Henry M. Morris, *History of Modern Creationism* (San Diego, CA: Master Book Publishers, 1984), 17–18.

11 See, for example, Pieper 1:467–80, 515–77; P. E. Kretzmann, *The Historical Books of the Old Testament: Genesis to Esther*, Popular Commentary of the Bible: The Old Testament (St. Louis: Concordia Publishing House, 1923), 1:7–10; Arthur W. Klinck, *Old Testament History: A Survey of the Old Testament* (St. Louis: Concordia Publishing House, 1933), 17–21.

12 See L. Fuerbringer, *Exegesis of Messianic Prophecies* (St. Louis: Concordia Seminary, 1937/1938), 6, 8.

13 *Brief Statement of the Doctrinal Position of the Missouri Synod* (St. Louis: Concordia Publishing House, n.d.), 4–5.

14 See the following by Graebner: *Evolution: An Investigation and a Criticism* (Milwaukee: Northwestern Publishing House, 1922); *Essays on Evolution* (St. Louis:

in the United States, as did Paul Bartz, Thomas Handrich, Walter Lammerts, Walter Lang, Alfred Rehwinkel, Wilbert Rusch, Paul Zimmerman, and John Klotz.[15] Several books defending a literal six-day creation were written by LCMS authors during the third quarter of the twentieth century, such as John Klotz's *Genes, Genesis, and Evolution*.[16]

Historical Background: The Winds of Change

But change had been in the cultural air. The eighteenth-century Enlightenment brought negative changes for Christianity and the church, including a subjective and rationalist view of the Bible. Knowledge was thought to come from worldly experiences rather than from sacred texts. Human reason was elevated over Scripture. Rationalist theologians viewed the Bible in a more secular way. Their theological thought became critical of the Bible. Teachings such as the inerrancy of Scripture, its authority, historicity, and truthfulness, began to be questioned more and more.[17]

During the years after the Enlightenment, a more scientific view of the world arose, as did theories of evolution set forth by Charles Darwin and others. Eventually a view of life arose called *scientism*, which believes that science holds the answers to all of life's questions.[18] Some see connections

Concordia Publishing House, 1925); and *God and the Cosmos: A Critical Analysis of Atheism, Materialism, and Evolution*, 3rd ed. (Grand Rapids: Eerdmans, 1946).

15 Ronald L. Numbers, *The Creationists: From Scientific Creationism to Intelligent Design* (Cambridge, MA: Harvard University Press, 2006), 125–25, 130–35, 140, 150, *et passim*; and Morris, *History of Modern Creationism*, 113–15, 121, 132–37, *et passim*.

16 John W. Klotz, *Genes, Genesis, and Evolution* (St. Louis: Concordia Publishing House, 1955). See also Alfred W. Rehwinkel, *The Flood in Light of the Bible, Geology, and Archeology* (St. Louis: Concordia Publishing House, 1951); and these books edited by Paul A. Zimmerman: *Darwin, Evolution, and Creation* (St. Louis: Concordia Publishing House, 1959); *Rock Strata and the Bible Record* (see above, p. 170 n. 4); and *Creation, Evolution, and God's Word* (St. Louis: Concordia Publishing House, 1972).

17 Carl S. Meyer, "The Historical Background of *A Brief Statement*," *CTM* 32 (July 1961): 403–28, esp. 415–18. Also see chapters 1–3 in Roy A. Harrisville and Walter Sundberg, *The Bible in Modern Culture: Theology and Historical-Critical Method from Spinoza to Kasemann* (Grand Rapids: Eerdmans, 1995).

18 Bruce Shieman, *An Atheist Defends Religion: Why Humanity Is Better Off with Religion Than without It* (New York: Alpha Books, 2009), 102–6, 151–84; Matthew Becker, "The Scandal of the LCMS Mind," *The Daystar Journal* (November 10,

between the rise of an historical-critical view of the Bible and an evolution-ary view of creation.[19] Others see the Copernican revolution as a factor that helped the above ideas gain greater prominence.[20] Evolution and scientism not only changed much of the world's perspective on the origins of the universe and the existence of human beings but also led to conflicting views concerning the early chapters of Genesis and whether creation occurred as recorded there.

Protestantism had to face these influences. In 1880 it was estimated that half of the major denominations in the United States no longer believed in an historical Adam. Most did not attach any theological importance to how God did His creative work.[21] By 1920, many Christian denominations accepted an evolutionary view of creation. Churches variously thought that (1) God created the world in six days, or that (2) the days were much longer periods of time (an old earth, day-age view incorporating eons of time), or that (3) God used evolutionary processes to create the world (theistic evolution).[22]

Theistic evolution incorporates much of scientific evolutionary thinking. A purely evolutionist view sees creation as having come about by chance as human beings developed from pre-humanoid creatures. These evolutionary processes are supposed to have happened over millions of years. Death

---

2013): 19–21, http://thedaystarjournal.com/the-scandal-of-the-lcms-mind/. Accessed 9/12/2022; Richard N. Williams and Daniel N. Robinson, eds., *Scientism: The New Orthodoxy* (London: Bloomsbury Academic, 2016); CTCR, *In Christ All Things Hold Together: The Intersection of Science and Christian Theology* (St. Louis: LCMS, 2015), 5–13, 78–81; Angus Menuge, "Making the Case against Scientism," *Logia: A Journal of Lutheran Theology* 30 (Holy Trinity 2021): 27–34.

19 See *Anatomy*, 137; and Hausmann, *Science and the Bible in Lutheran Theology*, 74–86.

20 Hausmann, *Science and the Bible in Lutheran Theology*, 41–71; Heiko A. Oberman, "Reformation and Revolution: Copernicus' Discovery in an Era of Change," in Heiko A. Oberman, *The Dawn of the Reformation: Essays in Late Medieval and Early Reformation Thought* (Edinburgh: T&T Clark, 1986), 179–203.

21 Matthew Barrett and Ardel B. Caneday, "Introduction: Adam, To Be or Not to Be?" in *Four Views on the Historical Adam*, ed. Matthew Barrett and Ardel B. Caneday (Grand Rapids: Zondervan, 2013), 16.

22 Barrett and Caneday, "Introduction," 17; Morris, *History of Modern Creationism*, 56–61; J. B. Stump, ed., *Four Views on Creation, Evolution, and Intelligent Design* (Grand Rapids: Zondervan, 2017). See also Walter A. Maier III, "Theological Observer: A Response to Day-Age Creationism," *CTQ* 83 (July/October 2018): 281–89; and J. P. Moreland, Stephen C. Meyer, Christopher Shaw, Ann Gauger, and Wayne Grudem, eds., *Theistic Evolution: A Scientific, Philosophical, and Theological Critique* (Wheaton, IL: Crossway, 2017).

putatively existed long before the appearance of human beings. God is not seen as involved in these evolutionary processes. While theistic evolution believes much of what evolutionists believe, it adds the thought that God *is* involved. He created matter. Then, this thinking goes on, He set in motion and even guided the lengthy evolutionary processes by which plants, animals, and human beings developed. Theistic evolutionists regard their views as in accord with Scripture. There is an approach to Genesis 1–11 that supports the tenets of theistic evolution. It understands these chapters not as history but instead as "pre-history," and/or views them as saga or legend, and in a rather symbolic or mythological way.[23]

To better understand the extent to which evolutionary views had embedded themselves in North American Christianity by the mid-twentieth century, one need only consider the publication of John Whitcomb and Henry Morris's book, *The Genesis Flood*.[24] Two evangelical publishing houses declined to publish it. One is reported as having passed on the book to avoid offending current and potential customers. *The Genesis Flood* reportedly proved an embarrassment for some evangelicals. After it appeared, however, more evangelicals began accepting a six-day creation.[25]

In the LCMS through the 1940s, seminary students were taught to oppose evolution. Beginning in the 1950s, though, some in the LCMS were no longer treating Genesis 1–3 or the fall as real history, nor were they seeing Adam and Eve as real people, and they were embracing theistic evolution as a way of explaining the origins of the world.

How did this come about? A few seminary graduates engaged in further study in various scientific disciplines. Some, such as Carl Krekeler, became convinced that the scientific evidence and the text of Genesis 1–2 stood at odds with each other. When Krekeler became a professor at Valparaiso University, he found other faculty members there sympathetic to his evolutionary views. They felt that the incontrovertible facts of evolution could not be reconciled with the Synod's teaching about creation in six days.[26]

---

23 See Charles Halton, ed., *Genesis: History, Fiction, or Neither: Three Views on the Bible's Earliest Chapters* (Grand Rapids: Zondervan, 2017).

24 John Whitcomb and Henry Morris, *The Genesis Flood* (Philadelphia: Presbyterian & Reformed Publishing Co., 1961).

25 Barrett and Caneday, "Introduction," 19–20. See also Numbers, *The Creationists*, 211–38; Morris, *History of Modern Creationism*, 153–85.

26 Carl Krekeler, "On Creation and Evolution," *The Daystar Journal*, November 11, 2013, 3–6, http://thedaystarjournal.com/category/article/author/carl-krekeler/. Accessed 9/6/2022. The *Daystar Journal*'s dozen or so articles on faith and science

Krekeler wrote a critical review of *Genes, Genesis, and Evolution*.[27] This led to his involvement with a panel discussion on *Natural Science and Revealed Religion* sponsored by The Lutheran Academy for Scholarship and the LCMS Student Service Commission. It was reported that at this meeting there was little support for the view that God created the world in six days.[28] Furthermore, presentations at a 1959 meeting of Lutheran College and University Workers in New England reportedly favored an evolutionary view, as did many participants there. The LCMS view of creation was characterized as indefensible, scientifically and intellectually. One participant at this conference gave almost the same presentation, favorable to evolution, at a Northern Illinois District Pastoral Conference a few days later.[29] In the early 1960s, Krekeler and Bill Bloom published a biology textbook that promoted theistic evolution.[30] Another LCMS individual published a book expressing an evolutionary view of life.[31]

In 1961 the LCMS Board for Higher Education held a meeting at the Synod's headquarters in St. Louis. John Klotz, Paul Zimmerman, and Wilbert Rusch spoke in favor of the Synod's position on creation and evolution, which from one participant's perspective was a position unfavorably received.[32] Thus already during the 1950s evolutionary views had been presented and were gaining a foothold within the LCMS.

This acceptance of evolutionary views within the Synod coincided with a changed view of the biblical text of Genesis 1–3. This resulted from an historical-critical study of the Scriptures that viewed Genesis 1–3 as something less than factual history. Broadly speaking, Lutheran seminary education in North America had changed after World War II. The teachers at Lutheran colleges and seminaries had themselves been "exposed to contemporary biblical research" and "contemporary theologians." As a result, students at all Lutheran seminaries were taught "a new brand of Lutheranism which was

---

from a moderate or liberal Lutheran perspective should be read and studied. See also Numbers, *The Creationists*, 332–35.

27 Carl Krekeler, review of *Genes, Genesis, and Evolution*, by John W. Klotz, *The Cresset* 19 (January 1956): 44–45.

28 Krekeler, "On Creation and Evolution," 7–9.

29 Krekeler, "On Creation and Evolution," 9–12.

30 William W. Bloom and Carl H. Krekeler, *General Biology: A Unified Text Manual* (Princeton: D. Van Nostrand, 1963). See also Numbers, *The Creationists*, 333–35.

31 Harold F. Roellig, *The God Who Cares: A Christian Interpretation of Time, Life and Man* (Bayside, NY: Branch Press, 1971). See also Hausmann, *Science and the Bible in Lutheran Theology*, 94, 100, 105.

32 Krekeler, "On Creation and Evolution," 15–17.

similar in all [the] schools" including institutions in Chicago, Minneapolis, Philadelphia, and the Missouri Synod seminary in St. Louis.[33]

Noting this shift at St. Louis in particular, one author observed that German higher criticism made its way into the seminary's classrooms as newer professors used the historical-critical method, leaving students with theological "question marks" rather than "periods."[34] That a number of professors at the St. Louis seminary and elsewhere in the LCMS were advocates of historical criticism is evident from books they published during the 1970s.[35]

The LCMS during the 1960s and 1970s

The 1960s

A succession of conventions. Through the 1960s the LCMS officially continued to affirm her traditional historic views of creation, Adam and Eve, the fall into sin, the first Gospel promise, and Holy Scripture. Its 1962 convention in Cleveland, Ohio, affirmed Scripture as the verbally inspired and inerrant Word of God. Resolutions concerning Scripture at this convention came as a response to the "Synod's concern about the use of the so-called historical-critical method by some of the [St. Louis] seminary professors."[36]

The Synod's next convention, in 1965 in Detroit, Michigan, reflected growing doctrinal unrest. One memorial desired that the Synod produce "clear and simple answers" to questions about the days of creation, the literal historicity of creation, Adam and Eve, and the fall into sin. The newly formed CTCR reported that it was dealing with doctrinal issues such as scriptural inspiration, inerrancy, and authorship, as well as the doctrine of creation and its relationship to science. The convention noted that the St. Louis seminary was a significant source of the Synod's doctrinal controversies. The convention reaffirmed the teaching that the Bible is the inspired, inerrant Word of

---

33 E. Clifford Nelson, *Lutheranism in North America 1914–1970* (Minneapolis: Augsburg Publishing House, 1972), 164–65.

34 James C. Burkee, *Power, Politics, and the Missouri Synod: A Conflict that Changed American Christianity* (Minneapolis: Fortress Press, 2011), 24.

35 Edgar Krentz, *The Historical-Critical Method* (Philadelphia: Fortress Press, 1975); Norman Habel, *Literary Criticism of the Old Testament* (Philadelphia: Fortress Press, 1971); Ralph W. Klein, *Textual Criticism of the Old Testament: From the LXX to Qumran* (Philadelphia: Fortress Press, 1974); Walter E. Rast, *Tradition History and the Old Testament* (Philadelphia: Fortress Press, 1972); Paul G. Bretscher, *After the Purifying* (River Forest, IL: Lutheran Education Association,1975).

36 *Exodus*, 2.

God, that Old Testament messianic prophecies are fulfilled in Christ, and that Moses wrote the Pentateuch.[37]

Before the 1967 convention, the Synod's immediate past president, John Behnken, authored a document entitled "Some Questions concerning Some Statements of God's Holy Word." He stated that some LCMS professors viewed the text of Scripture as "legend," "myth," "parable," or "symbol" rather than as history. He referred to evolution and theistic evolution as influencing these views of Scripture. These trends moved Behnken to address twenty-eight questions to the St. Louis faculty, the first several of which asked about Genesis 1–3. The former president wanted to know whether the faculty taught that Genesis 1 and 2 were factual history, or were these chapters to be understood through the lens of theistic evolution? Did the devil speak through the serpent? Was the Garden of Eden a real historic place or merely a legend? Did Adam and Eve actually eat the forbidden fruit and plunge the world into sin, or was that story a myth or legend? Was the first Gospel promise in Genesis 3:15 a true and factual promise of the coming Savior, or merely a legend in the nonhistorical symphony of creation?[38] Behnken did not receive a response to his questions.

In response to essays raising doubt about the historicity of Genesis 1–2 and continued synodical unrest, the Synod's 1967 convention in New York affirmed the Lutheran Confessions' teaching that Adam and Eve were real historical people and that the fall into sin was a real historical event that plunged the world into sin.[39] Although the Synod in convention continued to affirm her traditional doctrine of creation, a movement continued toward a more evolutionary view of creation and toward understanding Genesis 1–3 in a more mythological and figurative way.

A succession of writings. This movement is evident in St. Louis professor Norman Habel's 1963/1965 essay, *The Form and Meaning of the Fall Narrative*. Habel contended that Genesis 3 could be described as symbolic religious history.[40] This essay was understood as putting forward the idea that the snake might not have spoken and that the words of the text were not

---

37   *Exodus*, 2–3; Zimmerman, 20–23.

38   John W. Behnken, "Some Questions concerning Some Statements of God's Holy Word," CHI, William J. Schmelder papers, box 3, file 114. See also John W. Behnken, *This I Recall* (St. Louis: Concordia Publishing House, 1964), 194; *Exodus*, 11–12; *Watershed*, 14, 44–45; Blue Book (Zimmerman, 209).

39   *Exodus*, 3.

40   Norman C. Habel, *The Form and Meaning of the Fall Narrative* (St. Louis: Concordia Seminary Press, 1965), 9, 28–42.

as important as the religious truths that the story symbolized.[41] Habel indicated that his interpretation of the text was a recasting of the meaning and nature of Genesis 3 and that his interpretation was not universally accepted in the LCMS.[42] Many saw Habel's essay as an example of the new approach to biblical studies at the St. Louis seminary, and some were quite critical of it.[43] A more favorable response to the essay from Habel's department chairman, Martin Franzmann, still faulted it for questioning Genesis 3:14–15 as the *Protevangelium*.[44]

The hesitancy to see Genesis 3:15 as the first messianic Gospel promise in the Bible was part of the theological perspective of the St. Louis seminary faculty majority. The 1972 faculty document *Faithful to Our Calling, Faithful to Our Lord* stated that God's promise gave Adam "a new lease on life," but it did not identify Genesis 3:15 as the first Gospel promise of the coming God-man Deliverer.[45] Earlier that year, Concordia President John Tietjen noted that the Blue Book incorrectly understood Genesis 3:15 as a messianic prophecy and stated that the faculty majority believed Genesis 3:15 to be prophetic, but not messianic.[46] This lack of understanding of Genesis 3:15 as a messianic prophecy is part of an historical-critical view of Scripture which holds that the Old Testament should be understood primarily on its own terms rather than how it might be understood from the New Testament.[47]

---

41   See James E. Adams, *Preus of Missouri and the Great Lutheran Civil War* (New York: Harper & Row, 1977), 116–17, 189; Habel, *Form and Meaning of the Fall Narrative*, 46 n. 18.

42   Habel, *Form and Meaning of the Fall Narrative*, second unnumbered page of Preface.

43   For negative reaction to Habel's essay, see two essays by John Warwick Montgomery in *Crisis*: "Theological Issues and Problems of Biblical Interpretation Now Facing the Lutheran Church—Missouri Synod" (1:86–89, 105–9) and "Current Theological Trends in the Lutheran Church—Missouri Synod" (1:117–18). For a more positive view of Habel's essay, see Hausmann, *Science and the Bible in Lutheran Theology*, 107–9.

44   Martin H. Franzmann, "Hermeneutical Principles Involved in the Appraisal of the 1963 Essay on Genesis 3," 29–36, CHI, Richard LaBore Research Materials, Franzmann materials folder.

45   *Faithful* 1:28.

46   John H. Tietjen, *Fact Finding or Fault Finding? An Analysis of President J. A. O. Preus' Investigation of Concordia Seminary* (St. Louis: Concordia Seminary, 1972), 10–11, 20, 24.

47   See Claus Westermann, ed., *Essays on Old Testament Hermeneutics*, trans. James Luther Mays (Atlanta: John Knox Press, 1979), 11. See also Eugene F. Klug, review of *Faithful to Our Calling, Faithful to Our Lord*, Part I by the Faculty of Concordia Seminary, St. Louis, *Spr* 37 (June 1973): 71–72.

The historical-critical approach to Genesis 1–3 was being practiced not only at Concordia Seminary during the 1960s but also in other LCMS institutions. *Concordia Theological Monthly*, the journal of Concordia Seminary, published an article by Ralph Gehrke, a professor at Concordia Teachers College, River Forest, Illinois, entitled "Genesis Three in the Light of Key Hermeneutical Considerations."[48] Gehrke wrote of the sources used to construct the Genesis texts.[49] He stated that an "announcement of salvation" appears in Genesis 3:15.[50] He added, however, that the association of Christ with this passage comes from the way the passage is understood in the New Testament.[51]

Gehrke further argued that Genesis 2 and 3 are unclear as to historical fact and meaning. He left as open questions whether the Garden of Eden and the trees are factual features of the account. Gehrke affirmed original sin as an historical fact even though he viewed the garden and the serpent as symbols used by the sacred writer.[52] He also stated that the original sinless condition of human beings and the beginning of human sin are matters of faith that cannot be proved or disproved empirically.[53]

St. Louis professor Walter Wegner wrote that Genesis 1 and 2 contain two different creation accounts, which were compiled by different writers.[54] Wegner's article stated that the theological purpose of these chapters does not deal with a "description of the origin of the world or of man," nor do these chapters contain "chronological information" about creation. According to Wegner, the early chapters of Genesis are not about the time duration of God's creative work. Nor are they about the order of the days. Rather, Wegner claimed that the days themselves as well as the number of days formed a poetic or literary device designed to teach certain theological truths. They

---

48 Ralph D. Gehrke, "Genesis Three in the Light of Key Hermeneutical Considerations," *CTM* 36 (September 1965): 534–60. See also Hausmann, *Science and the Bible in Lutheran Theology*, 104–5, 109.

49 Gehrke, "Genesis Three in the Light of Key Hermeneutical Considerations," 540–51.

50 Gehrke, "Genesis Three in the Light of Key Hermeneutical Considerations," 557, 559.

51 Gehrke, "Genesis Three in the Light of Key Hermeneutical Considerations," 558.

52 Gehrke, "Genesis Three in the Light of Key Hermeneutical Considerations," 553–57, 559.

53 Gehrke, "Genesis Three in the Light of Key Hermeneutical Considerations," 559, 560.

54 Walter Wegner, "Creation and Salvation: A Study of Genesis 1 and 2," *CTM* 37 (September 1966): 520–30.

would not be statements of literal, objective fact. Wegner held that the method and chronology of creation are open questions.[55] His essay referred to Genesis 1–11 as primal history or prehistory, whereas Genesis 12 is the beginning of real history and the beginning of God's promise of the Messiah.[56] The article referred to the fall, Abraham, the Gospel promise, and how all this relates to Christ—but without reference to the first Gospel promise in Genesis 3:15. Rather, the Gospel was reportedly tied to God's promise to Abraham in Genesis 12. For Wegner, God's mercy and grace in Genesis 3 was about allowing Adam to live longer and making provisions for Adam's earthly life (food, clothing, etc.).[57] Depicting themes in Genesis 1–11 on a chart, Wegner placed Genesis 3:14–19 under the category of "Judgment/Death."[58]

Wegner's interpretation of Genesis 3:15 falls in line with Habel's view, placing the first Gospel promise in the realm of judgment (Law) rather than understanding it as Good News of the Messiah to come.[59] In another essay Habel identified God's grace in Genesis 3 as God clothing Adam and Eve, yet Habel made no statement about a messianic prophecy in Genesis 3. Instead, he wrote that God's promises to Abraham in Genesis 12 "stand at the beginning of a history of promise that culminates in the surprise ending of the Christ event."[60] From this critical perspective, God's promise of salvation in the Messiah begins with Genesis 12, not Genesis 3.[61]

There were also other essays in official Synod publications that followed the lead of prominent critical theologians, many of them European, promoting views of Scripture, messianic prophecy, creation, the days of creation, and the understanding of Genesis 1–11 that differed from the historic synodical positions.[62] The above-mentioned essays serve as representative examples of the way some theologians were interpreting the Scriptures in the LCMS

---

55 Wegner, "Creation and Salvation," 526–27, 531.

56 Wegner, "Creation and Salvation," 531–37.

57 Wegner, "Creation and Salvation," 533.

58 Wegner, "Creation and Salvation," 541.

59 See Habel, *Form and Meaning of the Fall Narrative*, 21–25, 40–41.

60 Norman C. Habel, "The Gospel Promise to Abraham," *CTM* 40 (June, July–August 1969): 26–27, 35.

61 See Walther Zimmerli, "Promise and Fulfillment," trans. James Wharton and Hans Walter Wolff; "The Hermeneutics of the Old Testament," trans. Keith Crim, in Westermann, *Essays on Old Testament Hermeneutics*, 92–93, 189–90.

62 E.g., Albert E. Glock, "The Study and Interpretation of the Old Testament," *CTM* 38 (February 1967): 90–108; John Reumann, "Methods in Studying the Biblical Text Today," *CTM* 40 (November 1969): 655–81; and Edgar Krentz, "Hermeneutics and the Teacher of Theology," *CTM* 42 (May 1971): 265–82.

beginning already during the 1960s. Other LCMS theologians wrote essays opposing the critical theology that was being promoted by some professors in the Synod.[63]

"*Day.*" As in Wegner's essay, a less historical view of Genesis 1–3 often also involved viewing the days of creation as something other than normal days. The Hebrew word for *day* is *yom*. The biblical basis for *yom* meaning what we understand as a normal day is found in Genesis 1–2; Exodus 20:8–11; 22:30; 23:12; 31:14–17; 34:21; 35:2; 40:2; and other Bible passages. Exodus 31:14–17 perhaps best illustrates this truth.

Exodus 31 reports God's instructions to the children of Israel concerning the Sabbath day, noting that for "six days" the children of Israel were to work, then rest on the seventh, the day "of solemn rest." For "in six days the LORD made heaven and earth, and on the seventh day He rested and was refreshed." *Yom* is the word for *day*, as in Genesis 1 and 2. Exodus 31 states that the days of creation are the pattern for Israel's daily life. God's people were to work for six days, then rest on the seventh, following His own work in creation. If in Genesis 1–3, "day" is figurative or mythological, really meaning long periods of time, then in Exodus 31, God was telling Israel to work for six lengthy periods of time and rest for a seventh.

Furthermore, Genesis 1 says that evening and morning constituted a day. The exchange of dark and light indicates what would be understood as a normal day.[64] Even Norman Habel, who viewed Genesis 1–3 in a more figurative way, pointed out that understanding *yom* to mean a long period of time would have been foreign to the original author's mind.[65] Some mainline liberal

---

63 Raymond F. Surburg, "The Mythical Interpretation of the Early Chapters of Genesis," in *Evidences for Creation* (Caldwell, ID, and Arnold, MO: Bible-Science Association & Shield Press, 1969), 59–94; Fred Kramer, "The Biblical Account of Creation," in *Rock Strata and the Bible Record*, ed. Paul A. Zimmerman (St. Louis: Concordia Publishing House, 1970), 98–106; Raymond F. Surburg, "Implications of the Historico-Critical Method in Interpreting the Old Testament," and Robert D. Preus, "Biblical Hermeneutics and the Lutheran Church Today," in *Crisis* 2:48–80, 81–120.

64 Pieper 1:470–75; Raymond F. Surburg, "In the Beginning God Created," in *Darwin, Evolution, and Creation*, ed. Paul A. Zimmerman (St. Louis: Concordia Publishing House, 1959), 57–64; Paul Zimmerman, "Creation and Evolution— The Convention Essay," in *God Our Maker* (Chicago: Proceedings of the Northern Illinois District Convention, LCMS, 1962), 30–32; David G. Hagopian, ed., *The Genesis Debate: Three Views on the Days of Creation* (Mission Viejo, CA: Crux Press, 2000).

65 Habel, *Form and Meaning of the Fall Narrative*, 45 n. 5.

biblical scholarship from about the same time as Habel's essay also acknowledged that *yom* in Genesis 1 means what is understood as a normal day.[66]

The 1970s

The Blue Book. President J. A. O. Preus's September 1972 report to the
Synod on the St. Louis seminary indicated that many of its professors practiced
historical-critical Bible study.[67] Adherence to historical criticism affected the
teaching of creation, leading some professors to question or to allow the questioning of the historicity of the creation accounts, Adam and Eve, the fall into
sin, and original sin.[68] Some St. Louis faculty members questioned whether
there was predictive messianic prophecy in the Old Testament.[69] The FFC,
appointed by Preus, also found that some professors allowed for the possibility of theistic evolution. The special creation of human beings in the image of
God (sinless) and the real historical fall into sin were not affirmed at times.
Original sin or human rebellion against God was affirmed, but this was often
done without reference to an historic fall event. The fall was at times depicted
as a symbolic event.[70]

Shortly after the appearance of the Blue Book, Concordia Seminary's
faculty published *Faithful to Our Calling, Faithful to Our Lord: An
Affirmation in Two Parts.* Part II consisted of statements by individual professors. In some of these statements, adherence to historical criticism was
evident.[71] Some members of the faculty accepted a less historical and more
symbolic understanding of the accounts of creation, the fall, and the historicity of Adam and Eve. There was also ambivalence about original sin and a lack
of mention of the first Gospel promise in Genesis 3:15.[72] In one statement,
Genesis 3 was described as an example of disobedience and rebellion against
God and of broken relationships.[73] Genesis 3 does speak of disobedience and
rebellion against God, but it also sets forth the first promise of the Gospel

---

66 George Arthur Buttrick, ed., *The Interpreter's Dictionary of the Bible* (New York:
   Abingdon Press, 1962), 1:183, s.v. "Day"; George Arthur Buttrick, ed., *The
   Interpreter's Bible* (New York: Abingdon Press, 1952), 1:471.

67 Blue Book (Zimmerman, 225–31, 280–328).

68 Blue Book (Zimmerman, 300–304, 332–42).

69 Blue Book (Zimmerman, 311–13, 320).

70 Blue Book (Zimmerman, 332–42).

71 *Faithful* II, 7, 15, 27, 37, 54–56, 59–61, 64–65, 67, 77–78, 96, 98, 102–3, 125, 140,
   149–51.

72 *Faithful* II, 33–35, 37–38, 68, 71, 95, 103–4, 119–20, 125, 126, 131–32.

73 *Faithful* II, 144.

183

in Genesis 3:15. *Faithful* II refers to Genesis 12 as the beginning of God's promise of a Savior, which was fulfilled in Christ.[74]

Original sin. Earlier in 1972, President Preus had released *A Statement of Scriptural and Confessional Principles*, in which an entire section was devoted to the affirmation of the doctrine of original sin and its grounding in the historic event of the fall of Adam and Eve.[75]

The doctrine of original sin has significant relevance for Christian theology. As Claus Harms stated: "He who rejects Original Sin overthrows the whole Christianity."[76] The Lutheran Confessions speak in this same way: "Knowledge of original sin is a necessity. For we cannot know the magnitude of Christ's grace unless we first recognize our malady" (Ap II 33).[77] As one summary of the Confessions put it: "The description of the fall into sin serves as the background for the main thesis of justification, that man in himself lacks all prerequisites for his salvation."[78] The Confessions tie original sin to the fall in Genesis 3.[79]

The loss of an historic fall by Adam and Eve negatively impacts the doctrine of original sin and undermines Scripture's teachings about the cause of sin, death, hell, the image of God, the need for regeneration (new birth), the

---

74   *Faithful* II, 144–45.

75   For *A Statement*, see below, pp. 265–77, esp. part V, pp. 272–73. For classical Lutheran expositions of original sin, see Herman A. Preus and Edmund Smits, eds., *The Doctrine of Man in Classical Lutheran Orthodoxy*, trans. Mario Colacci, Lowell Satre, J. A. O. Preus Jr., Otto Stahlke, and Bert H. Narveson (Minneapolis: Augsburg Publishing House, 1962), 141–95; Theodore F. A. Nickel, "Sin," in *The Abiding Word*, ed. Theodore Laetsch (St. Louis: Concordia Publishing House, 1947), 2:150–58.

76   Quoted in J. L. Neve and George I. Fritschel, *Introduction to the Symbolical Books of the Lutheran Church*, 2nd ed. (Columbus: Lutheran Book Concern, 1926), 123.

77   K-W, 117.

78   Holsten Fagerberg, A *New Look at the Lutheran Confessions, 1529–1537*, trans. Gene J. Lund (St. Louis: Concordia Publishing House, 1972), 133; see also 134–61. See Theodore F. Nickel, "Tietjen Case Letters and Documents," 1–5, CHI, Library, St. Louis, Concordia Seminary, History, Controversy, Documents, Theodore J. Nickel folder.

79   Ap II 46; FC Ep I 2–4, 8–10; FC SD I 7, 11–13, 20, 23–24, 27–29, 34, 38, 42. See *Lectures on Genesis* (1535–45), AE 1:160–82, for Luther tying original sin to the Genesis 3 fall. See also J. B. Stump and Chad Meister, eds., *Original Sin and the Fall: Five Views* (Downers Grove, IL: IVP Academic, 2020). For attempts at reconciling original sin with evolution, see Loren Haarsma, *When Did Sin Begin? Human Evolution and the Doctrine of Original Sin* (Grand Rapids: Baker Academic, 2021).

Holy Spirit's work of regeneration, Baptism, the necessity of the preaching of the Gospel, and a correct understanding of justification.

Response and counterresponse. In a document entitled *Fact Finding or Fault Finding?* Seminary president Tietjen stated that the Blue Book was *"unfair," "unreliable," "untrue," "less than scriptural,"* and *"un-Lutheran."*[80] On the other hand, the Synod continued to provide documents, primarily from the CTCR, which upheld her traditional scriptural beliefs in the area of creation, the historicity of Adam and Eve, their original sinlessness (the image of God), the fall, sin entering the world as a result of the fall, and the first Gospel promise.[81] Other documents dealt with messianic prophecy, the doctrine of Scripture, and Moses' authorship of the Pentateuch.[82] Several St. Louis faculty members helped write *A Call to Openness and Trust* and requested that the CTCR review it. The CTCR found that the document encouraged "doctrinal latitude" in relationship to "the creation of the universe."[83] The CTCR also produced a brief evaluation of the St. Louis faculty's *Faithful to Our Calling, Faithful to Our Lord,* Part I, stating that this document's faulty understanding of the authority, inspiration, and inerrancy of Scripture was reflected in the way it treated the Bible's account of creation and the fall.[84]

In *Faithful* I, the St. Louis faculty had stated that the debate about Genesis 2–3 was a debate about "the kind of literature found in the text" rather than "its doctrinal content." It claimed that Genesis 2–3 was neither an eyewitness report nor "a historical account" of the events. Rather, this biblical text was something more like a sermon, a theological document in "narrative form" addressed to ancient Israel. Original sin was maintained in *Faithful* I, but it was generally not tied to the historic fall. There was discussion of the fact that human sinfulness is "our own fault," which raised questions about

---

80 Quoted in *Memoirs,* 112 (italics original).

81 CTCR, *Creation in Biblical Perspective* (St. Louis: LCMS, 1970).

82 CTCR, *A Study Document on The Witness of Jesus and Old Testament Authorship* (St. Louis: LCMS, 1970); *A Lutheran Stance toward Contemporary Biblical Studies* (St. Louis: LCMS, 1972); *Gospel and Scripture: The Interrelationship of the Material and Formal Principles in Lutheran Theology* (St. Louis: LCMS, 1972); *A Comparative Study of Varying Contemporary Approaches to Biblical Interpretation* (St. Louis: LCMS, 1973).

83 CTCR, *An Evaluation of "A Call to Openness and Trust"* (St. Louis: LCMS, 1970), 1, 5. See Blue Book (Zimmerman, 212).

84 CTCR, *An Evaluation of the Faculty Document "Faithful to Our Calling, Faithful to Our Lord, Part I: A Witness to Our Faith"* (St. Louis: LCMS, 1973), 2.

whether sinfulness had been inherited from Adam and Eve.[85] Positively, *Faithful* I stated that any widely held scientific theory about the creation of the world should not be binding on the Christian. It also declared that discussions of the relationship of scientific theory to the biblical account of creation should be secondary to the Christian's being confronted with God's glory and goodness and the desire to recognize God's provision for our needs.[86]

Matters came to a head at the Synod's 1973 convention in New Orleans, Louisiana. In Res. 3-09, the Synod in convention stated that the St. Louis faculty majority position stood in violation of Article II of the LCMS constitution. The resolution stated the areas where theological violation had occurred. Those areas included the historicity of Adam and Eve, the fall into sin, original sin, and messianic prophecies in the Old Testament.[87]

The Difference This Makes

Why are biblical teachings about creation important? There has been a recent rising interest in atheism and a lessening of the influence of traditional religions, especially Christianity. Greater acceptance of atheism has coincided with an increased emphasis by some on the supposedly unresolvable conflict between religious faith and scientific knowledge.[88] Moreover, many young Christians leaving the church perceive Christianity to be against science and out of step with the modern scientific world. Some have reacted negatively to the creation versus evolution debate. Still other young Christians struggle to remain faithful to their religious beliefs as they live in a highly scientific world.[89]

---

85 *Faithful* I, 16–17. Contrast Kurt E. Marquart, "The Swing of the Pendulum: An Attempt to Understand the St. Louis 'Affirmations and Discussions,'" in *Truth, Salvatory and Churchly: Works of Kurt E. Marquart*, ed. Ken Schurb and Robert Paul, vol. 3: *Essays Historical and Historic* (N.p.: Luther Academy, 2018), 31–74; *Anatomy*, 97, 120–25, *et passim*.

86 *Faithful* I, 13–14.

87 *1973 Proceedings*, 133–39. See Zimmerman, 104, 108; *Memoirs*, 140–42. Part of 1973 Res. 3-09 can be found in *Exodus*, 54–56.

88 Sean McDowell and Jonathan Morrow, *Is God Just a Human Invention? And Seventeen Other Questions Raised by the New Atheists* (Grand Rapids: Kregel, 2010), 19–43, 57–131.

89 See David Kinnaman with Aly Hawkins, *You Lost Me: Why Young Christians Are Leaving Church ... and Rethinking Faith* (Grand Rapids: Baker Books, 2011), 131–48; and Charles Arand, "The Scientist as a Theologian of the Cross," *CJ* 43 (Summer 2017): 17.

Living in the present century, Christians will regularly be confronted with questions about the relationship between Christianity's teachings and the findings of science. We need deep knowledge of what the Bible teaches and to be able to confess and discuss these biblical teachings. Christians also need a sound understanding of scientific and evolutionary views so differences and similarities can be understood and conversations can take place based on knowledge instead of ignorance.

All of this applies to the LCMS. The Synod has officially maintained its traditional view of creation in six days; the historicity of Adam and Eve; the fall into sin; original sin; and the first Gospel promise in the Seed of the woman, who is the Second Adam. Nonetheless, questions occasionally arise in the Synod about the relationship of theology and science.[90]

The Gospel

From a theological standpoint, a proper understanding of the relationship of science and religion is important because of Christ, His Gospel of salvation for all sinners, and God the Father's love for the sinful world. "In a world devastated by the fall into sin," it has been well-said that there is nothing in this world that does "not bear the mark of sinfulness. To deny the pervasiveness of sin is to deny both the gravity of the fall and the depths of Christ's sacrificial victory."[91]

If creation did not happen as revealed in Genesis 1–3, a whole range of questions present themselves. How did the world and human beings come to be? What is the relationship of human beings to the other creatures that exist? How did sin, death, and evil enter the world? Or is death innate to creation? Despite the biblical teaching reflected in AC XIX, is God the cause of sin and the author of evil? If the fall was not a real historical event and the ensuing corruption of creation by sin did not really occur, why did Christ come? What need is there for the Gospel? And if the first Adam was not a real person, what does this say about Christ who is confessed as the Second Adam?

God's Word tells us that the world was created in perfection, without sin. The first Adam fell into sin, corrupting God's perfect creation, bringing sickness and death. Because of these things, the world needed the Savior who was

---

90   See, for example, *CJ* 43 (Summer 2017) and the follow-up in *CJ* 44 (Winter 2018): 7–14. It might be noted that in 2011, faculty members serving in the Missouri Synod's Concordia University System started their own creationist organization, the Society of Creation. See http://www.societyofcreation.org/.

91   Alberto L. Garcia and John A. Nunes, *Wittenberg Meets the World: Reimagining the Reformation at the Margins* (Grand Rapids: Eerdmans, 2017), 33.

promised to come: the Seed of the woman, the Second Adam, who would destroy the power of sin and death and bring grace and eternal life to human beings and the world. His second coming will usher in the new heavens and the new earth.

Stewardship of Creation and the Value of Human Beings

The account of God's creation of the world is important because of the command given to Adam and Eve to be fruitful and multiply, to replenish the earth, and to subdue it (Genesis 1:28). God has given human beings the vocation of being stewards of the earth He created. Christians should be in the forefront of helping to replenish the earth by being green in a godly sense. This means being in service to the God who created the earth and the universe and to all other human beings now living and for generations to come. This earth is God's physical gift to us as human beings. We are to nurture the earth, make it more fruitful, help to preserve all the creatures God has created, and pass this world along as a gift to the next generation of human beings.[92] Where we have failed to be the stewards God desires us to be, we need to be led to godly contrition and repentance and receive His grace and forgiveness in Word and Sacrament.

The doctrine of creation teaches that all human beings are made in God's image (Genesis 1:26–27). While all life is valuable in the Creator's sight, especially valuable are the lives of all human beings. All the different nationalities of people living on this earth are deserving of respect and dignity because God has created each one and has given each one life. This perspective on human beings should inhibit acts of violence toward other human beings or hatred of others because of the color of their skin or their different beliefs, even different religious beliefs. God's Word tells us that God so loved the world—every individual in the world—that He sent His only-begotten Son, Jesus Christ, to deal with the sins of every human being and to save all sinful human beings from their sins (John 3:16). Since God loves all and Christ died to save all, Christians should also love all other human beings and desire their spiritual and physical well-being. The world's wars, rumors of wars, and racism would be lessened if this perspective were held by all: "Love your neighbor as [much as you love] yourself" (Matthew 22:39). All human beings are equal in that all are sinners. All are also equal in that there is salvation for any of us only in Christ. Christians should understand that all human beings

---

92   The CTCR has produced an excellent resource: *Together with All Creatures: Caring for God's Living Earth* (St. Louis: LCMS, 2010).

have the potential to be spiritual brothers or sisters in Christ and should love them as Christ has loved us.[93]

Eminently applicable as these truths are in the contemporary world, they are hardly new. In fact, the above statements simply paraphrase what the CTCR wrote in 1970, that

> the biblical teaching that man is God's creature gives man his true worth. . . . The biblical teaching that man is created in the image of God not only gives to each man his own individual worth but also reminds him that all other men have the same worth.

The CTCR emphasized that the doctrine of creation "is a powerful force for ethical behavior" for the Christian's private life and in society, and "a powerful condemnation of racism and of all other forms of social injustice." It reminds Christians "to respect" their fellow human beings and "to work for justice toward all men." The CTCR added that Christians should "cherish . . . God's good earth and seek to preserve it as a fit habitation for all of God's creatures . . . and to respect all of nature as His creation." The doctrine of creation "offers a true theology of hope" for believers and is "a powerful antidote for human anxieties of every kind."[94]

Science

Like all Christians, Lutherans should be thankful to God for the gift He has given in science. God has provided many blessings to human beings through scientific inquiry.

Sadly, though, over the years a rift has grown between some Christians and society at large. For some, there appears to be an irreconcilable conflict between science and religion. In more recent times, however, scholars have been noting that the portrayal of an abiding conflict between science and religion is not historically accurate.[95] Christians prominent in the advancement of science have included figures such as Johannes Kepler, Andre

---

93　See CTCR, *Racism and the Church: Overcoming the Idolatry* (St. Louis: LCMS, 1994).

94　CTCR, *Creation in Biblical Perspective*, 11–12.

95　See Ted Peters, "Science and Theology: Toward Consonance," in *Science and Theology: The New Consonance*, ed. Ted Peters (New York: Routledge, 2019), 11; Alvin Plantinga, *Where the Conflict Really Lies: Science, Religion, and Naturalism* (Oxford: Oxford University Press, 2011); Joshua M. Moritz, "The War that Never Was: Exposing the Myth of the Historical Conflict between Christianity and Science," *Theology and Science* 10 (May 2012): 113–23.

Ampere, and Louis Pasteur.[96] There is scholarly debate about the impact that the Reformation had on the development of modern science.[97] Today there is a great deal of positive interaction between science and religion, as is evident not only from books but also by way of the journals and organizations dealing with this interaction.[98] As Christians teach the biblical doctrine of creation, they should also be diligently learning more about God's work of creating this wonderful world and more about the gifts God continues to give to us through science. Science truly is one of God's gifts to the human race.[99]

Where there are differences and disagreements between science and religion, there is the need to state those disagreements with honesty and humility while avoiding sinful pride, animosity, and evil thoughts toward those who view the world differently. Fairly and humbly studying the views of others shows the respect that should be given in Christian love. Such an approach by Christians toward the findings of science preserves friendships and leads to understanding of the views of others. It might even help each to learn

---

96   Stanley Jaki, *The Savior of Science* (Grand Rapids: Eerdmans, 2000); Alvin J. Schmidt, *How Christianity Changed the World* (Grand Rapids: Zondervan, 2004), 218–42; Henry M. Morris, *Men of Science, Men of God: Great Scientists of the Past Who Believed the Bible*, 21st printing (Green Forest, AR: Master Books, 2012).

97   B. A. Gerrish, "The Reformation and the Rise of Modern Science: Luther, Calvin, and Copernicus," in *The Old Protestantism and the New: Essays on the Reformation Heritage* (London: T&T Clark, 2004), 163–78; John Warwick Montgomery, "Luther and Science: Cross, Constellation, and Crucible," in *Defense of Martin Luther* (Milwaukee: Northwestern Publishing House, 1970), 87–114; G. B. Deason, "The Protestant Reformation and the Rise of Modern Science," *Scottish Journal of Theology* 32 (May 1985): 221–40.

98   Organizations include the Zygon Center for Religion and Science, The International Society for Science and Religion, The Creation Research Society, Institute for Creation Research, and the Society of Creation. Journals include *Zygon: Journal of Religion and Science*; *Theology and Science*; *The European Journal of Science and Theology*; *Creation Research Quarterly*; and the *Journal of Creation*. Books include John Ashton, ed., *In Six Days: Why Fifty Scientists Choose to Believe in Creation* (Green Forest, AR: Master Books, 2001); Steve Donaldson, *Dimensions of Faith: Understanding Faith through the Lens of Science and Religion* (Cambridge: Lutterworth Press, 2015); and S. Joshua Swamidass, *The Genealogical Adam and Eve: The Surprising Science of Universal Ancestry* (Downers Grove, IL: IVP Academic, 2019). S. Joshua Swamidass has also written "A Lutheran Voice in Science," *CJ* 43 (Summer 2017): 82–87.

99   Michal Valco and Armand J. Boehme, "Christian Faith and Science: Can Science Enhance Theology?" *European Journal of Science and Theology* 13 (June 2017): 89–97.

Photograph by Paul Ockrassa

Dr. Walter Brueggemann, dean of Eden Seminary in St. Louis, receives the Concordia Seminary exiles. To his left are Gerald Miller, student body president; John S. Damm, former academic dean (wearing black coat and hat); and John Tietjen (behind John Damm and also in black coat and hat), who had been suspended as president of Concordia Seminary (February 19, 1974).

something from the other. The CTCR document *In Christ All Things Hold Together* is a good resource, as is an essay by Michael Young on science and religion.[100] Being a scientist is a godly and noble Christian vocation.[101] Not only have scientists and theologians been studying the intersection of faith and science, but the study of science has also led a number of people to belief in God and to be willing to listen seriously to the Gospel of Christ.[102] There

---

100 Michael Young, "On the Need for a Thoughtful, Distinctively Lutheran Perspective on Creation," *Logia: A Journal of Lutheran Theology* 30 (Holy Trinity 2021): 35–40. See also Benjamin T. G. Mayes, "Theological Observer: Creation, Science, and God's Omnipotence," *CTQ* 82 (July/October 2018): 290–301.

101 Angus Menuge, *Science and the Savior: The Calling of a Scientist* (St. Louis: Concordia Publishing House, 2004).

102 See, for example, Michael Quillen, *Believing Is Seeing: A Physicist Explains How Science Shattered His Atheism and Revealed the Necessity of Faith* (Carol Stream, IL: Tyndale Refresh, 2021); Michael E. O'Connell, *Finding God in Science: The Extra-Ordinary Evidence for the Soul and Christianity, A Rocket Scientist's Gripping Odyssey*

has also arisen the questioning of Darwinism within the scientific communi-ty.[103] Christians should study all aspects of these debates, including intelligent design and the big bang theory.[104]

The biblical teachings of creation and the fall are important because they show God's love for human beings as He provides them with this created world and all they need to support this body and life. God's Word tells us about the greatest blessing God provides for human beings: salvation from sin and damnation in hell, and the blessing of eternal life in the new heavens and the new earth. The true hope for sinful human beings is in the Seed of the woman (Genesis 3:15), Christ the Savior, who came born of the Virgin Mary as prophesied by Isaiah (Isaiah 7:14; Matthew 1:22–23). His sinless life, death, and glorious resurrection has brought salvation to sinners (Romans 5).

As the 1970 CTCR document put it, the teaching about God's creation of the world and human beings falling into sin should deepen our gratitude for God's gracious redemption offered in Christ Jesus. Thankfully, the grace of God calls sinners to put their trust in Jesus Christ. Through the work of the Holy Spirit, new creatures in Christ are brought forward. By faith in Christ, individual outlooks and lives are changed. The Gospel thus is God's creative force for the betterment of human relationships so that people view others more lovingly, live in a more godly manner, and have a more positive view of society and also of God's creation.[105]

The biblical doctrine of creation teaches that the human race was created by God. After Adam and Eve's fall, all human beings (except One) are born with original sin and without faith in God. They need the spiri-tual rebirth given in Baptism. As they live by faith in God, Christians have many vocations, and in those vocations they are to serve both God and their fellow human beings and to be stewards of the world that God has created.

(Orange County, CA: Eigen, 2020); and Anthony Flew, *There Is a God: How the World's Most Notorious Atheist Changed His Mind* (New York: HarperOne, 2009).

103 Alex Newman, "Over 1,000 Scientists Openly Dissent from Evolution Theory," https://thenewamerican.com/over-1-000-scientists-openly-dissent-from-evolution-theo ry/. Accessed 9/4/2022. David Cloud, "Evolutionists against Darwinism," https://www. wayoflife.org/reports/evolutionists_against_darwinism.html. Accessed 9/4/2022.

104 See William A. Dembski and Sean McDowell, *Understanding Intelligent Design: Everything You Need to Know in Plain Language* (Eugene, OR: Harvest House, 2008); and Stephen C. Meyer, *Return of the God Hypothesis: Three Scientific Discoveries that Reveal the Mind behind the Universe* (New York: HarperOne, 2021); for the big bang theory, see esp. 87–110.

105 CTCR, *Creation in Biblical Perspective*, 12.

Imperfect people cannot carry out vocational responsibilities perfectly. But God sent Jesus Christ to redeem lost sinners. Through faith in Christ, they will conquer sin, death, and the devil and reach their final home in heaven. This is the spiritual family history, revealed in Scripture, that God desires for all human beings.

For Discussion

1. Read Genesis 1 and 2. Summarize what these chapters say about how the world and human beings came into existence. What does Job 38:1–40:2 add to the picture? Which of God's words from Job should keep us humble when we speak about the creation of the world?

2. What did the fall into sin do to God's perfect creation? What effect did it have on Adam and Eve, and on us? What is lost if this fall is not a real historic event?

3. How did cultural trends lead to different understandings of Genesis 1–3?

4. What are the differences between the traditional teaching on creation in the Missouri Synod and the view of creation taught at Concordia Seminary and elsewhere during the synodical controversy in the 1960s and 1970s? Did those differences matter then? Why or why not? Do they still matter today? Why or why not?

5. What impact does an historical-critical view of Scripture have on predictive messianic prophecy in the Old Testament in general and in particular on the first Gospel promise of Christ in Genesis 3:15?

6. Why is it important for Christians to be informed not only on the traditional scriptural doctrine of creation but also about theistic evolution and an evolutionary view of the world?

7. Why is it important for Christians to view science as a gift from God and the vocation of scientist as a godly vocation?

Digging Deeper

Center for Care of Creation, Concordia Seminary, St. Louis. https://concordia theology.org/ccc/home.html. See especially "A Few Reflections on Creation in Genesis 1."

Espinosa, Alfonso. "Creation." Pages 113–46 in *The Lutheran Difference: An Explanation and Comparison of Christian Beliefs*. Edited by Edward A. Engelbrecht. St. Louis: Concordia Publishing House, 2010.
Use together with the Bible study: Espinosa, Alfonso O. *Creation: The Lutheran Difference*. St. Louis: Concordia Publishing House, 2007.

Halton, Charles, ed. *Genesis: History, Fiction, or Neither? Three Views on the Bible's Earliest Chapters*. Counterpoints: Bible and Theology Series. Grand Rapids: Zondervan, 2015.

CHAPTER NINE

SEMINEX AND THE SUPERNATURAL

Robert A. Dargatz

Faculty members who taught Old and New Testament
courses at Concordia Seminary, St. Louis, and later at Seminex
were committed to using the historical-critical method. Their
commitment to this method of biblical study caused some
of them, among other things, to deny the authenticity
of various biblical miracles and the genuine existence of angels
and demons. The present chapter addresses specifically
the topics of angels and miracles.

Introduction

What would you think if, in the hour of death, the Christian faith had
little to say to you that would involve the supernatural and the miraculous?
How good would this Good News be, for you or anyone else?

You might recall what St. Paul wrote to the Corinthians by inspiration of
the Holy Spirit:

> For if the dead are not raised, not even Christ has been raised. And if
> Christ has not been raised, your faith is futile and you are still in your
> sins. Then those also who have fallen asleep in Christ have perished. If
> in Christ we have hope in this life only, we are of all people most to be
> pitied. But in fact Christ has been raised from the dead, the firstfruits of
> those who have fallen asleep. (1 Corinthians 15:16–20)

If Christ were not raised, how could He really be the resurrection and the life
(John 11:25)?

An observer of modern theology asked, "How can it be that some people
swallow the camel of the resurrection but strain at the gnats of miracles like
walking on water?" In other words, if you believe in a God who raises the

dead, why would you not believe the same God when in His Word He tells you of other miracles He has done? And when the Bible teaches that there are powerful invisible creatures of God, angels—some of whom fell and became demons—why would you reject that?

During the third quarter of the twentieth century, the LCMS faced a great divide over two interpretive approaches for understanding the Bible, which contributed in a major way to the Walkout and the formation of Seminex. The contrast between these two approaches manifested itself with respect to the biblical teaching on angels. It also showed up concerning biblical reports of various miracles. Unlike the traditional historical-grammatical method of biblical interpretation, the historical-critical method rested on assumptions that disallowed the supernatural. Prominent among practitioners of historical criticism in the LCMS were professors at Concordia Seminary. President John Tietjen insisted that the method had to be used to teach at the seminary level.[1]

Satan, who truly does exist, often employs the tactic of using human philosophy to infiltrate the thoughts and teachings of men and make God's revelation appear foolish. Yet St. Paul wrote that "it pleased God through the folly of what we preach to save those who believe. . . . For the foolishness of God is wiser than men, and the weakness of God is stronger than men" (1 Corinthians 1:21 and 25). God's wisdom and grace is centered in the person and work of the Lord Jesus Christ. God has revealed this Savior in the Gospel proclaimed by the prophets and apostles and preserved for the church in the Holy Scriptures. The church must remain vigilant against any other "gospel," which will amount to a powerless substitute for the genuine Gospel (Galatians 1:6–8).

The present chapter tells of efforts in the LCMS during the early 1970s to pinpoint and resist incursions of human reason that ran counter to God's genuine Good News in the cases of angels and miracles. First, however, we should look back a bit.

Historical Background

Christianity and its truth have constantly been challenged by competing philosophies and false religions. Doctrinal theology and church history need to be aware of the prominent philosophical modes of thought throughout history.

---

1   See above, "Historical Introduction" and chapter 3, pp. 1–11, 59–82.

David Hume and the Enlightenment

One of these philosophies is Skepticism, which existed already during the time of the ancient Greeks. This philosophy raised serious doubts about what could genuinely be known as true. Elements of this system of thought became especially prominent in the philosophy of David Hume during the period of the Enlightenment, which began in the latter part of the seventeenth century and extended into the nineteenth century in Europe. Immanuel Kant (1724–1804) characterized the Enlightenment as the leaving behind of a self-caused immaturity that had plagued people because they lacked the determination and courage to use and depend upon their own intelligence without resting upon outside influences like tradition and dogma.[2]

David Hume (1711–76) dismissed supernatural phenomena. He devoted chapter 10 of his *Enquiry concerning Human Understanding* to miracles.[3] While some of his points might be worthwhile in avoiding complete gullibility, Hume threw out the proverbial baby with the bathwater. He defined miracles as violations of the laws of nature and dismissed them as unreasonable.

Part of Hume's problem was with his definition. By contrast, C. S. Lewis defined miracles as exceptions to the course of nature, not violations. He pointed out that while God brought about a miraculous conception in Mary, thereafter her pregnancy proceeded in all the natural ways that pregnancies and the births of newborns usually do.[4] Lewis recognized that it was foolish to suggest that God could not do wondrous things in "exceptional" miracles when so much that is commonly taken for granted in "nature" lies beyond the ability of humans fully to explain or comprehend.

Hume had assumed what he was trying to demonstrate, claiming in effect that miracles cannot occur, therefore they have not occurred. John Warwick Montgomery has noted this kind of fallacious circular reasoning on the part of those who dismiss the reality of miracles by their very definition. Such thinkers refuse to consider even eyewitness testimony if it runs contrary to their preconceived notions.[5]

To be sure, there are bogus claims of miracles. As one might expect, such claims are in the spiritual arsenal of the "father of lies" (John 8:44). Too, Christ Himself warned: "For false christs and false prophets will arise

---

2   Immanuel Kant, "What Is Enlightenment?" in *The Philosophy of Kant*, ed. Carl J. Friedrich (New York: The Modern Library, 1949), 132.

3   Robert Maynard Hutchens, ed., *Great Books of the Western World*, vol. 35, *Locke, Berkeley, Hume* (Chicago: Encyclopedia Britannica, 1952), 488–97.

4   C. S. Lewis, *Miracles* (New York: Macmillan, 1947), 56, 72.

5   John Warwick Montgomery, *History and Christianity* (Minneapolis: Bethany House 1964), 19–21.

and perform great signs and wonders, so as to lead astray, if possible, even the elect" (Matthew 24:24). This means that there will be also supernatural acts by which the church should not be misled, for they are demonic works seeking to rob people of salvation in Christ. Yet we must hear what Christ says about His own miracles: "Woe to you, Chorazin! Woe to you, Bethsaida! For if the mighty works done in you had been done in Tyre and Sidon, they would have repented long ago in sackcloth and ashes" (Matthew 11:21; Luke 10:13). People will be accountable for rejecting the signs of the genuineness of Christ. The miracles of Christ and His disciples served to authenticate the truth of their ministries and their message! (See John 2:11 and 23; 11:45; 12:10–11; Acts 2:22; 8:6.)

Twentieth Century: Rudolf Bultmann, Karl Barth, and John Dewey

Two modern European theologians who influenced the approach to the Bible taken by some of the eventual Seminex faculty members were Rudolph Bultmann (1884–1976) and Karl Barth (1886–1968).

Bultmann, who claimed to be a Lutheran, became (in)famous for subjecting Scripture to "demythologizing"—stripping away the "myths" in the Bible in an effort to attend to its alleged underlying meaning.[6] Ultimately, this procedure removed any sense that biblical miracles actually occurred in real time and space history, though Bultmann conceded that Jesus believed in them.[7] He also dismissed any real existence of angels and Satan.[8] It might be noted that the LCMS specifically repudiated "demythologizing" already at its 1959 convention.[9]

Bultmann was convinced that the early church had built nonhistorical narratives to enshrine various teachings as part of Jesus' legacy. He denied that Jesus actually made many of the statements that Scripture attributes to Him.[10] He sought to strip away what he regarded as fictional settings so he could

---

6   Rudolph Bultmann, *Jesus Christ and Mythology* (New York: Charles Scribner's Sons, 1958); Karl Jaspers and Rudolph Bultmann, *Myth and Christianity* (New York: Noonday Press, 1958), 57–71.

7   Rudolph Bultmann et al., *Kerygma and Myth*, trans. Reginald H. Fuller (New York: Harper & Row, 1961), 199; Rudolph Bultmann, *Jesus and the Word*, trans. Louise Pettibone Smith and Erminie Huntress Lantero (New York: Charles Scribner's Sons, 1958), 172.

8   Bultmann, *Jesus and the Word*, 56.

9   "Statement on Scripture," in *Heritage*, 6–8.

10   Bultmann, *Jesus and the Word*, 43, 62–63.

recover the original message of Jesus, so that message could now be shared with modern mankind.

In this, Bultmann was profoundly influenced by one of his colleagues at the University of Marburg, Martin Heidegger, a leading exponent of the philosophy known as existentialism. Existentialism calls upon people to find freedom in taking responsibility for their lives. Bultmann imposed his philosophical bias on the Bible. By treating the biblical Jesus and His ministry in the category of myth, he made of the Gospel not an historical and factual message but instead a moral example and encouragement for virtuous, meaningful, and authentic living. Bultmann's rendering of Christianity turned out to be far more man-centered than God-centered.

A second major influence was the Swiss theologian Karl Barth. Barth appeared more "conservative" than Bultmann because he did not make demythologizing a notable aspect of his interpretation of the Scriptures. As Kurt Marquart summarized:

> Barth's system seemed more biblical than it was. The Swedish scholar [Gustaf] Wingren observed drily: "Barth has the ability to a very large degree of being able to employ the language of scripture in a system that is totally foreign to the Bible." Barth realized that the historical-critical method could produce nothing but a few dead bones. But he thought that one could—indeed must—keep the method, and then pack living flesh and sinews onto the dead bones by means of "theological interpretation"—hence the "New Hermeneutic." Barth demanded "that we endeavor to see 'through and beyond history into the spirit of the Bible'. . . ."[11]

Barth is generally known as the father of "neoorthodoxy," which championed the idea that Scripture was authoritative only if it caused one to encounter the living God. This subjective approach had little concern for the actual, reliable historical character of the biblical accounts. One of the notions eventually rejected in *A Statement of Scriptural and Confessional Principles* (adopted by the LCMS in 1973) is: "That only those matters in Holy Scripture were inspired by the Holy Spirit which directly pertain to Jesus Christ and man's salvation."[12] Such "Gospel Reductionism" was a hallmark of Seminex theology.

John Dewey (1859–1952) was not a theologian but an American philosopher who exerted a massive influence on education in the United States. Although LCMS controversy rather prominently shows the impact

---

11   *Anatomy*, 104–5, quoting W. G. Kuemmel, *The New Testament: The History of the Investigation of its Problems* (New York: Abingdon, 1972), 363.

12   *A Statement*, part IV.A.3 (below, p. 267).

of European theological thinking, the sway of American influences such as Dewey's cannot be minimized or ignored. Dewey looked for religion to join with secular education in making a great intellectual readjustment and to abandon the supernatural in favor of "science."[13] The anti-supernatural sentiment that prominent confessional LCMS theologians were concerned about in European universities had also conspicuously infiltrated U.S. universities as well. This became increasing influential in the wider North American intellectual milieu that had an impact in all areas of thought in the United States, including theological institutions.

In The Lutheran Church—Missouri Synod

The LCMS had its own Karl Barth, who was president of the South Wisconsin District at the time of the Walkout. Later he was president of the post-Walkout Concordia Seminary. This Karl Barth opposed the use of the historical-critical method. He observed that practitioners of the method borrowed ideas from European theologians such as Bultmann and found themselves hard put to keep up with the changing winds of that theology.[14] In fact, already during the late 1920s there had been concerns within the LCMS about harmful outside theological influences—especially rationalism and unionism—potentially intruding when the Synod's college and faculty members pursued advanced degrees from other seminaries and universities.[15]

Whatever else might be said about these concerns, over time some of them proved to be valid. Dr. Frederick Danker, an accomplished Concordia Seminary New Testament scholar who participated in the Walkout, delighted in the way that outside theological emphases had been imported into the seminary library under the leadership of his biblical studies colleague Edgar Krentz and others.[16] John W. Behnken, LCMS president from 1935 to 1962, expressed concern toward the end of his tenure that European theology was intruding itself in the teaching of North American churches, including Lutheran churches.[17] David P. Scaer of Concordia Theological Seminary has written: "The ["pre-Walkout" St. Louis] seminary faculty approach can be

---

13   Editor's note: See John Dewey, *Reconstruction in Philosophy*, enlarged ed. (Boston: Beacon Press, 1957), 45–51, 73–74, 183–88, 210–13.

14   *Watershed*, 10.

15   Gerhard Bode and Erik Herrmann, "02d. 'What is our Identity and Purpose?': The Americanization of the LCMS Part 4," *Controversy in the LCMS* (2010). See citation at the end of this chapter.

16   Danker, 34.

17   Danker, 72.

characterized as a Lutheran form of neoorthodoxy that allowed for Rudolph Bultmann's radical position that the gospel did not depend on biblical history and for [the Swiss Karl] Barth's evasion of historical questions."[18]

The treatment of the supernatural was one of the notable divergences between Concordia Seminary's long-held traditional stance and a position tolerated—and in a number of instances promoted!—by those who formed Seminex.[19] Before the Walkout, it was the issue that caused the Synod's Board for Higher Education to overrule the seminary's renewal of Professor Arlis Ehlen's teaching contract in 1972. Issues had emerged concerning his position on angels and on at least one biblical miracle, Israel's exodus from Egypt.

Arlis Ehlen was a brilliant scholar with a Harvard doctorate. He had also studied at Brandeis University and at the University of Bonn in Germany. One of his students reported that he would write a Greek word on a blackboard with his right hand going left to right while simultaneously writing the corresponding Hebrew word underneath with his left hand going right to left.

Dr. Ehlen frankly acknowledged his commitment to the historical-critical method. In this respect, he was acting consistently with the posture of the "new" (since 1969) seminary administration of John Tietjen. President Tietjen thought there had been too much ambiguity regarding the seminary's changing approaches as compared with the traditional approach of "old" Missouri. He did not appreciate this lack of candor.[20] Things had changed significantly in the teaching of theology at Concordia Seminary, and Dr. Tietjen was willing to say so, to a greater degree than others. As president, Tietjen was able to create an *esprit de corps* that led faculty members to face opposition with a spirit of "one for all and all for one."

Dr. Ehlen was not actively teaching later in 1972 when most faculty members' personal confessions of faith were gathered into *Faithful to Our Calling, Faithful to Our Lord*, Part II. Still, Ehlen was "invited by the faculty to join in offering a confession of his faith to the church."[21] He first provided a statement about the "dualities" of Law and Gospel and then of divine and human. Then he made a candid statement regarding his exegetical (interpretive) approach to "Angels" and "The Deliverance at the Red Sea."[22]

---

18   David P. Scaer, *Surviving the Storms: Memoirs of David P. Scaer*, ed. Robert E. Smith (N.p.: Luther Academy, 2018), 137–38.

19   See the faculty majority's treatment of miracles in *Faithful* I, 18–20.

20   *Memoirs*, 23.

21   *Faithful* II, 156.

22   *Faithful* II, 45–50.

Angels

Regarding angels, Dr. Ehlen stated:

I believe that the Biblical statements about angels must be understood against the background of what other humans in ancient times were saying and thinking about supernatural beings. Much attention was devoted to such beings, their names and ranks and personalities were described in detail, and they were often actually worshiped.

He later added:

A faithful study of the human-divine Word has showed me that God *evidently* does not want us to become fascinated by the existence of angels in and of itself. Rather, he wants us to see these creatures too as involved in his all-important dealings with mankind in judgment and in mercy (law and gospel).[23]

In President J. A. O. Preus's Blue Book report to the Synod about Concordia Seminary, Dr. Ehlen was identified as "Prof. C." This report quoted pertinent transcripts of the interviews that Preus's FFC conducted with St. Louis seminary faculty members. Responding to a question about whether he personally believed in angels, Prof. C had said, "Well, as I said, I don't deny that there are angels." The committee pressed: "You don't deny, but you don't, you're not answering with a yes or no. You don't deny that there are, but do you affirm it?" Reply: "I don't believe in angels in the same sense that I believe in our Lord." The discussion continued in this way, then shortly afterward the FFC asked, "Do you believe in the existence of a personal devil?" The committee wondered whether the professor was saying that he did not deny a personal devil but did not necessarily affirm one either. Prof. C responded:

I certainly do not wish to deny the existence of these unseen powers both those that assist God and things that are powers of evil in His world. The question would be whether the preaching of a sermon on this would be of help to, well, to myself or to other 20th-century people. Under certain, in certain situations, I should think yes, certainly.

Prof. C went on to say that Luther had gone "quite a ways farther . . . than the Scriptures themselves in describing the devil as his enemy."[24]

---

23   *Faithful* II, 48 (italics original).

24   Blue Book (Zimmerman, 323).

Photograph by Paul Ockrassa

Students meeting in the fieldhouse on the Concordia Seminary campus vote to go into exile, beginning the Walkout (February 19, 1974).

The conversation returned to this topic later in the interview. Prof. C said that

> there are these ways of speaking about the devil, Satan, the accuser, and these ways change from Old Testament to the New Testament—and in fact within the confines of the Old Testament—so that these details of the way in which he is personalized . . . are not the major point of the doctrine. The doctrine, however, holds that there is, well, you can call it forces of evil, there is a very strong evil power in this world, contrary to the way God intended it, and that this is a great danger for the Christian in his life—a danger which can be described in terms of a personal enemy, as the Bible itself does in many places, but in other places it talks about it as powers and principalities and so on.

The FFC pointed to a specific incident involving Jesus and His encounter with demons (Matthew 8:28–34; Mark 5:1–20; Luke 8:26–39) in which Jesus allowed demons to enter a herd of pigs that rushed down a hill and drowned themselves. Prof. C said that "the text doesn't indicate a real connection with Satan." Later, he commented:

> . . . I do like to make that distinction between what a text teaches and what is incidental or assumed already, because I do think historically, according to a proper historical method, this is the way you determine what the original intent of a particular text is: that which it actually

203

proposes to teach and not what is part of the cultural background that didn't have to be taught because it was taken for granted by everyone.

The committee asked, "Would you say then that I could deny the factuality of this business of the pigs taking the big jump and still be a good Lutheran theologian?" Answer: "Yes, I think you could still be a good Lutheran theologian."[25]

Dr. Ehlen's views on angels were not shared by everyone on the St. Louis faculty, not even by all the professors who formed Seminex in 1974. Professor Dale Hartmann, who then served as librarian at Concordia Theological Seminary, remembers the last joint seminary faculties meeting before the Walkout. After adjournment, he overheard a vigorous debate between St. Louis professors regarding the existence of angels. As with several other matters, at issue was not what the seminary uniformly affirmed. Rather, problems arose over what the institution's doctrinal supervisors, its president and board, were willing to allow.

This ambivalence came at a time of uncertainty over this subject in the church at large. Sociological studies conducted during the late 1960s and early 1970s were asking people about, among other things, their belief in angels. Among members of LCMS congregations in one survey, 77 percent believed that the devil really existed, as compared with 49 percent of "American Lutherans" in general.[26] However, almost a quarter even of the LCMS respondents were, at best, not so sure. A somewhat later study found that of the Lutherans surveyed, only 53 percent believed in the actual existence of the devil.[27]

That same study also reported that 70 percent of the respondents accepted the miracles of the Bible as happening just the way they were presented therein.[28] With this, we now turn to the reliability of biblical miracle accounts.

Miracles

The word *miracle* is derived from the Latin *mīrāculum,*[29] which can be defined as "a wonderful thing, surprise."[30] Ecclesiastical Latin distinguishes

25 Blue Book (Zimmerman, 324).

26 Jeffrey K. Hadden, *The Gathering Storm in the Churches* (Garden City, NY: Doubleday, 1969), 47.

27 Merton Strommen et al., *A Study of Generations* (Minneapolis: Augsburg, 1972), 82.

28 Strommen, *Study of Generations*, 82.

29 *The Oxford English Dictionary*, second (1989) ed., s.v. "Miracle."

30 D. P. Simpson, *Cassell's New Latin Dictionary* (N.Y. Funk & Wagnalls, 1960), s.v. "*Miraculum.*"

between *mīrācula*, which deal with "strange or marvelous things or occurrences ... which can be done only by God," and *mirabilia*, which deal with "wonders, wondrous things; amazing, and even seemingly inexplicable occurrences that are not, however" done by God. These things can be done, for example, by angels and devils.[31] (See for example, in Deuteronomy 13:2–3.) Some modern Bible translations do not contain the word *miracle* as such. This word itself might best be seen as a category name for important biblical phenomena, much like the word *sacrament*.

The biblical words employed to deal with miracles in the Scriptures are many and varied, a hint as to their importance in the Bible's presentation of God's message to mankind. These words have their importance in communicating the many facets of this aspect of God's revelation of Himself. They are

'ôth	"sign"
môphēth	"wonder"
sēmeion	"sign"
thauma	"wonder" or "marvel"
dunamis	"powerful deeds" or "marvelous" works
and sometimes *erga*	"works"

Although these words normally deal with miracles, they do not in every case refer to an unusual intervention by God that was an "out of the ordinary" working of things.[32] For example, see the use of *môphēth* in Job 9:10 and 37:14 and 16. The *ôth*, or "sign," of God's judgment announced to Eli regarding the impending death of his sons seems to focus more on the prophecy of their demise than the manner in which it was to come, another example of emphasizing the timing and severity of an event rather than any supernatural character of it (1 Samuel 2:34). The use of *sēmeion*, or "sign," in Luke 2:12 in its immediate context does not give the shepherds something supernatural to look for but rather something that was unusual. Still, none of this undermines the truth that the Bible uses each of the five words mentioned above most often in reference to miraculous events.

---

31   Richard A. Muller, *Dictionary of Latin and Greek Theological Terms* (Grand Rapids: Baker, 1985), 193–94.

32   Merrill F. Unger and William White Jr., eds., *Nelson's Expository Dictionary of the Old Testament* (Nashville: Thomas Nelson, 1980), 478.

Two words referring to miracles, "signs" and "wonders," appear together ten times in the Pentateuch, then ten times in Acts.[33] Signs and wonders are thus emphasized as an especially significant part of God's revelation of Himself to humankind via both the prophets and the apostles, and these signs and wonders are recorded in the Bible. God uses these events that are often "miraculous" to authenticate His message and especially His ultimate Messenger. Nicodemus told Jesus, "Rabbi, we know that You are a teacher come from God, for no one can do these signs that You do unless God is with him" (John 3:2). Jesus Himself pointed to His miracles as authenticating His claim to be the Messiah. He said, "Believe Me that I am in the Father and the Father is in Me, or else believe on account of the works themselves" (John 14:11).

Some of the later world religious leaders, like Mohammed, have no miracles attributed to them. However, many of the ancient myths dealing with the false gods of the nations surrounding Israel include accounts of "miracles." Some of the pseudo-miracles of false religions are mentioned and debunked in the Bible and in the Old Testament Apocrypha (cf. Exodus 7:8–13, and Bel and the Dragon or Daniel 14 in Roman Catholic editions of the Bible). Christians should not believe every claim that is made regarding miracles. There are many modern television "evangelists" who try to attract people with alleged healings. Moses was inspired by the Spirit to speak to this kind of thing in Deuteronomy 18. Miracles and prophetic pronouncements are to be consistent with God's revealed Word. Moreover, predictions should come to pass. God is omnipotent and will never fail to deliver on His promises.

The biblical usage of the word *sign* is especially worth contemplation. In our society, with its many motor vehicles and roads, people are confronted with a multitude of signs. Many if not most of them must be heeded, or one's life is put in serious danger. Someone who ignores yield signs and stop signs will likely meet with a catastrophic collision. Likewise, those who disregard the signs that God provides put their souls in danger of forfeiting eternal life. The apostle and evangelist John uses "sign" as his normal choice of terms to characterize the seven miracles of Jesus that he recounts prior to the resurrection. Most of these were not mentioned in the Synoptic Gospels. John commented: "Now there are also many other things that Jesus did. Were every one of them to be written, I suppose the world itself could not contain the books that would be written" (John 21:25).

The "wonders" of the Bible invite people to raise their vision and their thinking above the "ordinary" and to recognize the One who is the true

---

33   Gioacchino Cascione, "Signs, Wonders and Numbers in the Bible" 2–3, 7–8, at
     www.lutherquest.org/redeemerpress/SignsWonders.pdf.

source of empowerment and provision. "The fool says in his heart, 'There is no God'" (Psalm 14:1; 53:1). "The fear of the LORD is the beginning of wisdom" (Psalm 111:10; Proverbs 1:7; 9:10; cf. Job 28:28). The spectacular nature of God's wonders, both "ordinary" and "extraordinary," reveals His existence and presence (Romans 1:19–30).

Whether called "signs," "wonders," or "works," biblical miracles are important. God revealed Himself through them, and He does not waste His efforts. The miracles are gifts from God to be cherished. Understandably, some who are outside of Christianity will try to deny all miracles as ancient fables, but it is sad indeed when the denial of miracles occurs within Christendom.

The Exodus from Egypt

Arlis Ehlen also drew attention in early 1972 for his treatment of a biblical miracle. With respect to Israel's exodus from Egypt, he had questioned the biblical account's complete historicity (that the events really happened without exaggeration as described) and facticity (that the details cited were accurate, honest, and reliable). In a March 3 letter to the Synod, President J. A. O. Preus reported on statements that Dr. Ehlen had made to Concordia Seminary's board. Preus characterized Ehlen as having indicated that

> although he [Ehlen] believed the Exodus account to be the Word of God and to be inspired, he did not believe certain miraculous events recorded in Scripture in connection with the Exodus had actually taken place.[34]

Prof. Ehlen later wrote a letter to *The Lutheran Witness* in which he stated, in part:

> I am happy to affirm ... [the] miracle by which God redeemed his people Israel from their bondage in Egypt and wrought a great deliverance for them at the Red Sea. However, various details which the Scriptures use to highlight these miraculous events are evidently meant to be taken in something more than a merely literal, factual sense. (Cf. Exodus 15:12; Psalm 114:4, 6.)[35]

In his letter to the Synod, President Preus had gone on to paint a larger picture. He wrote:

> Few, if any, among us would deny the possibility of miracles on principle. However, the use of a technique of biblical interpretation which leads in practice to the denial of the miraculous events in the Scriptures reminds us that it is only a short step from a denial of the miraculous

---

34   M[artin] W. M[ueller], "Preus, Tietjen Issue Statements," *LW*, March 19, 1972, 23.

35   Arlis J. Ehlen letter, *LW*, April 30, 1972, 34.

Photograph by Paul Ockrassa

Dr. John Tietjen addresses students as they disperse to LCMS congregations around the country for Operation Outreach (January 25, 1974).

elements surrounding the greatest redemptive act of the Old Testament (the Exodus) to a denial of the miraculous elements in the greatest redemptive act of all—the deliverance from sin, death, and hell. I am thinking in particular of the incarnation of our Lord Jesus Christ and of his resurrection from the dead.[36]

Dr. Ehlen affirmed Christ's resurrection in his letter to *The Lutheran Witness*.[37] However, Dr. Preus was asking: If the historical-critical method of interpretation were to be used with consistency, what could be made of *any* biblical miracle account—including the resurrection?

Jonah

One of the miracle accounts prominently questioned by several St. Louis professors was that of the prophet Jonah being swallowed alive by a large marine creature and then spewed forth, still alive, after three days. After the Walkout, Frederick Danker repeatedly noted his disdain for the insistence that the biblical book of Jonah be treated as an historical account instead of

---

36 Mueller, "Preus, Tietjen Issue Statements," 24. See Dean Wenthe, "The Theological Significance of the Passing through the Sea at the Exodus for Old Testament Theology," *Spr* 36 (June 1972): 54–58.

37 Ehlen letter, 34.

a parable.[38] President Tietjen showed a similar disdain.[39] Professor Alfred von Rohr Sauer was upset with the FFC for being concerned with his view that Jesus in talking about Jonah (Matthew 12:39–41; 16:4; Luke 11:29–32) could have been referring to an Old Testament parable rather than an historical account.[40] When Concordia Seminary student body leaders supporting the faculty majority organized an "outreach," sending students to churches nationwide to make the case for their dissent from actions of the post-New Orleans convention seminary board, a "factsheet" [*sic*] was prepared to provide talking points. One of these points was that the story of Jonah, like Jesus' story of the Good Samaritan (Luke 10:30–36), teaches a truth even if it is a parable and not an historical account.[41] All of this came in opposition to the official position of the LCMS, "To Reaffirm the Historicity of the Jonah Account" (1965 Res. 2-27).[42]

Two young pre-seminary students became good friends when they attended Concordia Senior College, Fort Wayne, Indiana, from 1970 to 1972. In fall 1972, one of them went to the seminary in St. Louis and the other to Springfield. At length, these friends compared notes about what they were learning in seminary. The St. Louis student said he was instructed in Old Testament class that after Jonah was examined on the basis of literary and form criticism, the conclusion to be drawn was that the book was best interpreted as a parable. The Springfield student had been taught by his Old Testament professor, Dr. Raymond Surburg, to use the interpretative principle "Scripture interprets Scripture" (or "Scripture is its own best interpreter"). Therefore one should make early use of Bible study tools such as a concordance and a cross-reference study Bible. These tools would lead the reader to see that the prophet Jonah, son of Amittai, had been mentioned also in 2 Kings 14:25. In fact, Luther made this observation in his preface to Jonah.[43] Thinking the matter through with "Lutheran presuppositions," it seemed extremely unlikely that in the biblical book of Jonah, God would have painted such a disparaging picture of an historical person if this book were a nonhistorical, illustrative parable. To do so would run against what Luther explained as the proper application of the Eighth Commandment. In a parable, God could have just as easily given a fictitious name to the "Jonah"

---

38   Danker, 11, 35, 54, 107, 136, 142, 325, and 353.

39   *Memoirs*, 72.

40   *Memoirs*, 129–30.

41   *Exodus*, 182.

42   *Exodus*, 2.

43   AE 35:323.

character, or He could have referred to this character without mentioning a name. The St. Louis student admitted that the "Springfield approach" had much in it to be commended.

The Virgin Birth of Jesus

Another miracle that drew attention was Christ's virgin birth. Bruce Linderman, a St. Louis seminary student at the time around the Walkout, remembered his instruction:

> The virgin birth was not as we have been taught—but that it was a girl of marriageable age who had sexual relations before conceiving Christ. The Isaiah passage [Isaiah 7:14] refers to an Old Testament time and event—not a prophesy [*sic*].[44]

This stands, once again, in sharp contrast to what Springfield seminary students were being taught by Dr. Surburg. He made the following observations regarding the Hebrew text of Isaiah 7:14–15:

1. The "sign" was divinely given by "the Lord Himself."

2. The "sign" was given to the house of David, not just to Ahaz. (The "to you" is plural.)

3. The text is concerned with a miraculous sign, not merely a human baby. God spoke of giving a sign "deep as *Sheol*" or "high as heaven." This implies a unique and stupendous miracle.

4. The sign was concerned with the perpetuation of the house of David until the preeminent sign of the ages should be realized.

5. It concerned a virgin (*'almah*). The context necessitates just this, a virgin. Moreover, the inspired word specifies a virgin. Matthew cited Isaiah 7:14 as a fulfilled messianic prophecy dealing with Jesus and His birth (Matthew 1:22–23). Matthew's Greek translation of the Hebrew text follows that of the Septuagint, using the Greek word *parthenos*. This Greek word means "virgin," not a "young woman of marriageable age." [In fact, it is so defined in Bauer's *Greek-English Lexicon of the New Testament and Early Christian Literature*, which Concordia Seminary-turned-Seminex professor Frederick Danker edited for a new edition.[45]]

---

44 Ted Mayes, ed., *Memories of the Walkout from Concordia Seminary, St. Louis, MO., February 1974* (N.p., 2021), 84.

45 *A Greek-English Lexicon of the New Testament and Early Christian Literature*, 2nd ed., revised and augmented by F. W. Gingrich and Frederick W. Danker from Walter Bauer's 5th ed. (Chicago: University of Chicago Press, 1979), 627.

6. The name "God with us," which is the literal translation of the Hebrew "Immanuel," involves the incarnation of Christ.[46]

A sizable and significant section of President Preus's Blue Book report is titled "Permissiveness: The Virgin Birth of Christ."[47] It contains transcripts of six interviews between the FFC and Concordia Seminary professors, plus a memo sent by a faculty leader to exegetical and systematic theology professors that contains reflections on "Demythologization, *Theologia Crucis*, and Christ's Virgin Birth." This section provides a clue to a contrast in the treatment of subjects like the virgin birth at the St. Louis and Springfield seminaries during the years leading up to the Walkout. The present writer attended seminary at Springfield, where the faculty seemed more focused on its assigned task of providing pastors who at the end of their seminary education would be well prepared to proclaim that they believed and were prepared to teach and confess the exposition of the faith found in the *Book of Concord*. The transcripts and memo in the Blue Book section on the virgin birth indicate that at St. Louis, a higher priority was placed on reputation within the scholarly community. The St. Louis faculty spent more time contrasting the importance of the resurrection of Jesus to the Bible's teaching about Christ's virgin birth. It also devoted significant amounts of attention to familiarizing students with problems that various scholars raised about the place of the virgin birth of Christ in the scriptural record, but it paid relatively little attention to equipping them to meet such objections. When a student might confess that he had difficulty accepting the doctrine of the virgin birth, some of the St. Louis professors said they would listen to him and talk with him about their concerns. Some transcripts imply that professors would leave it to the students to deal with the problem when they were asked to take their ordination vows. No professor mentioned his responsibility to raise a concern when the faculty had to consider certifying the student as a candidate for ordination. This is not to suggest that the Springfield faculty all wore white hats while the St. Louis faculty all wore black ones. Nor was it the case that all the Springfield professors were judgmental and unapproachable, in contrast to St. Louis professors being patient and "pastoral" with their students. Yet the aforementioned "permissiveness" manifested itself when the overwhelming majority of St. Louis faculty members supported one another's controversial views and joined together in the Walkout to form Seminex.

---

46 See Raymond F. Surburg, "The Interpretation of Isaiah 7:14," *Spr* 37 (September 1974): 110–18.

47 Blue Book (Zimmerman, 343–56).

How can a professed commitment to the Lutheran Confessions not result in a more serious concern for upholding an assertion from one of the universal creeds of the church, as contained in the *Book of Concord*? If the virgin birth of our Lord is largely dismissed as mythology, has the nose of the camel gone far enough into the tent that the Easter proclamation of the resurrection and atonement for sins is put in serious jeopardy? A pertinent question arises from the Bible itself, when God told Abraham that Sarah would bear him a son despite her advanced age. In Genesis 18:14, God asked: "Is anything too hard for the LORD?"

The Resurrection of Jesus

It seems unthinkable that any faculty member at a Missouri Synod seminary would question the miracle of the resurrection. And yet . . .

One of the more outspoken members of the St. Louis faculty majority was Dr. Walter Bartling Jr. He remarked at a Louisiana Pastoral Conference held on April 17–20, 1972:

> I can't answer the question, "Do you believe in the historicity of Adam and Eve?" Historicity and facticity are not even in my dictionary.
>
> One thing they caught most of us on is, were Adam and Eve historical persons? I don't know. I don't think so. It is not important. They caught most of us in some way on most of the points in Preus' "Statement."
>
> I believe that many of my Christian brothers have problems with the virgin birth of Christ.
>
> Don't ask me, "Do you believe in a 6 day creation?" . . . I have problems with the virgin birth, real presence, *bodily resurrection* . . . I can't bear the burden of Scriptural infallibility.[48]

Dr. Bartling's problem with the miracle of the resurrection was further attested by Richard Noack, a leader among the students who did not join in the Walkout: "I was hesitant to identify with the faculty majority especially since I heard Prof. Walter Bartling state in class that it made no difference to his faith whether or not Jesus' body physically was raised from death."[49]

Another student, Timothy Maschke (who went on to teach theology at Concordia University Wisconsin), remembered a similar statement by yet another New Testament professor.

> I was in an exegetical class with Bob Smith in which he said, "If there is a resurrection, WOW!" I was shocked. After class I stayed to ask him

---

48 *Exodus*, 56 (italics added).

49 Mayes, *Memories of the Walkout*, 41–42.

what he meant. He said he didn't see the resurrection affirmed in the Gospel of John, but he wouldn't say that to "Grandma Schmidt." I . . . never understood how he could not believe in the resurrection.[50]

A Christianity without the miracle of Jesus' resurrection brings no real Gospel and has little or no value. Remember Paul's words to the Corinthians: "If Christ has not been raised, your faith is futile and you are still in your sins" (1 Corinthians 15:17). The earliest preaching of the Gospel (that is, the *kerygma*) by Christ's apostles had the resurrection as its centerpiece (for example, Acts 1:22; 2:31; 4:2; 4:33; 17:3 and 18). More important, a non-rising of Jesus would negate His own claims about His mission and ministry (for example, Mark 8:31; 9:31; 10:34 and parallel passages; also Matthew 12:38–41; John 2:18–22). What kind of Christianity might that leave? What sense of adherence to the Lutheran Confessions could remain, in any sense of the word, without the resurrection?

The Difference This Makes

The above "case studies" of controversy over biblical accounts of angels and of miracles are distinct, yet related. Several lessons can be learned from them.

Don't distort the Gospel.

The Christian faith tells Good News from an almighty Creator God who intervenes in His creation. Among the reasons He does so is, foremost, to save sinners. The question arises: What, exactly, was the Gospel that the majority faculty claimed to be preserving? If that "gospel" was not based on something that the Lord actually did in real history, on what would faith rest? Faith that is bereft of its historical pillars turns into "fideism." Then faith simply puts faith in faith. Such "faith" is empty and worthless.

Don't undermine Christianity.

No true Lutheran ever suggested that only Lutherans would be in heaven. Christians from other denominations will be in heaven if they have saving faith in Christ, even though they may be beset with various doctrinal confusions or errors.

Cults are another matter, though. Their devotees will not be in heaven. They neither know nor believe in the Jesus who really is and who has revealed

---

50 Mayes, *Memories of the Walkout*, 30. See above, chapter 3, authored by Maschke, pp. 59–82.

Himself. They may imagine that they have some relationship with a "Jesus," but this is a Jesus who does not really exist and who cannot save them.

Christian teaching has to be careful not only about what it directly affirms but also about what it allows.

One of the famous questions asked during the early 1970s, contemporary with the seminary investigation and the ensuing Walkout, was from the Watergate scandal: "What did you know, and when did you know it?" Were all the members of the faculty majority fully aware of what their colleagues were saying in class? Perhaps not. Yet they contented themselves to allow a wider range of tolerance for various positions, among themselves and their students, than they should have.

Moreover, most of the contacts that the faculty members cultivated in the St. Louis area and elsewhere served as an "echo chamber" of support for the seminary and for the wide range of positions it was allowing. Would the sympathetic local pastors and staff members at synodical headquarters have wanted to go on record as supporting a "take it or leave it approach," say, to the actual physical resurrection of Jesus and the resurrection of the dead at His return?

Be watchful concerning those claims that influence you, especially those you seek out.

A related point is that all Christians need to be aware of the influence exerted upon them by other people. Camaraderie and loyalty are good qualities for co-workers, but it is possible to be loyal to a fault. Perhaps this is even more likely among extremely talented and capable people who find much to admire in one another. We have already mentioned Dr. Frederick W. Danker's scholarly contribution to English-speaking Christendom, that is, his work on revising what is arguably the most significant Greek-English lexicon (dictionary) for the New Testament in our time. He also wrote a book about the Walkout, *No Room in the Brotherhood.* The latter book shows that Danker picked which "brothers" he respected and with whom he sought to work in harmony. He told the FFC that he "must submit himself to the discipline of other scholars."[51] Danker dismissed traditional doctrinal theologians as stifling to modern-day biblical scholars.[52] He knowingly ignored resolutions adopted by his entire church body, if these resolutions took positions with which he and his scholarly brotherhood did not agree.

---

51 Danker, 68.

52 Danker, 33.

To conclude this chapter, the present writer cannot help observing that God's *angels* were with the LCMS, and He worked a *miracle* through which it survived and recouped.

For Discussion

1. What led members of the faculty majority to question or deny various biblical accounts of angels or miracles?

2. What damage would the denial of the real existence of angels do to Bible narratives such as Genesis 19:1–11 and Matthew 28:1–7?

3. Can one legitimately believe in some biblical accounts regarding angels but not others? Why or why not?

4. Satan is a fallen angel. If he doesn't really exist, then who and what are our enemies?

5. Can one deny creedal items such as the virgin birth and bodily resurrection and still claim to be a confessional Lutheran? Why or why not?

6. If there are no miracles, can there be an incarnation or resurrection? If there is no incarnation or resurrection, then who exactly is Jesus and what is the Gospel?

Digging Deeper

Bode, Gerhard, and Erik Herrmann. *Controversy in the LCMS* (2010). Video recordings archived at https://scholar.csl.edu/controversylcms.

Brown, Colin. *Miracles and the Critical Mind*. Grand Rapids: Eerdmans, 1984.

Geisler, Norman L., and Ronald M. Brooks. *When Skeptics Ask*. Wheaton, IL: Victor Books, 1990. Especially pages 75–99.

Lewis, C. S. *Miracles: A Preliminary Study*. New York: Macmillan, 1947.

Montgomery, John Warwick. *History and Christianity*. Minneapolis: Bethany House, 1964.

CHAPTER TEN

CHURCH AND MINISTRY

John C. Wohlrabe Jr.

The events leading up to and following the February 1974
Walkout at Concordia Seminary did not focus on the doctrines
of church and ministry. Still, concerns had been expressed over
these teachings. Moreover, positions proffered concerning church
and ministry as well as actions taken by members of the faculty
of Concordia Seminary and the synodical administration would
have far-reaching repercussions for the LCMS.

Introduction

Troubles at church are disturbing. Perhaps you have witnessed this.
Congregations experiencing unrest can be particularly vexed if people end
up sparring with one another not only *at* church but also *about* the church.
Whenever the church itself turns into an issue, it becomes more difficult to
deal with other matters.

In the Missouri Synod at the time of the Walkout, people were grappling
with issues across the church body and in countless congregations. To get
the fullest picture of the theological range involved, we should not fail to
notice that along with various matters that observers saw boiling over, "back
burner" confusion also existed with reference to: what constitutes the church,
together with the public office of the ministry; what the church and the ministry should be doing; and how church and ministry relate to each other.

When you were young, did you ever play on a seesaw or teeter-totter?
It's a simple piece of playground equipment, basically a board poised on a
fulcrum. Good use of a seesaw involves balance and consideration for your
playmate. If your playmate on the other side invites another friend to join him
or her in sitting there, you could end up with your feet dangling in the air for
a while. And if they both suddenly jump off their side, watch out! Seesaws

require balance and consideration. Church history demonstrates that the doctrines of church and ministry require balance and consideration as well.

Church and ministry had been at issue before the forebears of the Missouri Synod organized the church body in 1847. As with many biblical teachings, paradox is involved. Balance between two seemingly competing teachings must be maintained to uphold scriptural truth. Since 1851, the Missouri Synod had an established, accepted doctrinal position wherein such balance was maintained. During roughly the third quarter of the twentieth century, however, differing views were put forward within the Synod. One of the places where they emerged was Concordia Seminary.

In May 1956, for instance, the seminary's dean of students asked then-student Kurt Marquart to draw up a list of points about which he and other students were concerned. These were doctrinal matters at issue on campus. Regarding "Ministry and Ordination," Marquart wrote:

1. Whether the spiritual priests [members] of a Christian congregation are the original and immediate possessors of all Church power (i.e., administration of all the means of grace), or whether this power, or any part thereof, is originally and immediately vested in the ministerium [pastors, collectively].

2. Whether the office of the ministry is validly conferred by the call of a Christian Congregation, even without the imposition of hands by an ordained clergyman in Holy Ordination.

3. Whether God confers the ministerial office through the congregation's delegation of its priestly powers, or through the imposition of hands by a clergyman.[1]

Marquart was warning about the positions characterized in the second part of statements 1 and 3. He and others were concerned over an imbalance weighted toward the office of the ministry over against the church and the priesthood of all believers.

Another example, from a few years later: In April 1970, Concordia Seminary professor Martin Scharlemann wrote a letter to LCMS president J. A. O. Preus, with a copy to seminary president John Tietjen. Scharlemann listed items causing him deep disquiet, including: "An elastic use of the word 'ministry' which results in an apparent denigration of the pastoral office and glamorizing 'special ministries,' including involvement in radical social

---

1   Kurt E. Marquart, *Truth, Salvatory and Churchly: Works of Kurt E. Marquart*, ed. Ken Schurb and Robert Paul, vol. 3: *Essays: Historical and Historic* (N.p.: Luther Academy, 2018), 15–16.

action. . . ."[2] Here there appeared to be confusion over what church and ministry should be doing, as well as a belittling of the pastoral office. Now the seesaw was tilted in the other direction.

Historical Background

Lutherans coming to the new world faced a different situation in a land where there was no prince or king who would control and support the church, including the appointing of pastors. The Thirty Years' War (1618–48) ended with the Treaty of Westphalia, which upheld the 1555 Peace of Augsburg's settlement *cuius regio eius religio* ("whose realm, their religion"). The religion of rulers determined the religion of those ruled for years to come in Europe. But in the United States, since the First Amendment to the Constitution included freedom of religion, Lutheran immigrants needed to establish their church identity apart from the state.

The Saxon forebears of the Missouri Synod who settled in Missouri in 1838 believed that they were the one true church outside of which there is no salvation and that their identity as church and church governance rested upon their elected bishop, Martin Stephan, together with other clergy in the emigration company. Ordination and the authority of the ministry determined the proper preaching of the Word and the administration of the Sacraments. Here the seesaw was imbalanced, weighted heavily toward the ministry.

In May 1839, only months after their arrival, their bishop was deposed for immoral behavior. The Saxons faced a debilitating dilemma. Were they still part of the Christian Church? Were their pastors validly called? Could the Word of God be properly preached and the Sacraments rightly administered in their midst? Some of the laypeople claimed that the doctrine of the priesthood of all believers meant the church holds supremacy over the ministry. They saw the office of the ministry as only a public service growing out of the church's needs. Only when this office is committed to an individual by the laypeople of the church is it valid, they asserted, and the church can call and dismiss pastors at will. This constituted another imbalance, now weighted toward the church.

In April 1841, a public discussion took place between a leading layman and a young pastor named Carl Ferdinand Wilhelm Walther. In what became known as the Altenburg Debate, Walther showed that the Saxons indeed still were members of the Christian Church because the church, properly speaking, consists of all true believers in Jesus Christ who have been brought to faith by the power of the Holy Spirit working through God's Word and Sacraments.

---

2   Zimmerman, 33; *Exodus*, 151.

Photograph by Paul Ockrassa

Dr. Richard Caemmerer speaks at the return of the students from Operation Outreach (January 31, 1974).

Only God knows who these true believers are, so the church is called "invisible." Yet this true church exists wherever God's Word is purely taught and the holy Sacraments are rightly administered. (These are identified as the "means of grace" or the "marks of the church.") Even those visible gatherings where false doctrine is put forward (referred to as heterodox companies) are still church as long as enough of God's Word is put forth and the Sacraments are administered so children of God can come to saving faith by the power of the Holy Spirit. An orthodox church is to be judged by the public confession to which its members pledge themselves.[3] Although Walther's Altenburg Theses did not specifically address the ministry, they still presented a scriptural view of the church. They settled the Saxon immigrants' questions and paved the way for them to respond to other Lutherans who would take issue with them on church and ministry.

The Missouri Synod was established in April 1847, after the Saxon Lutherans of Missouri were approached by other Lutherans who settled in Indiana, Michigan, and Ohio. Even before this, however, the Saxons had been approached by Pastor J. A. A. Grabau, the head of a company of Lutherans who fled religious persecution in their homeland, Prussia. Beginning in 1817,

---

3   Walter O. Forster, *Zion on the Mississippi: The Settlement of the Saxon Lutherans in Missouri 1839–1841* (St. Louis: Concordia Publishing House, 1953), 523–25.

the Prussian king Frederick Wilhelm III issued edicts declaring that Lutheran and Reformed churches in his territories were to be united. Lutheran pastors who refused to comply were imprisoned. A group of refugees from such treatment had been led by Pastor Grabau to New York and Wisconsin. Grabau wrote the Saxons that the orthodox Lutheran Church was the true visible church on earth outside of which there is no salvation and that validity of the means of grace depends upon properly ordained pastors. He held that these pastors are to be obeyed in all things not prohibited by Scripture. The Saxon Lutherans saw in his position similarities to what they used to think when they followed Stephan. They disagreed with Grabau. Soon a Bavarian Lutheran pastor named Wilhelm Loehe, who trained and sent pastors to North America and supported both the formation of a seminary in Fort Wayne and the Missouri Synod itself, began taking issue with Walther on the doctrines of church and ministry, as well as with the Missouri Synod's "democratic" governance. Loehe attempted a mediating position, but agreed with Grabau on certain key issues. He then held that church and ministry were "open questions" according to the Lutheran Confessions, along with the doctrines of Sunday, the Antichrist, the millennium and the conversion of Jews (referred to as chiliasm). The dispute played out in various church periodicals in North America and in Germany. It became quite caustic. Eventually, Loehe broke with the synod that he had helped to establish. Grabau issued an edict of excommunication against the Missouri Synod as a whole.

To articulate its position and confess a balanced, scriptural view, the Missouri Synod at its 1851 convention adopted theses and explanations on church and ministry drawn up by Walther. This presentation was then published as *The Voice of Our Church on the Question of Church and Office*.[4] This book's contents are worth noting at some length:

In "Concerning the Church," nine theses maintained that the church in the proper sense consists of all true believers in Christ. Because only God knows who true believers are, the church properly speaking is invisible. Christ gave the Keys of the kingdom of heaven to this church of believers, so it is this church that possesses all "heavenly gifts, rights, authority, offices, and the like." Even though this church is invisible, yet it can be identified by the "pure

---

4   C. F. W. Walther, *The Church and the Office of the Ministry*, trans. J. T. Mueller, rev. and ed. Matthew C. Harrison, Walther's Works (St. Louis: Concordia Publishing House, 2012). For more on the history of the doctrines of church and ministry in the LCMS, see the dissertation on which this chapter draws in several places: John C. Wohlrabe Jr., "An Historical Analysis of the Doctrine of the Ministry in The Lutheran Church—Missouri Synod until 1962" (ThD diss., Concordia Seminary, 1987), online at https://scholar.csl.edu/cgi/viewcontent.cgi?article=1006&context=thd.

preaching of God's Word and the administration of the Sacraments according to Christ's institution." While the visible church contains hypocrites and evil people, yet those communities that gather around the preaching of God's Word and administration of His Sacraments can be called "churches" because within these visible assemblies there are true believers. Although the true church is to be found where God's Word and Sacraments "are not denied entirely . . . every believer is bound, at the peril of losing his salvation, to flee all false teachers [and] avoid all heterodox congregations." That said, "only fellowship in the invisible Church . . . is absolutely necessary" for salvation.[5]

Under "Concerning the Holy Preaching Office or the Pastoral Office," part two of the book discussed the doctrine of the ministry with ten theses. Here it was maintained that the office of the public ministry or the pastoral office is distinct from the priesthood of all believers; it exists by virtue of an explicit command of God. Because this preaching office (*Predigtamt*) has God's command, it is "not an optional office" but must exist where Christians gather around the means of grace. Yet this office does not elevate those who fill it above other Christians. It is "an office of service." The office deserves respect and obedience "when the preacher uses God's Word," but even in instances of excommunication, the pastor cannot act without "the preceding knowledge of the whole congregation." Also, the congregation, and not the pastor alone, is to decide ceremonies and other adiaphora (matters neither commanded nor forbidden by God). This preaching office is "the highest office in the church," the height of responsibility, the full office of the public ministry, which is conferred by the priesthood of all believers in a congregation through the divine call. In public office, pastors called by God exercise the spiritual priesthood's rights in the name of the congregation. Ordination is not divinely mandated; rather, it is "an apostolic, churchly order and only a solemn public confirmation of the call," and it should not be omitted. All other churchly offices flow from the pastoral office as the highest office. Although involved in the office of the ministry, those who serve in these other roles do not have the full office of the ministry. The concluding thesis gave the right to judge doctrine to both pastors and laymen, and both pastors and laymen could attend and vote in church courts and councils.[6]

These theses on church and ministry, forged in the fires of controversy, became a doctrinal standard. Pastors and congregations who wished to join

---

5   Quotations in this paragraph are from Walther, *The Church and the Office of the Ministry*, 3–4. See Walther's Western District convention essays, *All Glory to God* (St. Louis: Concordia Publishing House, 2016).

6   Quotations in this paragraph are from Walther, *The Church and the Office of the Ministry*, 5–6.

the Missouri Synod—and synods seeking fellowship with it—had to accept the doctrines as explained here. Here the doctrines of church and ministry were held in balance. The theses presented the relationship between the congregation as the place where the marks of the church or means of grace are administered and the pastoral office as the steward and administrator of these means of grace. They demonstrate the relationship between the office of the ministry and what the office does, that is, its function: the administration of the church's marks.[7]

The established position of the Missouri Synod on church and ministry was to be the position of the Lutheran church bodies that joined an umbrella organization, the Synodical Conference. Begun in 1872, it consisted of confessional Lutheran synods in doctrinal agreement and therefore in church fellowship. Originally it involved the Missouri Synod, the Ohio Synod, the Norwegian Synod, the Illinois Synod (which then merged with the Missouri Synod), and the groups that made up the Wisconsin Synod (including the Minnesota, Michigan, and Nebraska Synods).

However, a differing view on church and ministry arose within the Wisconsin Synod beginning in the early years of the twentieth century. Instead of identifying the church as the assembly in which the means of grace are administered, any gathering of those who confess Christ was now seen as church. In the Missouri Synod view, the means of grace were administered in a local congregation; therefore other groupings, including synods and synodical districts, were considered churchly but humanly devised organizations to assist congregations in doing what could not be done locally, including missions and the training of church workers. However, the Wisconsin Synod now considered organizations beyond the local congregation to be church. This understanding invested such other organizations as synods and districts with the Office of the Keys. Concerning the public ministry, Wisconsin Synod theologians maintained that Christ had established it in only an abstract form: that God's Word must be preached and taught and the Sacraments must be administered. According to this view, the assignment of functions to specific offices was purely an historical development, so it is always up to the church to decide how those functions are distributed. The pastoral office in a congregation was not considered to be the divinely instituted full public office of the ministry, but only one office that the church may establish and to which the church may assign various functions. Church and ministry were no longer balanced, for this view had matters weighted toward the church, and a different understanding of the church at that. Further, in the doctrine of the ministry the Wisconsin Synod separated the full function from the full

---

7   Cf. Wohlrabe, "Historical Analysis," 45–47, 83–84.

223

office.[8] The theologians of the Wisconsin Synod considered such differences with Missouri not as disagreements in doctrine, but rather merely divergence in application.[9]

Confusion on the Church at Concordia Seminary and Beyond

The first signs of doctrinal difference with respect to teaching on the church within the Missouri Synod occurred when forty-four Missouri Synod clergymen signed a document which they called "A Statement" on September 7, 1945. They took issue with the Synod's long-standing positions that the orthodox character of a church body is to be judged by the public confession to which its members pledge themselves and that believers are to flee false teachers and avoid heterodox congregations. The "Statement of the 44" caused considerable unrest. Although it was eventually withdrawn as a basis for discussion, it was never retracted. Among other things, it maintained:

1. That deviation in doctrine or practice from certain teachings of the Bible . . . is not divisive of church fellowship.

2. That not all acts of joint religious work and worship with persistent teachers of false doctrine or their adherents are to be regarded as religious unionism forbidden by God's Word.

3. That . . . Christians may meet and pray together if they do so for a good purpose.

4. That Romans 16:16–17 is not to be applied to all Christians who differ from us in certain points of doctrine, but that this passage is limited in its application to those who are not Christians.[10]

Five of the forty-four signers were professors at Concordia Seminary.

In an effort to calm waters that had been stirred by the forty-four and to bring about unity, the Synod's 1959 convention passed Resolution 9, maintaining that pastors, teachers, and professors of the Synod "are held to teach and act in harmony with" synodically adopted doctrinal statements. However, at the next convention in 1962, it was announced that the Synod's Committee

---

8 Cf. Wohlrabe, "Historical Analysis," 113–22, 197–220. See also John C. Wohlrabe Jr., *Ministry in Missouri until 1962* (private printing, 1992), 20–22, 38–39.

9 H. G. Brueggemann, "The Public Ministry in the Apostolic Age," together with "Editorial Preface," *CTM* 22 (February 1951): 81–109.

10 See Zimmerman, 14; also *Moving Frontiers*, 422–24, and online at http://www .projectwittenberg.org/etext/lcms/ST44/ST44.htm.

on Constitutional Matters had ruled Resolution 9 unconstitutional. This resolution was purported to have changed the confessional basis in Article II of the Synod's constitution, which was adherence to Scripture and the Lutheran Confessions. Instead of Resolution 9, the 1962 convention resolved: "That the Synod beseech all its members by the mercies of God to honor and uphold the doctrinal content of these synodically adopted statements."[11]

During the 1960s, the St. Louis faculty developed a more permissive attitude toward doctrinal disagreement.[12] After 1969, when John Tietjen was elected as president of the seminary, this permissive attitude progressed into outright rejection of the possibility of a unified confession within the church. In 1970, LCMS president J. A. O. Preus announced that he had appointed a Fact Finding Committee (FFC) to investigate what was being taught at Concordia Seminary. Then, in January 1971, the faculty majority formally stated that it had no commitment to teach according to synodically adopted doctrinal statements. Furthermore, the faculty majority held that all such statements should first be judged only by how well they agree with "the truth of the Gospel drawn from the Scriptures," but not by whether they agree with Scripture as a whole.[13] This was a case of "Gospel Reductionism."[14] In the faculty's opinion, then, doctrinal resolutions adopted by the Synod had no real weight. Moreover, the faculty reserved the right to evaluate the contents of these statements not in light of Scripture but in light of the Gospel that they drew from Scripture. How was doctrinal unity supposed to remain within the church?[15]

Propelled by a series of doctrinal discussions in postwar Germany (often referred to as the Bad Boll Conferences), together with the Ecumenical

---

11 *Moving Frontiers*, 432.

12 See James W. Mayer, "The Church as the People of God United in the Word of God," *CTM* 33 (November 1962): 667; and Herbert J. A. Bouman, "Some Thoughts on the Church in the Lutheran Symbols," *CTM* 39 (March 1968): 175–93.

13 "Statements Adopted by the Faculty of Concordia Seminary, St. Louis, Mo.," *CTM* 42 (January 1971): 46–47. See later articles: Arthur C. Repp, "The Binding Nature of Synodical Resolutions for a Pastor or Professor of The Lutheran Church—Missouri Synod," *CTM* 42 (March 1971): 153–62; Arthur Carl Piepkorn, "Possible Courses of Action Involving a Disaffected or Dissident Individual or Group of Individuals in the Church," *CTM* 42 (December 1971): 726–30; E. L. Lueker, "Doctrinal Emphases in the Missouri Synod," *CTM* 43 (April 1972): 198–211; John Constable, "Of Congregational and Synodical Authority," *CTM* 43 (April 1972): 212–31; and Horst W. Jordan, "Some Concerns about Current Confessional Statements," *CTM* 44 (January 1973): 27–34. See also the Excursus above, pp. 99–104.

14 See above, chapter 1, pp. 15–37.

15 Zimmerman, 38, 46, 52, 161.

Movement which was gaining momentum throughout the twentieth century, the St. Louis faculty dedicated more and more time to the doctrine of the church.[16] Eventually, an ongoing study of church and ministry was conducted through the Concordia Seminary School of Graduate Studies. This included the coordination of workshops, the presentation of papers, and further studies by both faculty and students.[17] What these studies seemed to focus on was the need for changing the understanding of church and ministry within the LCMS:

> To understand the problems of the church in the contemporary world it is necessary to realize that since the 1950s several forces have combined to produce change more radical than perhaps any known to history.... Some of the implications of these changes for the church include an emphasis on a variety of forms of the ministry, minimizing the importance of the church as an institution, a readiness to let the church sacrifice itself as a servant, emphasis on the church as all the people of God, greater use of the laity, flexibility in training ministers.[18]

The Synod's 1965 convention expedited change in the understanding of the church's nature when it adopted the Mission Affirmations, a document drafted by Martin L. Kretzmann and supported by most of Concordia Seminary's faculty.[19] The Mission Affirmations specifically identified the church with mission and mission with the church. Mission became a mark of the church, as later articulated by Oscar Feucht: "The priesthood-of-all-believers concept underscores our Christian doctrine of the church. To be that church, we must be living witnesses to Christ. The Gospel belongs to all Christians. *It becomes visible when God's people are on a mission where*

---

16   E.g., F. E. Mayer, "The Proper Distinction between Law and Gospel and the Terminology Visible and Invisible Church," *CTM* 25 (March 1954): 177–98; Arthur Carl Piepkorn, "What the Symbols Have to Say about the Church," *CTM* 26 (October 1955): 721–63.

17   Richard R. Caemmerer and Erwin L. Lueker, *Church and Ministry in Transition* (St. Louis: Concordia Publishing House, 1965), 8–9.

18   Erwin L. Lueker, *Change and the Church* (St. Louis: Concordia Publishing House, 1969), 51, 53. Also, Caemmerer and Lueker, *Church and Ministry in Transition*, 11, 18.

19   Res. 1-01A to 1-01F, 1965 *Proceedings*, 79-81. See Martin L. Kretzmann, "The Self-Understanding of the Church," *CTM* 36 (April 1965): 230–42, and "Editorial: Structure and Mission," *CTM* (November 1972): 643–44, as well as chapter 6 above, pp. 123–43.

they are![20] The problem with this "missional" focus is that here mission was understood as more than the proclamation of God's Word and the administration of the Sacraments (the marks of the church) resulting in the formation of Lutheran congregations. The mission of the church became identified with acts of mercy including disaster relief, medical support, feeding and clothing the destitute, teaching various secular subjects including English as a second language, and even social and political action.[21] The FFC eventually noted this as a concern, that

> . . . some faculty members placed the social action of the Church on a level of importance with preaching the Gospel. One man said that the Church is also "a sociological institution," giving it a dual role. Still another faculty member indicated that he felt that social work was on the same level of importance as preaching.[22]

Confusion on the Ministry: The High View

As mentioned earlier in this chapter, student Kurt Marquart expressed concern about what may be considered a high view of the ministry taught during the 1950s. This high view formed part of a larger Liturgical Movement within the Missouri Synod and North American Lutheranism, expressed in various publications and through various organizations. Two Concordia Seminary professors were active in this movement, Theodore Graebner and Arthur Carl Piepkorn.

Graebner was a member of the Society of St. James, which was involved primarily in matters of liturgical reform.[23] After this group held its last convocation at Valparaiso University in 1947, Valparaiso carried on annual "Institutes of Liturgical Studies."

Piepkorn belonged to the Fellowship of the Blessed Sacrament and regularly contributed to the publication *Una Sancta*. Some who were identified with the Fellowship of the Blessed Sacrament and *Una Sancta* advocated for the establishment of an episcopacy in the Missouri Synod. This episcopacy would be linked to apostolic succession, together with the necessity for authentic ordination from the hands of a bishop in the apostolic line— similar to what is practiced in both the Lutheran Church of Sweden and the

---

20 Oscar E. Feucht, *Everyone a Minister: A Guide to Churchmanship for Laity and Clergy* (St. Louis: Concordia Publishing House, 1974), 46 (italics original).

21 See the Mission Affirmations; also Richard Jungkuntz, "The Church's Responsibility in International Affairs: A Theological Appraisal," *CTM* 41 (March 1970): 146–52.

22 Zimmerman, 62; also see Zimmerman, 167.

23 Wohlrabe, "Historical Analysis," 177.

Anglican community. Here the Office of the Keys and the public office of the ministry do not rest with the priesthood of all believers and the church, which office is then conferred upon men through the divine call, with ordination as the public recognition of that call. Instead, the Office of the Keys and the validity of the Sacraments rest within the ministry itself, going back to the apostles. The office of the ministry is thought to be conferred by way of ordination through a bishop in the apostolic line. Arthur Carl Piepkorn did not hold that an apostolic succession was necessary, though he believed an episcopacy to be the preferred historic form of polity.[24]

Piepkorn did not agree with the understanding of ordination put forward by the Missouri Synod. For him, not only did ordination affirm the congregation's call, the rite, which typically and distinctively included the laying on of hands, it actually conferred the office:

> 28. Ordination is effective by divine right (*jure divino*) . . . 29. The term "sacrament" is applicable both to the Sacred Ministry as well as to Holy Ordination, the distinctive element of which is the imposition of hands by a pastor. . . . 32. The ordinary administrant of any Sacrament is an ordained clergyman. . . .[25]

A 1959 article in Concordia Seminary's theological journal discussed the blessings and dangers of the Liturgical Movement. On the positive side, the movement enhanced the place of worship in the eyes of believers, as well as the place of the sacraments, the ministry, and the Lutheran Confessions. In addition, participation encouraged ecumenical interests and dedication to achieving the goals of the Liturgical Movement. Negatively, participants ran the risk of becoming entrenched in formalism, sacramentalism, hierarchicalism, confessionalism, unionism, and factionalism. In regards to the office of the ministry, the movement tended to direct congregations away from viewing their pastors as "hirelings and firelings" to seeing them as servants of Christ properly called to the church's highest office in order to administer Christ's gifts to God's people. Yet there existed also the danger of valuing the

---

24 Arthur Carl Piepkorn, "The Catholicity of the Lutheran Church," *Una Sancta* 11 (St. Athanasius, Bishop, Confessor and Doctor, 1952): 8; and Arthur Carl Piepkorn, "What the Symbols Have to Say about the Church," *CTM* 26 (October 1955): 728.

25 Arthur Carl Piepkorn, "The Sacred Ministry and Holy Ordination in the Sacred Scriptures and in the Symbols and Liturgy of the Church of the Augsburg Confession," *Una Sancta* 12 (St. Michael's Day, 1955): 8–10. See Arthur Carl Piepkorn, "The Sacred Ministry and Holy Ordination in the Symbolical Books of the Lutheran Church," *CTM* 40 (September 1969): 552–73; Arthur Carl Piepkorn, "The Liturgical Movement and American Lutheranism," *Una Sancta* 17 (St. Luke the Evangelist, 1960): 13–17.

ministry (and ordination) for its own sake, not for the sake of God's Word and Sacraments.[26] Again, we see the need for balance and tension in the seesaw that is church and ministry.

At its 1959 convention, the Missouri Synod directed its theological faculties to provide a statement on the issue of apostolic succession.[27] In April 1962, the faculties complied. They made eight points backed by Scripture and the Lutheran Confessions. In summary, the joint faculty statement said that God had established the office of the ministry for the preaching of the Gospel and the administration of the Sacraments. Because there are no specifics in the New Testament for the kinds of ministers or for some specific form of succession and ordination, any differences in rank within the ministry or form of ordination are determined by human beings. Because the essence of the church and ministry is not defined by ministerial succession or a specific polity (for example, an episcopal form), churches remain free to determine these by human agreement.[28]

Confusion on the Ministry: The Low View

Although concern about a low view of the office of the ministry was not expressed in formal terms until 1970, and then by Martin Scharlemann in a letter to J. A. O. Preus, this view had been gaining traction within the Concordia Seminary faculty for some time. In part, it grew from the position that had developed within the Wisconsin Synod. This understanding was reflected in the seminary's journal, *Concordia Theological Monthly*.[29] According to this perspective, the pastoral office was not established by Christ through the apostles specifically for the public administration of Word and

---

26 Henry W. Reimann, "The Liturgical Movement, an Appraisal," *CTM* 30 (June 1959): 421–31.

27 1959 *Proceedings*, 194–95.

28 "Apostolic Succession," *CTM* 33 (April 1962): 224–28. For more on the Liturgical Movement and its effects on the doctrine of the ministry, cf. Wohlrabe, "Historical Analysis," 178–96.

29 This included a digest of M. Lehninger's essay "The Development of the Doctrinal Position of the Wisconsin Synod during the Century of Its History," by P.M.B. (Paul M. Bretscher), "Church and Ministry," *CTM* 21 (July 1950): 531–33; also an article advocating the Wisconsin position, with an "Editorial Preface" referring to reports from an Interim Committee of the Synodical Conference addressing growing differences between the Missouri and Wisconsin Synods on "the doctrine of the call, the ministry, and the Church, which for a number of years threatened the unity of the constituent bodies of the Synodical Conference ..." (H. G. Brueggemann, "The Public Ministry in the Apostolic Age," *CTM* 22 [February 1951]: 81–109).

Sacrament among a local gathering of believers (according to Titus 1:5). Nor was it the office from which are derived other offices that the church may designate. Rather, the concept of pastor was considered historically developed and determined by the needs of the church, together with all other offices that the church may develop to meet more specific needs.

> It is a mistake to identify the pastorate with the ministry or to speak of other church offices as auxiliary offices to the pastorate. To assume that the pastorate is the one divinely instituted office and that all other offices flow out of the pastorate is a misapprehension. The ministry of the Word is the one divinely instituted office, and the pastorate is a branch of that ministry, just as other church offices are a branch of the same ministry.[30]

Another influence on the Concordia Seminary faculty came by way of the Ecumenical Movement and the WCC in what has been described as the "rediscovery of the laity."[31] Both Professors William J. Danker and Richard R. Caemmerer adopted and put forward a new understanding of Ephesians 4:11–12:

> This has usually been understood to mean: God gave pastors to make saints perfect; pastors are to do the work of the ministry; pastors are to edify the body of Christ until each member of it is strong in the faith and is a perfect man. But take out the commas! He gave pastors and teachers for perfecting the saints for the work of the ministry which the saints are to do! The saints are the ministers, the servants! Their service is that they edify, build up, the body of Christ.... Ministry, in this sense, is the work of every Christian. The pastor as feeder and leader, then, is in the business of "perfecting" the saints.[32]

This view—that pastors did not hold a distinct office established by Christ to feed His flock with His Word and Sacraments but were rather

---

30 Brueggemann, "Public Ministry in the Apostolic Age," 99.

31 See Brent Kuhlman, "Oscar Feucht's Everyone a Minister: Pietismus Redivivus," *Logia: A Journal of Lutheran Theology* 8 (Reformation 1999): 31.

32 Richard R. Caemmerer, *Feeding and Leading*, The Witnessing Church Series, ed. William J. Danker (St. Louis: Concordia Publishing House, 1962), 38. A similar view was put forward by another seminary professor, Walter J. Bartling, "A Ministry to Ministers: An Examination of the New Testament *Diakonia*," *CTM* 33 (June 1962): 326–36. Contrast Henry P. Hamann, "The Translation of Ephesians 4:12—A Necessary Revision," *CJ* 14 (January 1988): 42–49; Philip J. Secker, "Ephesians 4:11–12 Reconsidered," *Logia: A Journal of Lutheran Theology* 5 (Eastertide, 1996): 59–62; and James W. Voelz, "Dark Omens of Change," *LW* 106 (May 1987): 21.

ministers to ministers, equipping church members themselves for the work of ministry—was repeated again and again by certain professors from Concordia Seminary.[33] It was reaffirmed in the Mission Affirmations of 1965. It culminated in a 1974 book by Oscar Feucht, then secretary of adult education for the Synod's Board of Parish Education, entitled *Everyone a Minister*.[34] In emphasizing the priesthood of all believers and the laity, this view elevated the church over the public office of the ministry. It also focused on the functions of the office over the office itself.[35] In so doing, it further diluted the function of the office so that the office no longer focused on the proclamation of God's Word and the administration of the Sacraments. Instead, the office came to encompass all kinds of service, including social action.[36] A further distraction was the proliferation of various specialized forms of ministry.[37]

Confusion on the Ministry: Other Matters Surrounding the Walkout

Ordination of Women

The ordaining of women was officially adopted in the Lutheran State Church of Denmark in 1948, then in the Lutheran State Church of Sweden in 1958.[38] Other church bodies in the LWF followed suit during subsequent

---

33 Harry G. Coiner, "The Pastor in the Church," in *Toward a More Excellent Ministry* (St. Louis: Concordia Publishing House, 1964), 14–15; William J. Danker, "Missionary Training at Concordia Seminary," in *Toward a More Excellent Ministry* (St. Louis: Concordia Publishing House, 1964), 116; William J. Danker, *Two Worlds or None: Rediscovering Missions* (St. Louis: Concordia Publishing House, 1964), 34; Richard R. Caemmerer and Erwin L. Lueker, *Church and Ministry in Transition* (St. Louis: Concordia Publishing House, 1964), 15–16; Maynard Dorow, "Church, Ministry, and Mission Fields," *CTM* 35 (September 1964): 455–69; Erwin L. Lueker, *Change and the Church* (St. Louis: Concordia Publishing House, 1969), 119; and John H. Tietjen, "Shape of a Seminary," *CTM* 43 (May 1972): 291–94.

34 Feucht, *Everyone a Minister, passim.*

35 Dorow, "Church, Ministry, and Mission Fields," 455–69.

36 C. Thomas Spitz Jr., "The Total Ministry of the Church," *CTM* 33 (January 1962): 24–31. See Zimmerman, 167, 191.

37 Lueker, *Change and the Church*, 53.

38 "The Place of Women in the Church," *CTM* 19 (June 1948): 466–67, and (July 1948): 546–47; "Ordination of Women in the Church of Sweden," *CTM* 29 (October 1958): 778–79.

years. In North America, both the LCA and the ALC declared women eligible for ordination at their respective conventions in 1970.[39]

The Concordia Seminary faculty did not advocate directly for the ordination of women prior to the Walkout in 1974. However, they prepared the way. Erwin Lueker wrote:

> The evidence of the New Testament, then, indicates that the church of today has liberty in forming ecclesiastical structures and ministerial arrangements and, at the same time, indicates precedents that should be followed. In some areas it gives no answers. It has no specific command to establish a special form of ministry. Paul refused to endorse women as leaders in the church, but they served as prophets and teachers in New Testament times . . . .[40]

Edward Schroeder concluded that "the clear consequence of the Gospel is that the orders of creation are nonpermanent."[41] Evidencing Gospel Reductionism, he wondered whether those who deny ordination to women were following in the tradition of Judaizers or Melanchthon (that is, those who maintain the third use of the Law) rather than falling in line with his understanding of Luther's supposed Gospel emphasis. Schroeder even asked: "Is the issue of women in the pastoral office *doctrinal* at all?"[42]

The FFC stipulated that it did not spend much time asking about the ordination of women. However, referring to three interviews in particular, the committee noted:

> Responses were unclear in two instances. In another the position was taken that the orders of creation (man first, then woman) and their theological implications were not permanent. Thus the ordination of women to the pastoral office is regarded as permissible. In a somewhat related matter, the entire range of the apostle Paul's ethical teachings was treated as being tied to his own time, with the unmistakable inference that modern man is not bound by them on that account.[43]

Prior to the Walkout, Martin Scharlemann described the impact that the use of the historical-critical method had on discussions of the ordination of

---

39 James H. Pragman, *Traditions of Ministry* (St. Louis: Concordia Publishing House, 1983), 158–68.

40 Lueker, *Change and the Church*, 120.

41 Edward H. Schroeder, "The Orders of Creation—Some Reflections on the History and Place of the Term in Systematic Theology," *CTM* 43 (March 1972): 175.

42 Schroeder, "The Orders of Creation," 177 (italics original).

43 Blue Book (Zimmerman, 381), introducing portions of transcripts from interviews with Professors N [Wi Jo Kang], U [Ralph Klein], and T [Edward Schroeder].

women. He noted that biblical study using scientific investigation and literary criticism in an effort to get behind the text resulted in scholars setting forth their own personal interpretations based on their present understanding of reality. Scharlemann opined that theologians representing the ALC did not take seriously such texts as 1 Corinthians 14:33–35. Rather, they came to their own view in light of cultural and sociological occurrences that transpired since Paul's day. With respect to relevant passages in 1 Timothy (2:11–14; 3:1–6), the ALC theologians simply questioned whether Paul actually wrote the Pastoral Epistles.[44] After the Walkout, the faculty of Christ Seminary—Seminex strongly endorsed the ordination of women to the pastoral office of the ministry.[45]

The Divine Call

Incidents involved in the Walkout at Concordia Seminary in 1974, as well as events that unfolded afterward, further impacted the office of the ministry. They raised questions regarding the divine nature of the call. In an apparent effort to defuse the explosive situation that was developing at Concordia Seminary and within the Synod, President John Tietjen was approached several times, beginning at the 1973 synodical convention in New Orleans, Louisiana, in an effort to get him to resign his call as seminary president. It was implied that this resignation would avert his forced removal from office. Among those approaching Tietjen were Synod president J. A. O. Preus, members of the seminary Board of Control, and several District presidents. The final proposal involved not only requesting his resignation but also included the promise of a congregational call in the English District from John Baumgaertner, in the Atlantic District from Rudolph Ressmeyer, or in the Missouri District from Herman Scherer.[46] Tietjen rejected all such offers as long as he was charged with false doctrine.

Unquestionably, ecclesiastical supervisors may ask for a called worker's resignation for false teaching, immoral life, or malfeasance of duty. But for ecclesiastical supervisors to coerce or manipulate workers with the promise of another divine call is problematic. Furthermore, in the doctrine and polity of the LCMS, the divine call is mediated by God through the congregation of

---

44 Martin Scharlemann, "Radical Orthodoxy: Answer to Missouri's Problems," https://scholar.csl.edu/synodhistory/Synodical_History/Year/32/. Listen especially from 46:00 to 54:00.

45 "For the Ordination of Women: A Study Document Prepared by the Faculty of Christ Seminary—Seminex," *Currents in Theology and Mission* 6 (June 1979): 132–43.

46 *Memoirs*, 155, 156, 167, 181–82. See also *Exodus*, 98–100.

believers gathered around Word and Sacraments (the marks of the church). A District president may recommend to a calling congregation the names of currently serving pastors who are on the LCMS clergy roster. However, the office of pastor is conferred not by the District president but by God through the congregation, the priesthood of believers gathered around the marks of the church. Backroom deals and political manipulation can occasion questions and skepticism about the divine nature of the call to the pastoral office.

On January 20, 1974, the seminary board suspended John Tietjen as president of Concordia Seminary. The next day, the majority of the students declared a moratorium on attending classes. The majority of the faculty also voted to strike, that is, not to teach any of their classes. They further claimed that by suspending John Tietjen, the Board of Control was guilty of "silencing the teaching of the Word of God."[47] The Board of Control met February 17–18, 1974, and announced that any faculty members not returning to their classrooms on February 19 would have their calls terminated. On that morning, "the majority of faculty members and students made their exodus from Concordia Seminary and marched into a self-imposed exile."[48] Which raises the question: if those serving in auxiliary offices of the public office of the ministry (theological professors at a seminary) have a divine call (which the Synod has maintained since 1851), do they have the right to "go on strike" and no longer fulfill the duties of their call? Or put another way, is this not a case of neglect and malfeasance regarding the divine call?

Ordentlichen Beruf / Rite Vocatus
("Rightly Called" / "Called According to Rite")?

After the Walkout, several District presidents placed and then ordained graduates of what was initially called Concordia Seminary in Exile (later changed to Christ Seminary—Seminex). The Missouri Synod has long allowed the Council of Presidents (the District presidents together with the president and vice presidents of the Synod) to place properly certified seminary graduates with the consent of the congregations who were extending the calls and receiving the new candidates. For years there had been a colloquy (interview) process for clergy who had not been examined and certified by the faculties of the Synod's seminaries yet who wished to be called as pastors of LCMS congregations.

Seminex graduates were not certified by either of the two LCMS seminaries (in St. Louis and in Springfield) to receive calls to LCMS congregations.

---

47 *Exodus*, 100.

48 *Exodus*, 119.

Even so, a number of District presidents allowed Seminex graduates to be called to congregations under their auspices and then ordained these candidates. The 1975 synodical convention authorized President Preus to remove from their offices those District presidents who persisted in placing and ordaining Seminex graduates who had not gone through the approved LCMS colloquy procedure.[49] Eventually, Preus removed four District presidents from office. There was confusion over whether the Seminex graduates they ordained had been properly trained, examined, and called according to Article XIV of the Augsburg Confession. Moreover, the conduct of these men raised questions about the proper role of all District presidents in governance and concord within the Synod. A schism soon followed, as approximately 250 congregations left the Missouri Synod to form the AELC.

The Difference This Makes

Pastors and teachers of the LCMS hold that the Lutheran Confessions are a true and faithful exposition of scriptural teaching to which they subscribe unconditionally. These Confessions, found in the *Book of Concord* of 1580, maintain that there is one holy, Christian Church, which consists of all true believers. Because human beings cannot know who truly believes, this holy, Christian Church is identified here and now by the pure proclamation of the Gospel and the right administration of the Sacraments.[50] Christians are not to be indifferent toward doctrine taught in the church.

Nor are they to be indifferent concerning the doctrine that is taught *about* the church. The church is not to be identified with missions if missions are understood as something apart from the pure proclamation of the Gospel and the right administration of the Sacraments. This was reaffirmed in *A Statement of Scriptural and Confessional Principles*:

> We believe, teach, and confess that the primary mission of the church is to make disciples of every nation by bearing witness to Jesus Christ through the preaching of the Gospel and the administration of the sacraments. Other necessary activities of the church, such as ministering to men's physical needs, are to serve the church's primary mission and its goal that men will believe and confess Jesus Christ as their Lord and Savior.[51]

Despite all the study devoted to church and ministry by the faculty majority of Concordia Seminary prior to the Walkout, confusion was sown regarding

---

49 Res. 5-08, 1975 *Proceedings*, 126–27.

50 AC and Ap VII and VIII; FC SD II 50; X 31.

51 *A Statement*, part III (cf. below, p. 266).

the nature of the church, which fostered confusion concerning church fellowship, the ministry, missions, and more.

Throughout, the Lutheran Confessions emphasize that we are saved by God's grace through faith in Jesus Christ "when we believe that Christ has suffered for us and that for his sake our sin is forgiven and righteousness and eternal life are given to us."[52] The Augsburg Confession goes on:

> To obtain such faith God instituted the office of preaching, giving the gospel and the sacraments. Through these, as through means, he gives the Holy Spirit who produces faith, where and when he wills, in those who hear the gospel. It teaches that we have a gracious God, not through our merit but through Christ's merit, when we so believe.[53]

In addition, in Article XIV the Augsburg Confession holds that: "Concerning church government it is taught that no one should publicly teach, preach, or administer the sacraments without a proper [public] call."[54]

Because the call comes from God through the church, the church and the ministry are maintained in balance and tension. The Lutheran Confessions also identify the ministry in terms of both function and office. Both of these are also maintained in balance and tension when focused on proclamation of the Word and administration of the Sacraments. The dignity of the divine call should be upheld together with the scriptural requirements for those who are rightly called to the office. Yet the faculty majority of Concordia Seminary prior to, during, and following the Walkout fostered confusion regarding church and ministry within the LCMS.

For Discussion

1. What is the tension and balance between the understanding of church and ministry that was established in the Missouri Synod in 1851 and maintained since that time?

2. What is the tension and balance between office and function within the understanding of ministry that was established in 1851 and maintained since that time?

3. How did the teaching of some faculty members at Concordia Seminary prior to the 1974 Walkout disrupt the balance in the understanding of the church?

---

52   AC IV 2 (K-W, 40).

53   AC V 1–3 (K-W, 40).

54   AC XIV (K-W, 46).

4. What are the marks of the church, according to the Lutheran Confessions? List some problems involved with trying to locate the church apart from the marks of the church.

5. What dangers may arise from stressing function over office or office over function in the doctrine of the ministry?

6. Does the order of redemption as articulated in Galatians 3:28 negate the order of creation and the order of the fall as found in Genesis 1–3 and identified by the apostle Paul regarding the office of the ministry in 1 Corinthians 14:33–35 and 1 Timothy 2:11–15; 3:1–6?

7. According to 1 Timothy 3:1–13 and Titus 1:5–9, what is expected of those who receive a divine call and are placed in the public office of the ministry? What actions could call into question the divine nature of the call?

Digging Deeper

CTCR. *The Ministry: Offices, Procedures, and Nomenclature.* St. Louis: LCMS, 1981.

Harrison, Matthew C., and John T. Pless, eds. *Women Pastors? The Ordination of Women in Biblical Lutheran Perspective.* St. Louis: Concordia Publishing House, 2008.

Marquart, Kurt E. *The Church and Her Fellowship, Ministry, and Governance.* Volume 9 of *Confessional Lutheran Dogmatics.* Edited by Robert D. Preus and John R. Stephenson. Fort Wayne, IN: International Foundation for Lutheran Confessional Research, 1990.

Walther, C. F. W. *The Church and the Office of the Ministry: Kirche und Amt: The Voice of Our Church on the Question of Church and Office.* Translated by J. T. Mueller. Edited by Matthew C. Harrison. St. Louis: Concordia Publishing House, 2012.

CHAPTER ELEVEN

AFTER THE WALKOUT

Publications by the Faculty of Seminex

John T. Pless

This chapter examines some significant and representative writings from the men who left Concordia Seminary in 1974. Considering the range of material that includes not only books and scholarly essays but also short articles and blog posts, this endeavor is highly selective. The focus falls mostly on several key professors. The theology of Seminex was not monolithic; there were nuances and different accents among its faculty members. This chapter endeavors to let respective professors speak for themselves so that today's readers might gain an undistorted view of the doctrinal and ecumenical themes with which they occupied themselves after February 1974.

Introduction

Prior to the Walkout, members of the Concordia Seminary faculty majority were, to say the least, discontented with certain traditional theological positions of the LCMS. Nor were they pleased with efforts made by the Synod and its officials to exercise discipline over them and their teaching. For instance, Old Testament professor Ralph Klein remembered an article that he had published in the seminary's official journal not long before the Walkout. It was titled "The Yahwist Looks at Abraham." Klein noted: "This clear denial of the Mosaic authorship of the Pentateuch was anathema to the synodical hierarchy."[1]

---

1   Ralph Klein, "*Currents in Theology and Mission*: A History," *Currents in Theology and Mission* 43 (January 2016): 3.

Klein and his faculty majority colleagues had been pushing the Missouri Synod envelope, as it were, with such writings. When they left Concordia Seminary, however, they relieved themselves of a great deal of resistance against which they had been laboring. They did not have to answer to that seminary's board anymore. Most of them left the LCMS altogether. What did they write after they were no longer responsible to the Synod's doctrinal supervision? This is the subject of the present chapter.

From *Concordia Theological Monthly* to *Currents in Theology and Mission*

Before the Walkout and the formation of Seminex, St. Louis seminary professors benefited from a variety of outlets for their writings within the Missouri Synod. These included the various products of Concordia Publishing House, as well as *The Lutheran Witness* magazine. Especially did the faculty have access to the theological journal that the seminary produced, *Concordia Theological Monthly* (*CTM*).

In 1973, shortages of both money and time to engage in the editorial process caused a reduction in the journal's frequency to five issues a year. No longer a "monthly," it retained as its title the letters *CTM*, which no longer stood for anything. As a publication, the new *CTM* made no secret that it no longer stood for positions championed by *Concordia Theological Monthly* since its first issue in 1930. The first *CTM* carried an article in which an LCA New Testament professor, John Reumann, made a case for the ordination of women.

CTM produced only a few issues, in 1973 and early 1974. During its brief career, however, it showed the innovative path on which the majority of professors had embarked. They embraced a method of biblical interpretation unencumbered by earlier assumptions about divine inspiration, as exemplified by the above-referenced articles. They also preferred ecumenical sensitivities to confessional restrictions. This was shown in the publication of seminary president John Tietjen's "Theological Education in Ecumenical Perspective," a response to an honorary doctorate conferred on him in 1973 by Eden Seminary (United Church of Christ) in St. Louis.

Tietjen's speech appeared in what turned out to be the last issue of *CTM*, in January 1974. The journal ended with the Walkout. Soon thereafter, the Seminex faculty started publishing a new journal, *Currents in Theology and Mission*—also often abbreviated as *CTM*. Ralph Klein, who edited this journal from 1974 to 2009, never called it by those letters, though. He wanted to highlight it, he later remembered, as

> something new, something addressing the wider Lutheran and ecumenical audience. . . . So we sought articles on biblical studies, especially the three-year lectionary, worship renewal, social justice, pastoral care, the full inclusion of women in the leadership of the church, and the like.[2]

During its early years, the new journal, published quarterly, boasted nearly 4,000 subscribers. In 1983, when Seminex was incorporated into the LCA's Lutheran School of Theology at Chicago, *Currents* became the official journal of the Chicago school and two of its sister seminaries.

Richard R. Caemmerer Sr.

Especially during the first decade of its existence, *Currents* served as a major outlet for literary contributions by Seminex faculty members. The elder churchman among them, Richard R. Caemmerer Sr. (1904–84), was a living link with the Missouri Synod's past. Having himself studied under Francis Pieper, Caemmerer joined the St. Louis faculty in 1940 and soon thereafter emerged as a magnetic teacher for the next generation of the Synod's clergy. In 1945 he signed the "Statement of the 44." After the Walkout—in which he participated together with most of his faculty colleagues, almost all of them his former students—he continued to teach courses in homiletics at Seminex for several years.

In 1978, *Currents in Theology and Mission* devoted much of its October issue to Caemmerer's autobiographical essay "No Continuing City: A Memoir of Change toward Deepening Growth in Jesus Christ." The essay bespoke Caemmerer's gratitude for the legacy he had received as a child of second-generation German Lutheran immigrants. He recalled with affection and appreciation the content and manner of Francis Pieper and W. H. T. Dau in the seminary classroom, and highly approved of Pieper's emphasis on Christ's vicarious atonement rather than the authority of Scripture as the guiding and unifying principle of Christian doctrine.[3]

A year after the Walkout, Caemmerer published a short essay in *Currents*, "A Glance at 'A Stance,'" a response to the CTCR document *A Lutheran Stance toward Ecumenism*. Caemmerer expressed appreciation for the document's mild tone but went on to criticize what he saw as its legalistic orientation, attributing unwarranted authority to synodical resolutions. He faulted

---

2   Klein, "*Currents in Theology and Mission*: A History," 3.

3   Richard R. Caemmerer Sr., "No Continuing City: A Memoir of Change toward Deepening and Growth in Jesus Christ," *Currents in Theology and Mission* 5 (October 1978): 279.

the CTCR report for falling prey to a "dogmatic reductionism" (no doubt a play on the countercharge of "Gospel reductionism"), that is, making claims for the authority of the Scriptures and doctrinal orthodoxy superior to the liberating Gospel.[4] Caemmerer seems to have pitted against each other Scripture and Gospel, also confession and love, failing to note that the only Gospel the church has is the one preached according to Scripture. Caemmerer's critique continued a trajectory set in the "Statement of the 44" which he had signed more than three decades earlier.

Like that "Statement," Caemmerer's "Glance" essay sought what Hermann Sasse identified as an "inclusive Lutheranism" grounded not in the marks of the church (as noted in AC V) but rather in a broad understanding of the Gospel embracing fellow believers in love.[5] Concern for doctrinal purity was regarded as contaminating relationships between those who are equally members of Christ's kingdom and hindering the mission of extending His reconciliation to the world. Unlike the 1945 "Statement," which had affirmed the inerrancy of Scripture as "the great Lutheran principle,"[6] Caemmerer's essay made no mention of the authority of Scripture anchored in the fact that it is God's inerrant Word. Rather, he portrayed Scripture's authority only in terms of its capacity to deliver the faith-creating message of the cross.

Ordination of Women as an Early Indicator

Currents in Theology and Mission soon became a vehicle to promote the ordination of women. A year and a half after the Walkout, it carried the article "A Study of the Ordination of Women" by Harry G. Coiner (1912–92), a former St. Louis seminary professor, who argued that the New Testament understood the pastoral office to be basically a matter of carrying out various functions and that women could not be excluded from it.[7]

In fall 1978, the Seminex faculty discussed a series of position papers on the ordination of women. Out of this discussion, the faculty adopted "For the Ordination of Women: A Study Document Prepared by the Faculty of Christ Seminary—Seminex." The document aimed to show oneness with

---

4   Richard R. Caemmerer Sr., "A Glance at *A Stance*," *Currents in Theology and Mission* 2 (June 1975): 174.

5   See the 1966 essay "Inclusive Lutheranism," in *The Lonely Way: Selected Essays and Letters by Hermann Sasse*, vol. 2: *1941–1976*, trans. Matthew C. Harrison et al. (St. Louis: Concordia Publishing House, 2002), 341–45.

6   *Moving Frontiers*, 422; the "Statement of the 44" is also available at http://www .projectwittenberg.org/etext/lcms/ST44/ST44.htm.

7   Harry G. Coiner, "A Study of the Ordination of Women," *Currents in Theology and Mission* 2, no. 4 (August 1975): 221–27.

other Lutherans in the ALC and LCA, as well as Christians globally who had already opened the ministry to women. It also provided a theological rationale for women's ordination. Largely following the work of John Reumann and also Krister Stendahl (a Harvard Divinity School professor who went on to become the bishop of Stockholm in the Church of Sweden), the document pointed to Galatians 3:28 as the evangelical "breakthrough" overriding texts that seem to place limitations on female involvement in church leadership.[8]

From this toehold, the document kept climbing toward women's ordination. Referring to Stendahl, it asserted that "Jesus' maleness is not a constitutive factor in what is meant when the church calls him 'Son of God.'"[9] It added that because the Lutheran Confessions do not explicitly limit public ministry to males and since the issue of authority "is not a proper concern in considering the pastoral office," contemporary Lutherans may ordain women.[10]

What of counterarguments? Those based on the order of creation were dismissed from consideration. Potential negative ecumenical implications were not deemed weighty enough to stand in the way of fully including women in the ministry. The document allowed: "Ordaining women may indeed be a break with tradition. But breaking tradition is itself in the best of the Christian tradition if—and that is always a big if—the break is occasioned by the Gospel."[11] The Seminex faculty claimed that the Gospel frees the church to ordain women.

Frederick W. Danker

Frederick Danker (1920–2012) was born in Frankenmuth, Michigan, the son of Lutheran teachers. Danker joined the Concordia Seminary faculty in 1954 while completing a doctorate in classical Greek. An understudy of William Arndt, Danker would take his place alongside F. W. Gingrich on the editorial team of *A Greek-English Lexicon of the New Testament and Other Early Christian Literature*. He continued this work on editions published in 1979 and 2000.

Following in the footsteps of Arndt, Danker would also write a commentary on Luke for a Concordia Publishing House commentary series. His manuscript was accepted by the editors but rejected by a subcommittee

---

8 "For the Ordination of Women: A Study Document prepared by the Faculty of Christ Seminary-Seminex," *Currents in Theology and Mission* 6, no. 3 (June 1979): 134.

9 "For the Ordination of Women," 139

10 "For the Ordination of Women," 138.

11 "For the Ordination of Women," 136.

because, according to Danker, "the work included too many biblical citations, especially to the Book of Wisdom in the Old Testament, as well as references to non-canonical Jewish writings."[12] That did not stop Danker. Instead, he founded Clayton Publishing House, which published his Luke commentary in 1972 under the title *Jesus and the New Age: A Commentary on the Third Gospel*. Clayton Publishing House would also print Danker's book *Benefactor: Epigraphic Study of a Graeco-Roman and New Testament Semantic Field* in 1982.

In 1989, Augsburg Publishing House released a lay-level commentary that Danker had written on 2 Corinthians.[13] He treated the letter in its cultural context, examining Paul's literary devices, particularly attentive to the function of a civic benefactor. While Danker endorsed historical-critical approaches to the Scriptures, he focused on the literary character of the scriptural texts. He sought to elucidate the meaning of the biblical message by means of short word studies and through tracing literary parallels in the world of Graeco-Roman antiquity.

Danker's bibliography of books and articles on biblical themes is vast, both before and after 1974. In 1977 Clayton Publishing House released Danker's book of a completely different genre, *No Room in the Brotherhood: The Preus-Otten Purge of Missouri*, a fast-paced partisan telling of the events leading to Seminex and the immediate fallout occasioned by the Walkout. Danker's account is not one of a detached historian but rather of a soldier in a battle fighting for his own reputation. The book has something of the character of a diary, giving ample evidence of the emotional involvement of the writer. Danker saw himself as fighting for a righteous cause, the freedom of the Gospel and a Christian community characterized by diversity of theological expression. However, his sarcasm and cynicism color his narrative of the events he attempted to report.

John H. Tietjen

Another book authored by a key participant in Seminex is John H. Tietjen's *Memoirs in Exile: Confessional Hope and Institutional Conflict* published by Fortress Press in 1990. Tietjen (1928–2004) was called to the seminary as president in 1969 after he had served as a parish pastor, an editor (of *The American Lutheran*, a forerunner of *Lutheran Forum*), and a public relations director. With a doctorate from Union Seminary, where his dissertation

---

12 Danker, 55.

13 Frederick W. Danker, *II Corinthians*, Augsburg Commentary on the New Testament (Minneapolis: Augsburg, 1989).

dealt with efforts toward Lutheran unity in North America, Tietjen was celebrated as the man who would lead the Synod's premier seminary into a more expansive ecumenical future. His book reflects the events leading up to his election as seminary president, the turbulence of his almost five years in that office, and the aftermath of the Walkout.

Tietjen saw himself as a victim of LCMS president J. A. O. Preus, and he portrayed Preus as a clever operator presiding over a well-organized ecclesiastical-political machine. There was no recognition that deep and genuine theological concerns motivated Preus. Tietjen perhaps demonstrated how much of a theologian of glory he really was by his certainty in identifying how God was at work in these events. As Gilbert Meilaender pointed out in a perceptive review of *Memoirs in Exile*, the book lacks both a sense of humor and humility.[14] Tietjen's hubris was all too transparent as he sought to justify his actions leading up to the Walkout and beyond.

Edgar Krentz

Edgar Krentz (1928–2021) was a New Testament scholar. According to the entry on his faculty page at the Lutheran School of Theology at Chicago, he remained indebted to Ernst Käsemann: "In 1963 he spent a sabbatical year at the University of Tübingen, Germany, where Ernst Käsemann taught him that it was possible to combine committed Lutheranism with radical New Testament interpretation, a position he adopted for the rest of his career."[15]

Krentz, trained in classics at Washington University, would return to Germany for another sabbatical in 1973–74. Not on campus when the Walkout occurred, he resigned from Concordia Seminary when he returned to St. Louis and joined his colleagues at Seminex.

Krentz's sabbatical, funded by a John Behnken Fellowship from Aid Association for Lutherans, resulted in the publication of *The Historical-Critical Method* by Fortress Press in its Guides to Biblical Scholarship series in 1975. This little book had greater significance than its length of 88 pages might suggest. In it, Krentz attempted to provide a concise but actual description of what had come to be labeled as the historical-critical method. As the use of this method was a major item in the LCMS controversy, Krentz's work was timely.

The value of Krentz's monograph is that he set the method in the context of the history of biblical interpretation and demonstrated how it arose from

---

14 See Gilbert Meilaender, "How Churches Crack Up: The Case of The Lutheran Church—Missouri Synod," *First Things* 14 (June–July 1991): 38–42.

15 www.lstc.edu/news/article-615. Accessed 12/31/2021.

the Enlightenment. He paid special attention to Johann August Ernesti (1707–81), who applied to the New Testament the kind of method used in editing other ancient texts, which devoted attention not only to words and their meanings but also to historical considerations. Krentz approvingly cited Franz Lau's pronouncement that Ernesti became "the father of profane scientific interpretation" of the Bible.[16]

Johann Salomo Semler (1725–91) is usually designated as the father of the historical-critical method. While Ernesti did not believe that divine Scripture could err, for Semler divine inspiration gives way "to a purely historical-philological interpretation of the Bible, in the light of the circumstances surrounding the origin of the various books, without any concern for edification."[17] According to Krentz, a seminal essay written in 1898 by Ernst Troeltsch (1865–1923), "On Historical and Dogmatic Theology," formulated the foundational principles of the historical-critical method:

> (1) the principle of criticism or methodological doubt, which implies that history only achieves probability. Religious tradition must also be subjected to criticism . . . . (2) The principle of analogy makes criticism possible. Present experience and occurrence become the criteria of probability in the past. . . . (3) The principle of correlation (or mutual interdependence) implies that all historical phenomena are so interrelated that change in one phenomenon necessitates a change in causes leading to the effects it has. Historical explanation rests on this chain of cause and effect.[18]

Krentz deftly narrated the nuances in the development of the historical-critical method, lauding the way that secular historical research sharpened and defined the techniques of biblical studies in the nineteenth century and early twentieth century. He concluded: "By the end of the Second World War historical criticism was firmly established, not to be dislodged by any attack. . . . Today historical criticism is taken for granted; we cannot go back to a precritical age."[19]

For Krentz, this meant that the methods of the biblical scholar are those of historians in general. Like the historian, the biblical scholar "tries to answer the questions 'what actually happened' and 'Why?' about events reported in

---

16 Edgar Krentz, *The Historical-Critical Method* (Philadelphia: Fortress Press, 1975), 18.

17 Krentz, *Historical-Critical Method*, 19.

18 Krentz, *Historical-Critical Method*, 55.

19 Krentz, *Historical-Critical Method*, 32–33.

the Bible."[20] Just as historians attempt to get behind the assemblage of "facts" reported in a narrative, so the biblical scholar must strive to get behind the reports and penetrate to the earlier stages of the telling of the story of Israel or of Jesus. Historical criticism outfits the biblical interpreter with the tools and techniques for this task.

Krentz offered ten points that in his mind validated the use of the historical-critical method.[21] (1) Critical scholarship has provided research aids such as grammars, lexicons, commentaries, and more. (2) Historical and geographical study provided by the method has further revealed the life of Israel and the early Christian communities. (3) Because of these first two points, the "original grammatical and *historical sense* of the Bible," greatly valued by the Reformation, has become more clear.[22] (4) The method indicates the "time-conditioned, historical character of the Bible," which (5) appropriately makes "the Bible seem *strange and foreign*" to modern readers.[23] (6) The method brings the biblical text to the fore, separate from overlays imposed by dogmatic tradition or church history.[24] (7) More recent scholarship challenges and modifies older results. "Historical criticism," therefore, "is *self-correcting*."[25] (8) The method brings about "significant change in *theological insight*," as it highlights that variety in Scripture.[26] (9) It also changes theological method, for "the Bible must be read historically and then interpreted for our own age."[27] (10) "Historical criticism produces only probable results."[28]

Having laid out what he saw as the historical-critical method's legitimate and positive uses in the life of the church, Krentz addressed the drawbacks of

---

20 Krentz, *Historical-Critical Method*, 37.

21 See Krentz, *Historical-Critical Method*, 63–67.

22 Krentz, *Historical-Critical Method*, 64 (italics original).

23 Krentz, *Historical-Critical Method*, 64 (italics original).

24 Krentz, *Historical-Critical Method*, 65.

25 Krentz, *Historical-Critical Method*, 66 (italics original).

26 Krentz, *Historical-Critical Method*, 66 (italics original).

27 Krentz, *Historical-Critical Method*, 66.

28 Krentz, *Historical-Critical Method*, 67. It might be noted that already almost a decade earlier, in 1966, Concordia Publishing House had released a short book by Krentz, *Biblical Studies Today*. There he painted a positive picture of the landscape of biblical studies at mid-century. Also see his article, "Hermeneutics and the Teacher of the Church," *CTM* 42 (May 1971): 265–82. After the Walkout, Krentz wrote "Historical Criticism and Confessional Subscription," *Currents in Theology and Mission* 15 (February 1988): 128–36; and "Biblical Interpretation in Crisis: The Ratzinger Conference on the Bible and the Church," *Currents in Theology and Mission* 20 (February 1993): 54–56.

the method and the worries in the minds of those who regard it as destructive of saving faith. Krentz did not glibly dismiss these concerns. He recognized the potential of using the method for destructive ends. But in keeping with the old principle that an abuse does not destroy a proper use (*abusus non tollit usum*), Krentz contended for a reception of the historical-critical method used according to basic Christian (and in his case, Lutheran) presuppositions. Krentz's book not only described the historical-critical method but also defended its use in the church. This was not the first time that Krentz had defended the use of the historical-critical method, nor would it be his last word on the subject.[29]

Commenting on Krentz's book, the Norwegian theologian Knut Alsvåg observes:

> The one thought that seemingly never entered the heads of the leading Protestant theologians under modernity was that the foundation upon which the edifice was built was flawed from the outset. Seen in this light, the problem of historical-critical Bible research is not that it is critical; the problem is that it is not sufficiently critical, as its own basic assumptions are looked at with a similar kind of reverence as the one inerrancy advocates reserve for the Bible.[30]

In other words, historical criticism has become as sacred to biblical critics as the Scriptures are to Christians who refuse to engage in such criticism! In a footnote, Alsvåg explains a bit. He refers to Krentz's sentence: "Today historical criticism is taken for granted; we cannot go back to a precritical age." Quoting Krentz a bit more, Alsvåg writes: "The fact that 'biblical scholars use the methods of secular history on the Bible' ([Krentz,] p. 48) does not invite Krentz to any kind of critical awareness."[31]

Ralph Klein

Ralph Klein (1936–2021) grew up in a Missouri Synod parsonage. After graduating from the St. Louis seminary, he completed a doctorate in Old Testament at Harvard. Before coming onto the seminary faculty, he served as an instructor at the Synod's senior college in Fort Wayne, Indiana. He was perhaps the most prolific writer among his post-Walkout colleagues. In

---

29 See Knut Alsvåg, "'These Things Took Place as an Example for Us': On the Theological and Ecumenical Significance of the Lutheran *Sola Scriptura*," *dialog* (2016): 206. This article can be found at https://onlinelibrary.wiley.com/doi/10.1111/dial.12256. Accessed 8/19/2022.

30 Alsvåg, "'These Things Took Place as an Example for Us,'" 206.

31 Alsvåg, "'These Things Took Place as an Example for Us,'" 209 n. 52.

addition to more than 1,300 articles, short notes, and book reviews, Klein wrote significant books in Old Testament studies.[32]

On the occasion of his death in December 2021, Klein's longtime colleague Kurt Hendel wrote: "Dr. Klein was a leading and influential proponent of the historical-critical study of Scripture, the ecumenical movement, and the ordination of women, all of which inspired significant debate and division within the Lutheran Church—Missouri Synod during the 1960s and 1970s. He was also an ardent supporter of the civil rights movement and a vocal opponent of the Vietnam War."[33]

In a 2011 article, Klein reflected on changes in his own thinking since 1974:

> I still use my historical and linguistic training as primary research tools, but all of us have been affected by the many new methodological approaches, such as narratology, social scientific criticism, and the like. We recognize more and more that the final form of the text also has an important meaning, even if we can detect stages through which a text has passed in oral tradition or literary redaction. We have also all been impacted by feminism, womanism, and post colonial criticism, and we are keenly aware that the social location of the biblical interpreter—and even of the biblical author—must be taken into account as we try to understand what texts meant then and what they mean now. I am much more aware now than I was in 1974 about how pervasive patriarchy was in the biblical world and the biblical text. It colors its view of the human situation and of God.[34]

Klein went on that before Seminex, he and his colleagues attempted to counter the Missouri Synod's teaching on inerrancy by asserting the sufficiency of the Gospel: "We were faced with the questions of inerrancy, which

---

32   These include two Fortress Press *Hermeneia* volumes: *1 Chronicles—A Commentary*, ed. Thomas Krüger (Minneapolis: Fortress Press, 2006), and *2 Chronicles—A Commentary*, ed. Paul D. Hanson (Minneapolis: Fortress Press, 2012); also: "The Books of Ezra and Nehemiah: Introduction, Commentary, and Reflections," in vol. 3 of *New Interpreter's Bible* (Nashville: Abingdon Press, 1999), 661–851; *1 Samuel*, 2nd ed., Word Biblical Commentary 10 (Grand Rapids: Zondervan, 2000); *Israel in Exile: A Theological Interpretation* (Philadelphia: Fortress Press, 1979); and a contribution to the Fortress Guides to Biblical Scholarship series. As indicated above, Krentz had written a book in this series on the historical-critical method. Klein's volume was *Textual Criticism of the Old Testament: From the Septuagint to Qumran* (Philadelphia: Fortress Press, 1974).

33   https://www.lstc.edu/news-events/news/article-618. Accessed 1/4/2022.

34   Ralph Klein, "How My Mind Has Changed," *Currents in Theology and Mission* 38 (April 2011): 126.

we tried to change into the question about the sufficiency of the gospel." However, the ELCA "is not bothered about the inerrancy question, Adam and Eve, and all the rest." The ELCA faces other challenges.

> The ELCA is still trying to break out of its own version of fundamentalism or the assumption that what the Bible says on controvertible ethical questions is clear (it usually is not) or valid for all time (in the Bible people got married at 14 or 15 years of age, and thanks to decisions made by the couple's parents. Patriarchy predominates in almost all of the Bible's statements about sexuality).[35]

Klein saw the Scriptures' endorsement of patriarchy as a problem for the contemporary church to overcome. His fixation with this issue can be seen in his staunch advocacy for women's ordination and later in his endorsement of the blessing of same-sex unions and the ordination of gay and lesbian persons.

As already mentioned, the Seminex faculty embraced the ordination of women very early in its history. In a published interview with Gloria Weber, the second woman ordained in the ALC, Klein noted that the traditional passages (1 Corinthians 14:34–36; 1 Timothy 2) used by the Missouri Synod to support a male-only pastorate do not speak to ordination in their original context and may not be applied to the question.[36] Instead, Klein suggested that other sections in the Pauline epistles, especially 1 Corinthians 11 and Galatians 3, would seem to legitimate it. For Klein, the biblical interpreter has to make a distinction between the original meaning in its historical/cultural context and the application that is made for the life of the church today.

Klein would also be a champion of the full inclusion of gay and lesbian people in the public ministry of the church. Leading up to the 2009 decision of the ELCA on this issue, Klein added his signature to that of other "teaching theologians" in that church body who urged this position.[37] To say the least, he readily identified himself with this cause.

Klein's commitment to both women's ordination and his endorsement of homosexuality became evident in his review article from 2012, "Competing Contemporary Lutheran Study Bibles," which examined study Bibles with very similar titles published in 2009: *Lutheran Study Bible* from the ELCA's Fortress Press and *The Lutheran Study Bible* from Concordia Publishing

---

35 Klein, "How My Mind Has Changed," 127.

36 See Ralph Klein and Gloria Weber, "Interview on Women's Ordination," *Currents in Theology and Mission* 4 (June 1977): 151–57.

37 The text of the petition may be found at https://web.archive.org /web/20070918233252/http://prophetess.lstc.edu/~rklein/Doc3/statement.htm. Accessed 9/18/2022.

House of the LCMS. Klein wisely referred to the two books by naming their parent denominations.

After commenting on various features of layout and appearance, Klein noted the greatest contrast between the two study Bibles, which was "theological and methodological." He continued:

> The ELCA uses historical criticism and other critical methods and offers an insightful article on faithful reading through cross-cultural and inter-religious lenses. The LCMS maintains the anti-critical posture it turned to (or returned to) in the late '60s and early '70s of the last century. The position is often so extreme that anyone wishing help with difficult passages, wanting to know how to deal with modern scientific or cultural questions, or hopeful of finding the fruits of biblical research will go away sorrowing. The LCMS treatment of current biblical scholarship is often misleading and even deceptive.[38]

Klein rehearsed the differences between the two study Bibles in questions of authorship and messianic prophecies. For the most part, he approved the ELCA study Bible's handling of the texts on homosexuality as an abuse of power rather than as an expression of idolatry and habitual sin implying a life incompatible with the holiness of the kingdom of God, as articulated in the LCMS study Bible. Regarding women in the church, Klein reported how the ELCA volume notes that 1 Corinthians 14:34 (women should be silent in the church) might be a non-Pauline textual addition to the letter, or else it is inconsistent with the whole of Paul's theology. On the other hand, Klein wrote: "The LCMS again assumes a hard line: The biblical revelation does not permit women to serve as priests or pastors. Paul's command that women be silent in the churches must be understood, in part, as countercultural and anti-syncretistic."[39]

Klein's conclusion is not surprising:

> In my judgment the LCMS volume is unacceptable. Readers are not given up-to-date, helpful information, and the views of critical scholars are often distorted. The ideological dogmatism is so strong that it often undercuts the possibility of the Bible bringing fresh perspectives. The ELCA version is much better and can lead to very fruitful insights. It is written by competent and responsible scholars, who admit many open questions and let readers decide for themselves.[40]

---

38 Ralph Klein, "Competing Contemporary Lutheran Study Bibles," *Currents in Theology and Mission* 39 (October 2012): 370.

39 Klein, "Competing Contemporary Lutheran Study Bibles," 373.

40 Klein, "Competing Contemporary Lutheran Study Bibles," 373.

Robert H. Smith

A native of Holyoke, Massachusetts, Robert H. Smith (1932–2006) was called to Concordia Seminary's faculty in 1968. He had come from a ten-year pastorate in Chappaqua, New York, during which he finished his doctorate in New Testament at the St. Louis seminary.

Smith wrote numerous articles and books.[41] Perhaps his most significant book after the Walkout was on accounts of Jesus' resurrection in the four Gospels.[42] Early on in this volume, he declared that "this book is not another attack, nor on the other hand it is not one more defense of the historical truth of Easter."[43]

Smith made good on this claim. He did not engage the question of the historical veracity of the resurrection itself. Instead, he offered a study of the resurrection narratives contained in each of the four Gospels, examining literary techniques employed by each of the evangelists as they sought to accent theological themes and motifs interpreting the Passion, death, and resurrection of Jesus. To do so, Smith provided verse by verse commentary on each of the four Gospel accounts. Although his primary concern was not to get at the events testified in these narratives by uncovering earlier oral traditions and/or documents, he did clearly engage to an extent in such form criticism as he interpreted the accounts of the empty tomb and the appearances of the risen Jesus.

Smith maintained that the central goal of the New Testament is not to defend the resurrection but to bear testimony to the saving significance of the resurrected Christ. He wrote:

> Luke comes closer than the other evangelists to asserting and defending the reality of Jesus' resurrection (Luke 24:36–43), and yet even he has other and more basic concerns. John is terribly misunderstood when Thomas (20:24–29) is viewed as a modern skeptic, questioning miracles and demanding empirical evidence. Too much of the wrong thing has been made of Matthew's remark about the rumor of the theft of Jesus' body (28:15).[44]

---

41 Smith's books include the Concordia Commentary volume on *Acts* (St. Louis: Concordia Publishing House, 1970) and Augsburg Commentary on the New Testament volumes on *Hebrews* (Minneapolis: Augsburg, 1984) and *Matthew* (Minneapolis: Augsburg, 1989).

42 Robert H. Smith, *Easter Gospels: The Resurrection of Jesus according to the Four Evangelists* (Minneapolis: Augsburg, 1983).

43 Smith, *Easter Gospels*, 9.

44 Smith, *Easter Gospels*, 10.

252

Everett Kalin

Everett Kalin (b. 1929) came to the St. Louis faculty to teach New Testament after service as a pastor in the Atlantic District. An area of interest for him was the topic of canonicity, that is, which books belong in the Bible and why. In his Harvard doctoral work, he defended the assertion that the early church recognized many writings as inspired, but this did not qualify them all as canonical. Rather, "the inspired community" recognized particular writings as giving authentic witness to the Gospel of Jesus Christ.[45]

Elsewhere Kalin's use of redaction criticism is prominent. For example, in one article he tried to show how the author of the Gospel of Matthew in 9:18–26 shaped material from Mark 5:21–43 to tell the stories of a girl returned to life and of a woman cured from a flow of blood. According to Kalin, redaction criticism enables readers to see how the evangelist brought out the Good News of Jesus and His kingdom for a specific audience.[46]

Like many of his Seminex colleagues, he would come to support the ordination of gays and lesbians. In an article on Romans 1:26–27, Kalin argued that this text cannot be used to close today's discussion on homosexuality, as Paul was speaking in a different cultural context. Even if there are conflicting but strongly held views on the legitimacy of same-sex relations, Paul still calls on Christians to welcome one another (Romans 15:7).[47]

Robert Bertram

Robert W. Bertram (1921–2003) came from a prominent Missouri Synod family. His father, Martin, was a professor at the Synod's college in Fort Wayne and a prolific translator. Robert's maternal grandfather was W. H. T. Dau, a professor at St. Louis and later president of Valparaiso University, perhaps best-known as the compiler and translator of C. F. W. Walther's classic work on the distinction between Law and Gospel.

---

45 For the phrase "inspired community," see an article Kalin wrote already prior to the Walkout: "The Inspired Community: A Glance at Canon History," *CTM* (September 1971): 541–49. Thirty years later, Robert Smith reported that Kalin thought Martin Luther King's "Letter from Birmingham Jail" ought to be included in the biblical canon and read in church assemblies. See Robert H. Smith, "Oh, Brother! A Tribute to Everett Kalin," *Currents in Theology and Mission* 26 (December 2001): 546.

46 E.g., Everett Kalin, "Matthew 9:18–26: An Exercise in Redaction Criticism," *Currents in Theology and Mission* 15 (February 1988): 47.

47 Everett Kalin, "Romans 1:26–27 and Homosexuality," *Currents in Theology and Mission* 30 (December 2003): 432.

Robert Bertram received his doctorate from the University of Chicago, where he had studied under, among others, then-Missourian Jaroslav Pelikan. After teaching for years in the theology department at Valparaiso, he joined the St. Louis faculty in 1963. He became known for his intellectual depth and his creative and engaging use of traditional Lutheran categories.

Bertram was concerned to connect the confession of Christ with life in the church and the world. His "crossing" way of doing theology bears some resemblance to Paul Tillich's "method of correlation." Bertram saw Christian witness taking place as the Law is used to diagnose the problem of sin expressed personally and socially in multiple ways, as life is bent inward in unbelief. In 2004, Bertram summed up his understanding of the Law's two functions:

> To put the matter in the old Lutheran jargon, precisely as the first function of the law, its *usus civilis* [civil use], begins to succeed in us, socializing us and improving our behavior, simultaneously its second function, its *usus theologicus* [theological use], takes over and "accuses" us, like a reality check, reminding us once more of how far we fall short.[48]

The Gospel comes as a liberating word by which sin is forgiven and human beings are set right with God to live in freedom within the world for the good of their fellow human beings and the whole creation.

For Bertram, the exclusive task of the church is to confess this Gospel. He viewed the confession made in 1530 at Augsburg as a model for the act of confessing today. Not surprisingly, Bertram participated in the U.S. Lutheran— Roman Catholic Dialogue.[49]

After the Walkout, Bertram cofounded the Crossings Community with his colleague Edward Schroeder. Crossings was to apply theology to life. Like Schroeder, Bertram dealt with a variety of topics, though he tended to pay

---

48 Robert Bertram, "Faithful Teaching, but Religious?" in *By Faith Alone: Essays on Justification in Honor of Gerhard O. Forde*, ed. Joseph A. Burgess and Marc Kolden (Grand Rapids: Eerdmans, 2004), 331.

49 Among the essays that Bertram contributed were "Faith Alone Justifies: Luther on *Iustitia Fidei*" and "Recent Lutheran Theologies on Justification by Faith: A Sampling" (both published in *Justification by Faith: Lutherans and Catholics in Dialogue VII*, ed. H. George Anderson, T. Austin Murphy, and Joseph A. Burgess [Minneapolis: Augsburg, 1985], 172–84, 241–55) and "Luther on the Unique Mediatorship of Christ" (in *The One Mediator: The Saints, and Mary, Lutherans and Catholics in Dialogue VIII*, ed. H. George Anderson, J. Francis Stafford, and Joseph A. Burgess [Minneapolis: Augsburg, 1992]: 249–62).

close attention to homiletical application and pastoral practices. For example, he provided a critique of "infant Communion."[50]

After Bertram's death, his former student Michael Hoy collected some of his many essays on confession into a volume in the *Lutheran Quarterly* Books series, a book that includes an extensive bibliography of Bertram's writings. These essays deal with examples of Christians crossing worldly authority to make confession: Black churches in the U.S. civil rights movement, South African Christians opposed to Apartheid, Dietrich Bonhoeffer in Nazi Germany, and the revolution of the 1980s in the Philippines. One chapter is devoted to the birth of Seminex as a "confessional movement" over and against what Bertram deemed an abuse of authority in the Missouri Synod's confusing of Law and Gospel.[51] These provocative essays raise a question: for all of his good intentions of distinguishing the Law from the Gospel, didn't Bertram himself confuse the two as he cast the Gospel as an agency of civil righteousness?

Edward H. Schroeder

Like his senior colleague Robert Bertram, Edward H. Schroeder (1930–2019) taught at Valparaiso University before joining the St. Louis faculty in 1970. Bertram and Schroeder had collaborated on a new theology curriculum at Valparaiso, and they would again work in tandem in St. Louis.

While Bertram commuted to Chicago after he and other Seminex professors relocated there in 1983, Schroeder remained in St. Louis to work with the Crossings Community. This work included retreats, seminars, and the weekly newsletter *Thursday Theology*. This electronic series would contain more than five hundred issues, stretching over a ten-year period. In *Thursday Theology*, the feisty Schroeder provided comments on church life (both in the ELCA and the LCMS), book reviews, observations on ecumenical developments, suggestions for preaching, discussion of mission theology, and his own opinions on political and ethical matters. It was in this final category that Schroeder demonstrated himself to be a champion of the position on same-sex relationships ultimately adopted by the ELCA. Rejecting any appeal to the orders of creation or the place of God's Law in creation, Schroeder argued that the Gospel liberates those who identify as heterosexual or as homosexual to live out their sexual identities in Christ. For Schroeder, the distinction

---

50 Many of Bertram's essays were published in the *Crossings Newsletter* and can be accessed online at www.crossings.org/newsletter.htm.

51 Robert W. Bertram, *A Time for Confessing*, ed. Michael Hoy (Minneapolis: Fortress Press, 2017).

between Law and Promise pushes the church to bless same-sex unions and ordain gay and lesbian candidates for public ministry.[52]

An overview of Schroeder's theology is to be found in a 2016 book that contains several essays by Schroeder's former students.[53] He himself wrote the first three chapters, however, which provide a picture of his theological method. Schroeder reported that he sought to establish the work of the theologian in preaching the wisdom of the cross alone, as in Luther, so that the gift of salvation in the crucified Christ would be fully magnified and broken sinners would be given full consolation. He believed that this approach recast the question of history so that it was not so much one of historicity (that is, what really happened) but how the promise of the Gospel overcomes the history of the threat of the Law and the power of sin in human existence.

Norman Habel

Norman Habel (b. 1932) is an Australian who came to teach at Concordia Seminary in 1960 while completing a doctorate in Old Testament there. He returned to Australia in 1974 after the Walkout. He wrote two commentaries on Job, one in the Cambridge Commentary on the New English Bible series and the other in Westminster's Old Testament Library series.[54] Habel has also contributed to *The Earth Bible Commentary*, a series that seeks to view the Scriptures through the lens of ecology.[55]

Habel has also written a memoir in which he reflects on his life and career. He includes his controversial tenure as an early promoter of Old Testament form criticism at the St. Louis seminary. He further notes how he was under

---

52 For a fuller treatment and critique of Schroeder on this issue, see John T. Pless, "The Use and Misuse of Luther in Contemporary Debates on Homosexuality: A Look at Two Theologians," in *Pastor Craft: Essays and Sermons by John T. Pless* (Irvine, CA: New Reformation Publications, 2020), 499–518.

53 Edward H. Schroeder et al., *Gift and Promise: The Augsburg Confession and the Heart of Christian Theology*, ed. Ronald Neustadt and Stephen Hitchcock (Minneapolis: Fortress Press, 2016).

54 *The Book of Job* (Cambridge: Cambridge University Press, 1975), and *The Book of Job: A Commentary* (Philadelphia: Westminster Press, 1985).

55 *The Birth, the Curse, and the Greening of the Earth: An Ecological Reading of Genesis 1–11* (Sheffield: Sheffield Phoenix Press, 2011), and *Finding Wisdom in Nature: An Eco-Wisdom Reading of the Book of Job* (Sheffield: Sheffield Phoenix Press, 2014).

great suspicion and was not allowed to teach or preach in the Lutheran Church in Australia for several years after his return to his native land.[56]

Habel's fascination with ecology pushes him to a position that appears to be close to pantheistic. Even Matthew Becker, who is generally sympathetic to Habel and the theology of Seminex more broadly, writes of Habel's memoirs:

> Even non-fundamentalist Lutherans might find some material objectionable here. While the author is to be commended for his frequent return to the theme of *sola gratia*, which serves as the book's *cantus firmus*, how Lutheran can one be, if one denies the doctrinal content of Article II of the Augsburg Confession [on original sin] or affirms what appears to be a form of animism? Still, Habel has a wonderful way with words, and there is much to ponder in his fine story-telling.[57]

The Difference This Makes

In an interview, Edgar Krentz remarked that teaching at Seminex was a liberating experience. He no longer had to carefully weigh his words for fear that some student was taking notes for the purpose of reporting him to Synod officials for the content of his lecture.[58] Similarly, after Seminex started, the books and articles written by its faculty were published in large part by non-LCMS publishers and so were not subject to LCMS doctrinal review. No longer beholden to the Synod, the professors found themselves free to write more clearly, without nuancing their words to meet doctrinal criteria expected by the LCMS.

In other words, their post-Walkout writings reflect their theological commitments with greater clarity. Prior to the Walkout, positions implicitly held were not always explicitly stated. At that time, a concerted effort had been made to convince clergy and laity that no one had changed the fundamental doctrine of the Synod. The faculty's post-Walkout writings demonstrate that this was not the case. These writings by Seminex professors make it clear that their theological convictions and teachings had indeed changed from those traditionally embraced by the Missouri Synod.

Their theology was, in large part, shaped by the academy more than the church. Unlike their Saxon ancestors who would have wanted nothing to do with the Prussian Union in the nineteenth century, the theologians of

---

56 Norm Habel, *Why on Earth Are You Still a Lutheran? Memoirs of a Heretic* (Eugene, OR: Wipf & Stock, 2016).

57 Matthew Becker, review of *Why on Earth Are You still a Lutheran?* by Norman Habel, *Lutheran Quarterly* 31 (Winter 2017): 467.

58 Interview with Edgar Krentz, http://vimeo.com120244026. Accessed 12/31/2021.

Photograph by Paul Ockrassa

Two days into the student moratorium, Dr. Robert Preus, acting vice president of academic affairs, addresses the Concordia Seminary community concerning plans for classes (January 23, 1974).

Seminex valued ecumenical respectability over confessional fidelity. Freedom of thought and of expression took precedence over submission to an inerrant Bible. The change of direction which had been more nuanced and subtle in the 1960s and '70s became increasingly clear after 1974.

Observers outside of the LCMS recognized this as well. Carl Braaten (b. 1930), who was on the faculty of the Lutheran School of Theology at Chicago when Seminex professors relocated there in 1983, observed: "Having been condemned as liberals and heretics by their home church, they became advocates of progressive agendas in their new ecclesial setting. The poison of political correctness spread into every aspect of seminary life."[59] Roy Harrisville (b. 1922) of Luther Seminary, St. Paul, Minnesota, commented on the former Missourians: "When the umbilical cord was cut those dissidents tended to run amok."[60]

It appears that many of the Seminex faculty wanted to make it clear that whatever their theology was, it was not that of the Missouri Synod. In varying

---

59 Carl Braaten, *Because of Christ: Memoirs of a Lutheran Theologian* (Grand Rapids: Eerdmans, 2010), 120.

60 Roy Harrisville, *A Memoir: That Reminds Me* (Roseville, MN: Eclipse Press, 2020), 209.

258

degrees, their writings after the Walkout show the trajectory they had set for themselves while they were still at Concordia Seminary, a trajectory that would continue and even intensify in their new church home.

For Discussion

1. What is the relationship between academic freedom and confessional fidelity in the Missouri Synod's universities and seminaries?

2. How did the theological positions taken by the Seminex theologians shape the stance on sexual ethics taken by the ELCA?

3. It is clear that the Seminex theologians wanted to engage the world outside of the LCMS. How did these theologians attempt to do this? Were they successful? What lessons might we learn from their experience?

4. What do you think the Missouri Synod would look like today if the Walkout had never happened?

Digging Deeper

Braaten. Carl E. "Robert W. Bertram and Edward H. Schroeder." Pages 11–28 in *A Harvest of Lutheran Dogmatics and Ethics: The Life and Work of Twelve Theologians 1960–2020*. Delhi, NY: ALPB Books, 2021.

Klein, Ralph W. "*Currents in Theology and Mission*: A History." *Currents in Theology and Mission* 43 (January 2016): 3–7.

Pless, John T. "Taking the Pulse of Theology in the Missouri Synod." *Concordia Theological Quarterly* 83 (January–April 2019): 27–41.

Sasse, Hermann. "Inclusive Lutheranism." Pages 341–45 in *The Lonely Way: Selected Essays and Letters by Hermann Sasse*. Volume 2: *1941–1976*. Translated by Matthew C. Harrison et al. St. Louis: Concordia Publishing House, 2002.

A SINGULAR EVENT WITH AN ABIDING EFFECT

The 1974 Seminary Walkout

Dean O. Wenthe

A key interpretive principle for a Lutheran confession is that *sola gratia* precedes *sola fide* and *sola Scriptura*. It is God's grace that bestows faith in the blessed and holy Trinity and trust in Sacred Scripture through the activity of the Holy Spirit. From the 1960s to the present, God's abiding grace has blessed the confession and theological life of the LCMS. Her clear affirmation of the authority and infallibility of Scripture and of a *quia* rather than a *quatenus* subscription to the Lutheran Confessions[1] is a great gift and treasure from God. In a time when denomination after denomination has abandoned two thousand years of Christian teaching and practice, especially on ethical issues, but also on central tenets of Christology and theology, the LCMS stands out for her commitment to Christian and Lutheran orthodoxy. For all of her human frailties, she has much for which to be grateful.

At the center, her uniqueness is a robust rejection of the historical-critical method. This method of scriptural study challenges the authority and clarity of Sacred Scripture by viewing the claims of Scripture as fluid and plastic, without enduring, objective meaning. With classical Lutheranism, the Missouri Synod continues to confess that Scripture provides a normative narrative from creation to consummation, with Jesus Christ as the center. The 1974 Walkout by the majority of the faculty and students of Concordia Seminary provides a dramatic display of the way the practice or rejection of

---

1   Editor's note: That is, that we subscribe to the Lutheran Confessions because (*quia*) they are a true exposition of the Bible, not merely insofar as (*quatenus*) they truly reflect God's Word.

the historical-critical method changed theologies and impacted lives. It was a singular, pivotal, and public event, the effects of which remain prominent in the life of the church.

As a student at the St. Louis seminary from 1967 to 1971, I directly observed: (1) the election of Dr. John Tietjen in 1969; (2) the teaching of the historical-critical method by the majority of the seminary faculty; and (3) the 1971 visit of President J. A. O. Preus's Fact Finding Committee. Also, while a student, I served as Dr. Martin Scharlemann's grader and benefited from the leadership of the faculty minority. Dr. Ralph Bohlmann and Dr. Robert Preus welcomed a group of confessional students to their homes every two weeks for conversation and encouragement. Their erudition and pastoral care for students in the theological minority on campus was a great gift.

When the Walkout occurred, I was serving as a Hebrew instructor at Concordia Theological Seminary. With Dr. Harold Buls, Dr. Walter Maier, and Dr. David Scaer, I traveled to St. Louis to teach the few students who remained for spring quarter, 1974. The campus seemed like a ghost town! There were some fifty of them, compared to more than seven hundred during the 1970–71 academic year. Yet the recovery of Concordia Seminary proved swift and remarkable. Gifted professors and capable students brought fresh and vibrant life and instruction back to the campus. Indeed, Dr. Robert Preus, who in mid-1974 became president of Concordia Theological Seminary, quietly relaxed recruitment for the benefit of the sister seminary.

Beyond my personal experience, however, is the Walkout's abiding theological significance. The departure of the leaders who were espousing and advocating for the historical-critical method made the recovery of biblical authority clear and swift. With ready hearts and minds, my students received the teaching of the early Lutheran fathers, namely, that the Sacred Scriptures are the *viva vox Jesu* ("the living voice of Jesus") through His prophets and apostles. The church has much for which to be grateful, as the various contributions in this volume indicate.

At the same time, we need to confess and use Sacred Scripture to meet new and significant challenges. Here are two that require attention and rejection.

First is the abiding influence of the historical-critical method not only on Sacred Scripture but also on all literature. It is as though the historical-critical method has reached its ultimate goal in French philosophers such as Jacques Derrida and Michel Foucault. As such thinkers have taught people to read texts, there is no longer any search for truth.[2] The resulting "deconstruction"

---

2   See Mark Bauerlein, "Truth, Reading, Decadence," *First Things* 314 (June/July 2021): 21–26.

Photograph by Paul Ockrassa

Dr. Martin H. Scharlemann, acting president of Concordia Seminary, receives a copy of the student resolution regarding the moratorium from Seminarian David Reichert at the entry to the President's Office at Concordia Seminary (January 21, 1974).

of the various writings in the literary canon has negatively impacted the view of all texts, including the perception of the biblical canon. This, combined with growing dependency on electronic forms of communication, has reduced the capacity of succeeding generations seriously to engage and study a text. It is key that the church challenge the radical reduction in the knowledge of Sacred Scripture.[3]

In a world where countless young people suffer as they search for their identity, the Bible invites them to the wonderful truth that each and every human being is made in the image of God—the very apex of God's creative work—and is also the object of God's love and mercy in the incarnation, life, death, resurrection, and ascension of Jesus of Nazareth. Further, the Scriptures are more than truthful information. They are meant to be lived. They are the source of life as we understand who God is and who we are: "Your word is a lamp to my feet and a light to my path" (Psalm 119:105). The Collect for the Word rightly focuses on our need to be defined by and guided by the

---

3   See John W. Kleinig, "The Rags of Scripture Rather than the Robes of Reason: Johann Georg Hamann," *CTQ* 86 (July/October 2022): 339–50.

Scriptures: "Grant that we may so hear them, read, mark, learn, and inwardly digest them."[4]

A second significant challenge is the manner in which natural law has lost its traction in our culture. In previous generations, many who did not recognize Scripture's authority still affirmed the humanity of the unborn, that marriage was a bond between a man and a woman, etc. Carl Trueman describes our current context:

> Whereas the problems for Christian institutions in the early 20th century might be described as having been a crisis in the understanding of God—could he become incarnate, rise from the dead and reveal himself to his creatures—the problems of the early 21st century are different in kind. They can be characterized as a crisis in what it means to be human. Are embryos persons? Are sex differences morally significant? Is "gender identity" different from sex? It is ironic that disagreements about the creature may prove more devastating to the church than those about the Creator.[5]

May this volume with its historical insights further the witness of the church and deepen our affection for and belief in the Sacred Scriptures, "the living voice" of Jesus through the prophets and apostles. As the liturgy reminds us: "Jesus Christ is the Light of the world, the light no darkness can overcome."[6]

---

4   *LSB*, 308.

5   *The Wall Street Journal*, November 11, 2022.

6   *LSB*, 243.

A STATEMENT OF SCRIPTURAL AND CONFESSIONAL PRINCIPLES

I
Christ as Savior and Lord

We believe, teach, and confess that Jesus Christ is our Savior and Lord, and that through faith in Him we receive forgiveness of sins, eternal life, and salvation. We confess that "our works cannot reconcile God or merit forgiveness of sins and grace but that we obtain forgiveness and grace only by faith when we believe that we are received into favor for Christ's sake, who alone has been ordained to be the mediator and propitiation through whom the Father is reconciled" (AC, XX, 9).[1] We believe that Jesus Christ is the only way to heaven and that all who die without faith in Him are eternally damned. We believe that those who believe in Christ will enjoy a blissful relationship with Him during the interim between their death and His second coming and that on the last day their bodies will be raised.

We therefore reject the following:

1. That we may operate on the assumption that there may be other ways of salvation than through faith in Jesus Christ;

2. That some persons who lack faith in Christ may be considered "anonymous Christians";

3. That there is no eternal hell for unbelievers and ungodly men.

II
Law and Gospel

We believe that the two chief doctrines of Holy Scripture, Law and Gospel, must be constantly and diligently proclaimed in the church of God until the end of the world, but with due distinction (FC, SD, V, 24). The Law, as the expression of God's immutable will, is to be used by the church to bring men to a knowledge of their

---

1   Quotations from the Lutheran Confessions in this appendix are from *The Book of Concord: The Confessions of the Evangelical Lutheran Church*, ed. Theodore G. Tappert (Philadelphia: Fortress Press, 1959).

sins as well as to provide Christians with instruction about good works (FC, SD, V, 17–18). The Gospel receives the primary emphasis in the ministry of the New Testament, for it is the message that "God forgives them all their sins through Christ, accepts them for His sake as God's children, and out of pure grace, without any merit of their own, justifies and saves them" (FC, SD, V, 25).

We therefore reject the following:

1. That the Gospel is any message or action which brings good news to a bad situation.

2. That the Gospel is a norm or standard for the Christian life, or that the Gospel, in effect, imposes a new law upon the Christian.

3. That what God's Law declares to be sinful (for example, adultery or theft) need not be regarded as sinful in all times and situations.

4. That Christians, as men who have been freed from the curse of the Law, no longer need the instruction of the Law to know what God's will is for their life and conduct.

III
Mission of the Church

We believe, teach, and confess that the primary mission of the church is to make disciples of every nation by bearing witness to Jesus Christ through the preaching of the Gospel and the administration of the sacraments. Other necessary activities of the church, such as ministering to men's physical needs, are to serve the church's primary mission and its goal that men will believe and confess Jesus Christ as their Lord and Savior.

We therefore reject any views of the mission of the church which imply:

That an adequate or complete witness to Jesus Christ can be made without proclaiming or verbalizing the Gospel.

IV
Holy Scripture

A. *The Inspiration of Scripture*

We believe, teach, and confess that all Scripture is given by the inspiration of God the Holy Spirit and that God is therefore the true Author of every word of Scripture. We acknowledge that there is a qualitative difference between the inspired witness of Holy Scripture in all its parts and words and the witness of every other form of human expression, making the Bible a unique book.

We therefore reject the following views:

1. That the Holy Scriptures are inspired only in the sense that all Christians are "inspired" to confess the lordship of Jesus Christ.

2. That the Holy Spirit did not inspire the actual words of the Biblical authors but merely provided these men with special guidance.

266

3. That only those matters in Holy Scripture were inspired by the Holy Spirit which directly pertain to Jesus Christ and man's salvation.

4. That noncanonical writings in the Christian tradition can be regarded as "inspired" in the same sense as Holy Scripture.

5. That portions of the New Testament witness to Jesus Christ contain imaginative additions which had their origin in the early Christian community and do not present actual facts.

B. *The Purpose of Scripture*

We believe that all Scripture bears witness to Jesus Christ and that its primary purpose is to make men wise unto salvation through faith in Jesus Christ. We therefore affirm that the Scriptures are rightly used only when they are read from the perspective of justification by faith and the proper distinction between Law and Gospel. Since the saving work of Jesus Christ was accomplished through His personal entrance into our history and His genuinely historical life, death, and resurrection, we acknowledge that the recognition of the soteriological purpose of Scripture in no sense permits us to call into question or deny the historicity or factuality of matters recorded in the Bible.

We therefore reject the following views:

1. That knowing the facts and data presented in the Scripture, without relating them to Jesus Christ and His work of salvation, represents an adequate approach to Holy Scripture.

2. That the Old Testament, read on its own terms, does not bear witness to Jesus Christ.

3. That it is permissible to reject the historicity of events or the occurrence of miracles recorded in the Scriptures so long as there is no confusion of Law and Gospel.

4. That recognition of the primary purpose of Scripture makes it irrelevant whether such questions of fact as the following are answered in the affirmative: Were Adam and Eve real historical individuals? Did Israel cross the Red Sea on dry land? Did the brazen serpent miracle actually take place? Was Jesus really born of a virgin? Did Jesus perform all the miracles attributed to Him? Did Jesus' resurrection actually involve the return to life of His dead body?

C. *The Gospel and Holy Scripture*
(Material and Formal Principles)

We believe, teach, and confess that the Gospel of the gracious justification of the sinner through faith in Jesus Christ is not only the chief doctrine of Holy Scripture and a basic presupposition for the interpretation of Scripture, but the heart and center of our Christian faith and theology (material principle). We also believe, teach, and confess that only "the Word of God shall establish articles of faith" (SA, II, ii, 15), and that "the prophetic and apostolic writings of the Old and New Testaments are the only rule and norm according to which all doctrines and teachers alike must be appraised and judged" (FC, Ep, Rule and Norm, 1) (formal principle). The Gospel which is the center of our theology is the Gospel to which the *Scriptures* bear witness, while the Scriptures from which we derive our theology direct us steadfastly to the *Gospel* of Jesus Christ.

We reject the following distortions of the relationship between the Gospel and the Bible (the material and formal principles):

1. That acceptance of the Bible as such, rather than the Gospel, is the heart and center of Christian faith and theology, and the way to eternal salvation.

2. That the Gospel, rather than Scripture, is the norm for appraising and judging all doctrines and teachers (as, for example, when a decision on the permissibility of ordaining women into the pastoral office is made on the basis of the "Gospel" rather than on the teaching of Scripture as such).

3. That the historicity or facticity of certain Biblical accounts (such as the Flood or the Fall) may be questioned, provided this does not distort the Gospel.

4. That Christians need not accept matters taught in the Scriptures that are not a part of the "Gospel."

D. *The Authority of Scripture*

We believe, teach, and confess that because the Scriptures have God as their author, they possess both the divine power to make men wise unto salvation through faith in Jesus Christ (causative authority), as well as the divine authority to serve as the church's sole standard of doctrine and life (normative authority). We recognize that the authority of Scripture can be accepted only through faith and not merely by rational demonstration. As men of faith, we affirm not only that Holy Scripture is powerful and efficacious, but also that it is "the only judge, rule, and norm according to which as the only touchstone all doctrines should and must be understood and judged as good or evil, right or wrong" (FC, Ep, Rule and Norm, 7).

We therefore reject the following views:

1. That the authority of Scripture is limited to its efficacy in bringing men to salvation in Jesus Christ.

2. That the authority of Scripture has reference only to what the Scriptures *do* (as means of grace) rather than to what they *are* (as the inspired Word of God).

3. That the Scriptures are authoritative for the doctrine and life of the church, not because of their character as the inspired and inerrant Word of God but because they are the oldest available written sources for the history of ancient Israel and for the life and message of Jesus Christ, or because they were written by the chosen and appointed leaders of Israel and of the early church, or because the church declared them to be canonical.

4. That the Christian community in every age is directly inspired by the Holy Spirit and is therefore free to go beyond the doctrine of the prophets

and apostles in determining the content of certain aspects of its faith and witness.

E. *The Canonical Text of Scripture*

We believe, teach, and confess that the authoritative Word for the church today is the canonical Word, not precanonical sources, forms, or traditions—however useful the investigation of these possibilities may on occasion be for a clearer understanding of what the canonical text intends to say.

We therefore reject the following views:

1. That there are various "meanings" of a Biblical text or pericope to be discovered at various stages of its precanonical history, or that the meaning a canonical text has now may differ from the meaning it had when it was first written.

2. That Biblical materials that are judged to be "authentic" (for example, "authentic" words of Jesus, "authentic" books of Paul, or "authentic" ideas of Moses) have greater authority than "non-authentic" Biblical statements.

3. That certain pericopes or passages in the canonical text of Scripture may be regarded as imaginative additions of the Biblical authors or of the early Christian community and therefore need not be accepted as fully authoritative.

4. That extracanonical sources may be used in such a way as to call into question the clear meaning of the canonical text.

5. That the essential theological data of Biblical theology is to be found in the precanonical history of the Biblical text.

6. That certain canonical materials have greater authority than other canonical materials because of their greater antiquity or because they are allegedly more "genuine" or "authentic."

7. That various statements of Jesus recorded in the Gospels may not actually be from Jesus and therefore lack historical factuality or the full measure of His authority.

F. *The Infallibility of Scripture*

With Luther, we confess that "God's Word cannot err" (LC, IV, 57). We therefore believe, teach, and confess that since the Holy Scriptures are the Word of God, they contain no errors or contradictions but that they are in all their parts and words the infallible truth. We hold that the opinion that Scripture contains errors is a violation of the *sola scriptura* principle, for it rests upon the acceptance of some norm or criterion of truth above the Scriptures. We recognize that there are apparent contradictions or discrepancies and problems which arise because of uncertainty over the original text.

We reject the following views:

1. That the Scriptures contain theological as well as factual contradictions and errors.

2. That the Scriptures are inerrant only in matters pertaining directly to the Gospel message of salvation.

3. That the Scriptures are only functionally inerrant, that is, that the Scriptures are "inerrant" only in the sense that they accomplish their aim of bringing the Gospel of salvation to men.

4. That the Biblical authors accommodated themselves to using and repeating as true the erroneous notions of their day (for example, the claim that Paul's statements on the role of women in the church are not binding today because they are the culturally conditioned result of the apostle's sharing the views of contemporary Judaism as a child of his time).

5. That statements of Jesus and the New Testament writers concerning the human authorship of portions of the Old Testament or the historicity of certain Old Testament persons and events need not be regarded as true (for example, the Davidic authorship of Psalm 110, the historicity of Jonah, or the fall of Adam and Eve).

6. That only those aspects of a Biblical statement need to be regarded as true that are in keeping with the alleged *intent* of the passage (for example, that Paul's statement about Adam and Eve in Romans 5 and 1 Corinthians 11 do not prove the historicity of Adam and Eve because this was not the specific intent of the apostle; or that the virgin birth of our Lord may be denied because the infancy narratives in Matthew and Luke did not have the specific intent to discuss a biological miracle).

7. That Jesus did not make some of the statements or perform some of the deeds attributed to Him in the Gospels but that they were in fact invented or created by the early Christian community or the evangelists to meet their specific needs.

8. That the Biblical authors sometimes placed statements into the mouths of people who in fact did not make them (for example, the claim that the "Deuteronomist" places a speech in Solomon's mouth which Solomon never actually made), or that they relate events as having actually taken place that did not in fact occur (for example, the fall of Adam and Eve, the crossing of the Red Sea on dry land, the episode of the brazen serpent, Jesus' cursing of the fig tree, John the Baptist's experiences in the wilderness, Jesus' changing water into wine, Jesus' walking on water, or even Jesus' bodily resurrection from the dead or the fact of His empty tomb).

9. That the use of certain "literary forms" necessarily calls into question the historicity of that which is being described (for example, that the alleged midrashic form of the infancy narratives in Matthew and Luke suggests that no virgin birth actually occurred, or that the literary form of Genesis 3 argues against the historicity of the Fall).

G. *The Unity of Scripture*

We believe, teach, and confess that since the same God speaks throughout Holy Scripture, there is an organic unity both within and between the Old and New Testaments. While acknowledging the rich variety of language and style in Scripture and recognizing differences of emphasis in various accounts of the same event or topic, we nevertheless affirm that the same doctrine of the Gospel, in all its articles, is presented throughout the entire Scripture.

We reject the view that Holy Scripture, both within and between its various books and authors, presents us with conflicting or contradictory teachings and theologies. We regard this view not only as violating the Scripture's own understanding of itself but also as making it impossible for the church to have and confess a unified theological position that is truly Biblical and evangelical.

H. *Old Testament Prophecy*

Since the New Testament is the culminating written revelation of God, we affirm that it is decisive in determining the relation between the two Testaments and the meaning of Old Testament prophecies in particular, for the meaning of a prophecy becomes known in full only from its fulfillment. With the Lutheran Confessions, we recognize the presence of Messianic prophecies about Jesus Christ throughout the Old Testament. Accordingly, we acknowledge that the Old Testament "promises that the Messiah will come and promises forgiveness of sins, justification, and eternal life for His sake" (Apology, IV, 5) and that the patriarchs and their descendants comforted themselves with such Messianic promises (cf. FC, SD, V, 23).

We therefore reject the following views:

1. That the New Testament statements about Old Testament texts and events do not establish their meaning (for example, the claim that Jesus' reference to Psalm 110 in Matthew 22:43–44 does not establish either the psalm's Davidic authorship or its predictive Messianic character).

2. That Old Testament prophecies are to be regarded as Messianic prophecies, not in the sense of being genuinely predictive, but only in the sense that the New Testament later applies them to New Testament events.

3. That the Old Testament prophets never recognized that their prophecies reached beyond their own time to the time of Christ.

I. *Historical Methods of Biblical Interpretation*

Since God is the Lord of history and has revealed Himself by acts in history and has in the person of His Son actually entered into man's history, we acknowledge that the historical framework in which the Gospel message is set in Scripture is an essential part of the Word. Furthermore, we recognize that the inspired Scriptures are historical documents written in various times, places, and circumstances. We therefore believe that the Scriptures invite historical investigation and are to be taken seriously as historical documents. We affirm, however, that the Christian interpreter of Scripture cannot adopt uncritically the presuppositions and canons of the secular historian, but that he will be guided in his use of historical techniques by the presuppositions of his faith in the Lord of history, who reveals Himself in Holy Scripture as the one who creates, sustains, and even enters our history in order to lead it to His end.

We therefore reject the following views:

1. That the question of whether certain events described in the Scripture actually happened is unimportant in view of the purpose and function of Holy Scripture.

2. That methods based on secularistic and naturalistic notions of history, such as the following, may have a valid role in Biblical interpretation:

   a. That the universe is closed to the intervention of God or any supernatural force.

   b. That miracles are to be explained in naturalistic terms whenever possible.

   c. That the principle of the economy of miracles may lead us to deny certain miracles reported in the Scriptures.

   d. That the doctrines of Holy Scripture are the result of a natural development or evolution of ideas and experiences within Israel and the early church.

   e. That the message of Scripture can be adequately measured by laws derived exclusively from empirical data and rational observation.

   f. That man's inability to know the future makes genuine predictive prophecy an impossibility.

3. That our primary concern in Biblical interpretation is not with explaining the meaning of the primary sources, namely, the canonical Scriptures, on the basis of the sources themselves.

4. That if the use of historical methods leads to conclusions at variance with the evident meaning of the Biblical text, such conclusions may be accepted without violating the Lutheran view of Scripture or our commitment to the Lutheran Confessions (for example, the claim that it is permissible to deny the existence of angels or a personal devil because of literary, historical, or theological considerations).

V
Original Sin

We believe, teach, and confess that God, by the almighty power of His Word, created all things. We also believe that man, as the principal creature of God, was specially created in the image of God, that is, in a state of righteousness, innocence, and blessedness. We affirm that Adam and Eve were real historical human beings, the first two people in the world, and that their fall was a historical occurrence which brought sin into the world so that "since the fall of Adam all men who are propagated according to nature are born in sin" (AC, II, 1). We confess that man's fall necessitated the gracious redemptive work of Jesus Christ and that fallen man's only hope for salvation from his sin lies in Jesus Christ, his Redeemer and Lord.

We therefore reject the following:

1. All world views, philosophical theories and exegetical interpretations which pervert these Biblical teachings and thus obscure the Gospel.

2. The notion that man did not come into being through the direct creative action of God, but through a process of evolution from lower forms of life which in turn developed from matter that is either eternal, autonomous, or self-generating.

3. The opinion that the image of God in which Adam and Eve were created did not consist of concreated righteousness, that is, a perfect relationship to God.

4. The notion that Adam and Eve were not real historical persons and that their fall was not a real historical event which brought sin and death into the world.

5. The opinion that original sin does not deprive all men of their spiritual powers and make it impossible for them to be in the right relationship to God apart from faith in Jesus Christ.

VI
Confessional Subscription

We reaffirm our acceptance of the Scriptures as the inspired and inerrant Word of God, and our unconditional subscription to "all the Symbolical Books of the Evangelical Lutheran Church as a true and unadulterated statement and exposition of the Word of God" (Constitution, Article II; cf. also Bylaw 4.21). We accept the Confessions because they are drawn from the Word of God and on that account regard their doctrinal content as a true and binding exposition of Holy Scripture and as authoritative for our work as ministers of Jesus Christ and servants of The Lutheran Church—Missouri Synod.

We accept the following clarifications of the nature of our confessional subscription:

1. We acknowledge that the doctrinal content of the Lutheran Confessions includes not only those doctrines of Holy Scripture explicitly treated in the Confessions but also those Biblical doctrines set forth somewhat indirectly or incidentally, such as the doctrines of Holy Scripture, creation, the Holy Spirit, and eschatology.

2. With the fathers, we recognize that not everything in the Lutheran Confessions is a part of its doctrinal content, but we reject all attempts to abridge the extent of this doctrinal content in an arbitrary or subjective manner. We recognize, for example, that subscription to the Lutheran Confessions does not bind us to all strictly exegetical details contained in the Confessions, or even to the confessional use of certain Bible passages to

support a particular theological statement. However, since the Confessions want to be understood as Biblical expositions, we reject the notion that we are not bound by our confessional subscription to the exposition of Scripture contained in the Confessions or to the doctrinal content which the Confessions derive from individual Bible passages.

3. We recognize that the Confessions must be read and studied in terms of the historical situations in which they were written, but we reject the view that our confessional subscription means only that we regard the Confessions as a historically correct response to the problems encountered by the church when the Confessions were written.

4. We recognize that the doctrinal content of the Confessions centers in Jesus Christ and the Gospel of our justification by grace through faith, but we reject the view that the doctrinal content of the Confessions includes only those confessional statements which explicitly and directly deal with the Gospel of Jesus Christ. Accordingly, we do not accept the idea that our subscription to the Lutheran Confessions permits us to reject such confessional positions as the existence of the devil and of angels or that Adam and Eve were real historical persons whose fall into sin was a real historical event.

5. We recognize that the Lutheran Confessions contain no distinct article on the nature of Holy Scripture and its interpretation, but we acknowledge and accept the confessional understanding of the nature of Holy Scripture and of the proper theological principles for its interpretation.

6. We recognize the Lutheran Confessions as a true exposition of Holy Scripture and therefore reject the opinion that our subscription to the Lutheran Confessions leaves us free to reject any doctrinal statements of the Confessions where we feel there is no supporting Biblical evidence.

7. We acknowledge that our subscription to the Lutheran Confessions pledges us to preach and teach in accordance with the entire Holy Scripture. We therefore reject the opinion that all Biblical matters not explicitly treated in the Lutheran Confessions are open questions.

8. We confess that the Holy Scriptures are the only rule and norm for faith and life, and that other writings "should not be put on a par with Holy Scripture" (FC, Ep, [Rule and Norm,] 1–2). We therefore reject the notion that it is legitimate to maintain the doctrinal conclusions of the Confessions without accepting their Biblical basis, or to regard formal confessional subscription as an adequate safeguard against improper exegetical conclusions.

9. Finally, we affirm that our acceptance of the Lutheran Confessions means not only that we tolerate the doctrinal content of the Lutheran Confessions as a viable option for Lutheran Christians today but that we in fact preach, teach, and confess the doctrinal content of the Lutheran Confessions as our very own.

Conclusion

The 1971 convention of The Lutheran Church—Missouri Synod reaffirmed the Synod's desire to abide by its doctrinal position as stated in its constitution (Article II). The Synod clearly stated its conviction that its confessional base is as broad as Holy Scripture and that the Synod accepts anything and everything that the Scriptures teach. Moreover, the Synod declared its right as a Synod to apply its confessional base definitively to current issues, and thus conserve and promote unity and resist an individualism which breeds schism.

This Statement expresses the Synod's Scriptural and confessional stance on a number of important topics. It is hoped that the endorsement of this Statement will be of assistance to the Synod in the "conservation and promotion of the unity of the true faith" (Constitution, Article III).

The Resolution of the Missouri Synod Adopting
A Statement of Scriptural and Confessional Principles

In its July 6–13, 1973, synodical convention, The Lutheran Church—Missouri Synod officially adopted A Statement of Scriptural and Confessional Principles *as a "statement of belief" which "expresses the Synod's position on current doctrinal issues." The full text of the convention's action is as follows:*

Preamble

The Formula of Concord, in the Lutheran Confessions, mentions Doctor Luther as asserting that "the Word of God is and should remain the sole rule and norm of doctrine, and that no human being's writings dare be placed on a par with it, but that everything be subjected to it." The next paragraph begins: "This, of course, does not mean that other good, useful, and pure books such as interpretations of the Holy Scriptures, refutations of errors, and expositions of doctrinal articles, should be rejected. If they are in accord with the aforementioned pattern of doctrine they are to be accepted and used as helpful expositions and explanations." (FC, SD, Summary, paragraphs 9–10)

Doctor Walther's "Thirteen Theses," which emerged during the Predestinarian Controversy in America, surely fit into this category. The first of these theses appeared in *Der Lutheraner*, 15 January 1880, and the last in the 1 May 1880 issue. The entire 13 were approved one year later by a vast majority at the synodical convention in Fort Wayne, 11–12 May 1881 (Missouri Synod Proceedings, 1881, pp. 35–36, 41)

Our Synod has continued to be greatly concerned with doctrine, as past convention resolutions indicate (1950–1971). Also, in order to clarify the status of doctrinal statements, the Synod approved Resolution 5-24, "Status of Synodically Adopted Doctrinal Statements," at the Milwaukee convention, July 1971, which reads:

RESOLVED, That the Synod reaffirm the desirability of the formulation of doctrinal statements which clearly set forth the teachings of the Holy Scriptures and apply them to issues of our day; and be it further

RESOLVED, That the Synod clearly state that such doctrinal formulations are subordinate to the Lutheran Confessions; and be it further

RESOLVED, That the Synod distinguish between resolutions concerning doctrine formulated and adopted at a convention and more formal statements of belief which are produced by officially authorized groups, and which are then presented to the congregations and clergy of the Synod for study and discussion, and which are subsequently adopted by a synodical convention; and be it further

RESOLVED, That the Synod reaffirm the resolutions of recent conventions that the Synod "honor and uphold the synodically adopted statements as valid interpretations of Christian doctrine" (1969 Proceedings, p. 91); and be it finally

RESOLVED, That in the case of the aforementioned more formal and comprehensive statements of belief that the Synod declare

(1) its position that these statements, together with all other formulations of doctrine, derive their authority from the Word of God which they set forth from the Holy Scriptures;

(2) its insistence that the ministry of the church regard these formulations with special seriousness and that those who disagree with these formulations in part or in whole be held to present their objections to them formally to those officials whom the Synod has given the immediate supervision of their doctrine;

(3) its conviction that as a result of joint study of the Word of God the Holy Spirit will lead the Synod into all truth, that possible errors in the aforementioned statements will be discovered and corrected, that instances of failure to submit to the clear teaching of the Holy Scriptures will be evangelically dealt with on an individual pastoral basis, and that the Synod can speak with a voice that is Scriptural, Gospel-oriented, truly Lutheran, and that we will continue to "walk together" as a true Synod.

Accordingly, the following resolution is herewith submitted.

WHEREAS, A Statement of Scriptural and Confessional Principles, issued by the President of The Lutheran Church—Missouri Synod in consultation with the vice-presidents of the Synod, 3 March 1972, addresses itself to the doctrinal issues troubling the church today; and

WHEREAS, A Statement presents what the Synod throughout its history has confessed and taught on these issues, as witnessed to by synodical statements, catechetical expositions, and convention resolutions; and

WHEREAS, A Statement is, therefore, neither a new standard of orthodoxy nor a document "based on private writings, but on such books as have been composed, approved, and received in the name of the churches which pledge themselves to one doctrine and religion" (FC, SD, Comp. Summary, paragraph 2); and

WHEREAS, The Synod's Commission on Theology and Church Relations has evaluated A Statement as follows:

We find the doctrinal content of A Statement to be in accord with the Scriptures and the Lutheran Confessions and to contain nothing contrary to them. We also find the doctrinal content of A Statement of Scriptural and Confessional Principles to be in accord with the doctrinal position of The Lutheran Church—Missouri Synod as it has been taught historically and expressed in the official doctrinal statements of the Synod [Adopted 3 November 1972]; and

WHEREAS, A Statement, in its entirety, has been presented to the congregations and clergy of the Synod, and during the past 16 months has been studied and discussed throughout the church, and has been approved by various synodical boards (Board of Control, Springfield; Board for Higher Education) and congregations; and

WHEREAS, The Lutheran church in the past, when confronted with doctrinal controversy and crisis, has accepted expressions of belief which are in agreement with Scripture and the Lutheran Confessions, e.g., the Thirteen Theses of Doctor Walther, 1881; therefore be it

RESOLVED, That The Lutheran Church—Missouri Synod declare A Statement of Scriptural and Confessional Principles, in all its parts, to be Scriptural and in accord with the Lutheran Confessions, and therefore a formulation which derives its authority from the Word of God and which expresses the Synod's position on current doctrinal issues; and be it further

RESOLVED, That The Lutheran Church—Missouri Synod declare A Statement of Scriptural and Confessional Principles to be a "more formal and comprehensive statement of belief" in the sense of Resolution 5-24 of the 1971 Milwaukee convention, and that the Synod further declare that A Statement shall hold the status defined in said resolution (Preamble, above).

Action: Adopted
Resolution 3–01
1973 Proceedings, pp. 127–128

TOPICAL INDEX

PERSON INDEX

Scripture Index

288

LUTHERAN CONFESSIONS INDEX